TOO MUCH, TOO SOO

TOO MUCH,
TOO SOON

by Diana Barrymore

and Gerold Frank

Illustrated with Photographs

HENRY HOLT AND COMPANY
NEW YORK

To Robert, my husband,
who understood

And it is clear to me that Shakespeare sought to depict a great deed laid upon a soul unequal to the performance of it.

—From the Preface of
the Temple Edition of *Hamlet*

BOOK ONE

"**D**iana! Diana Barrymore!"

Somewhere a persistent beating at the base of my brain. And somewhere a voice, musical, magnificently grand, yet as from a great distance, over the heads of cheering audiences, across vast plains of stage, calling me. Was it my father's voice?

"Oh, Fig, darling. Come back!" *Fig, darling.* Only Daddy used that name, and to Mother. "Fig, my darling, don't leave me. The hounds run over my soul and rend it!"

But those were the despairing words he wrote to Mother when they separated . . . I was confused.

Then, suddenly, I was awake. I lay in a white-walled room. I felt strangely weak. My husband Bob knelt by my bed, rubbing my hands, saying over and over again, "It's all right now, Diana. Everything's all right now."

Had it been Bob's voice all the time? Painfully I let my eyes wander. I could not move my head. Objects came into focus. Shoes, a man's white shoes, white trousers . . . a doctor? Unable to see above or below, my eyes took in what they could. A chair. A table. My purse. Bob's hat. The letter from Actors' Equity warning me that I could be expelled if I appeared drunk on stage again . . . And the gray letter that came in the same mail. I remembered its words.

> Dear Diana . . . I enjoyed so much reading that you were to appear in Boston. I haven't heard of you for so long. You

won't remember me, but I knew you when you were a little girl in Newport, and I was a guest at your coming out party in 1938. How exquisite you were, how vital . . . What have you been doing these last years, Diana?

Shall I tell you, Dear Mrs. Unknown? Last night I tried to kill myself . . .

"Please, Miss Barrymore." The voice was gentle. "You must take this now——"

A strong hand was behind my head lifting me up, and like a child I obediently opened my mouth. A teaspoon appeared from nowhere. I felt the cold metal and then I was choking down an evil-smelling liquid. Someone put a glass of cold water to my lips. I drank, gratefully, and felt myself sink back into the pillows again.

"Take it easy," the voice said. "You've had a rough time." It paused. "Don't give us any more trouble now, promise?"

"I'll promise for her, Doctor," I heard Bob say. He seemed to be talking from far off. "Everything just piled up on her, poor kid. And I've been no help . . ."

I dozed, hearing their conversation as in a dream. Bob's voice: "I didn't believe it at first, Doctor. She's pulled this before, but it was always phony. The whole family's so damned theatrical—her father and mother put on the same act . . . If I hadn't come back and found her in time——" His voice trailed away.

I lay, floating, in another world, half awake, half asleep. The gray letter tugged at my memory. I remembered my coming-out party—not clearly, but like a film seen long ago. The brilliantly lit room, enormous gold and black, with one wall all mirrors. The lovely picture I made in the white satin dress that Captain Molyneux designed for me in Paris the summer before. I thought, I can hardly remember that girl standing in the receiving line. I remember Tony Duke, champagne glass in hand: "I give you the most beautiful, the most talented, the most exciting debutante of 1938!" Tony and I were going to announce our engagement that next spring. I remember Cholly Knickerbocker's columns about me—"Personality Deb. No. 1." I was very proud. I remember Mrs. Cornelius Vanderbilt taking my hands in hers: "Diana, the nicest compliment I can pay is to say that you are the image of your mother at her own début—you look lovely, the way every girl should look when she makes her bow. Stay as you are, my dear . . ."

My mind played tricks. Suddenly the mirrored room vanished, and it was last night, in the hotel room: Bob out walking the dog, while I lay in bed, watching the walls close in on me, unable to scream—only to think, *it's getting too much for me, I can't take it any more.* The travesty of a play I found myself in, the lurid posters outside the theater showing a half-naked girl everyone thought was me, the notices comparing me to a female Jerry Lewis . . . I was drunk, I staggered on stage, and everyone saw it. I felt like a chorus girl in a fifth-rate burlesque. How low could you sink, Diana, to sell the name of Barrymore so cheaply, making like a slapstick tart in a two-bit honky-tonk . . . When I think of what you've had and could have had . . . Let's face it, Diana. You're a has-been at thirty-four. You're broke. You're blacklisted in three-fourths of the theaters in the country. And you know you're not going to stop drinking completely, and Bob isn't going to stop drinking either, and if Equity kicks you out, that's the end because you'll never work any theater again . . . What's the point of going on? What else are you fitted to do? Sure, you could get a job at Macy's selling lingerie, but your name is Barrymore, and you can't do that . . .

It was then that I took the pills. I took the pills. I took the pills.

I opened my eyes.

Bob was standing there now, looking down on me. I thought, as I'd thought so often before, we're like two lost children in the woods, we don't know our way, we can only hold on to each other . . .

"It got too much for me," I said aloud.

Bob nodded. "I know, darling. But you're all right now. Please try to sleep."

I fell asleep, suddenly, soundly.

The shrilling telephone by my bed woke me. It was hours later. Ann Andrews, my mother confessor, was on the line from New York. She wasted no time in commiseration. "Well, darling, I'm told you made every front page in Boston with what you did last night."

I was myself again. I asked, "What did I make in New York?"

Ann, who gave up hope for me long ago, sighed. "Thank Christ, darling, only an inside page."

"Ooooh?" I said. "Really, they might have given me better billing."

"I must say," went on Ann, who was not amused, "I simply don't understand you. After all you've gone through, why go off the far end now? Don't tell me you really wanted to die?"

I thought about it. "No, I didn't want to die—but I didn't want to live either."

Ann clucked impatiently. She always tells me the truth as she sees it, which is one of her privileges. She knew my mother and father, she knows my beginnings and where I have come. She doesn't believe in self-pity. People, she feels, get what is their due. "Diana," she was saying, "dear girl, dear child, you make your own hell and carry it with you. Don't you know that . . . ?"

I thought of what she said as I lay recuperating in Boston General Hospital that day not so long ago, and I think of it now as I sit here wondering where—and how—to begin a story that needs so much explaining along the way. So much has been dreamed, so little done; there was so much promise and so much waste.

Looking back, it seems to me that I have lived three separate lives. First, that of a child reared by governesses in New York and Paris, who became the *enfante terrible* of Cholly Knickerbocker and El Morocco and Princeton week ends, and all the marvelous gold and tinsel of the high, fine world of the *Social Register*. Then, that of a young actress on Broadway and in Hollywood, who tried desperately to live up to a fabulous name in a world bounded by her father's escapades and her own confusion. And third, there is the life I have led since—a life which I often think needs the combined talents of a Tennessee Williams and a Dostoevski to explain, and the wisdom and compassion of a St. Augustine to forgive.

I shall try to tell it all as honestly as I know how. Perhaps in the telling I will come to some belated understanding of myself. There seems to be more than one Diana Barrymore— one I recognize and one I do not. One Diana has done outrageous things. She has drunk too much. She has made a public spectacle of herself. She has become involved in street brawls. More than once she's found herself on the front pages of tabloid newspapers and exposé magazines. She has been unlucky with men—and there have been many men. That Diana has been a bloody fool.

There is another Diana, the Diana who tells this story. I am always sober. I am the lady I was born and brought up to be. When I hear what Diana Barrymore has done—and in recent years when I picked up a morning newspaper I never knew what I might read about her—I am aghast. "How disgraceful!" I say to myself. I mean it. "She should be horsewhipped!" And my heart breaks a little for that girl who had everything—name, breeding, talent, opportunity after opportunity—and seems to have done her best to throw it away.

Sometimes, in my dark moments, when I pace the floor and play my records and dream my fantasies, I turn to the mirror and study the girl I find there. I search her face. Who is she, and what is she? I talk to her. I say, "Hello, Newport. Fine mess you've made of things, haven't you? You think that's great, Diana Barrymore? Diana, somewhere along the line you got off. You did wrong, obviously. Where? What happened? Why?"

CHAPTER ONE

I T ALL BEGINS, if it has a beginning, on a sunny April day in 1917 when my mother, then Mrs. Blanche Oelrichs Thomas of Newport, one of the most beautiful and spectacular women in the world, swept into Cartier's, the jewelers, in New York. She had gone to trade her diamond tiara—the only other like it was owned by the Empress of Russia—for a rope of matched pearls that she'd commissioned Mr. Cartier to find for her.

On her way to his private office she passed John Barrymore, the actor, bending over a showcase. Their glances met fleetingly and she remembered him later as "very slim and nervously poetic, with grayish eyes of immense fascination." He was the matinee idol of the day—as *Peter Ibbetson*, in his current Broadway hit, he personified glamour, romance, and manhood to countless women—and Mother couldn't help wondering what extravagance he might be buying and for which of his many favorites.

A few days later Mother was introduced to him at a Theatre Guild party to which she had been invited, both as Mrs. Thomas, the society leader, and as Michael Strange, her pen name as poet and playwright. She and Jack Barrymore looked into each other's eyes and fell violently in love—a love affair so full of exaltation and despair, of quarrels and reconciliations, of mutual threats of self-destruction, that a friend

17

described it as "a tennis match in Hell, with nobody missing the ball."

It *was* a mad love affair. Mother was married, with two small sons. He had just gotten over a disastrous marriage. Their friends warned them against each other. You don't mate whirlwinds without reaping destruction. Nothing helped. Even the gods smiled, Mother felt, upon the union of two such superbly attractive and talented human beings—he, the most electrifying personality on the American stage and one of the world's handsomest men; she, a woman of such beauty and personal magnetism that heads turned wherever she went. Ultimately, despite all her distraught family could do, Mother divorced Leonard Thomas and married John Barrymore. The wedding took place in New York on August 15, 1920, less than forty-eight hours after Mother's divorce became effective.

At that, it was none too soon. I was born March 3, 1921.

Often I think of these two fiery strains that met in me. I think of the tortured marriage between these two self-intoxicated personalities, one who fulfilled his promise as few men have, yet who always felt himself a fraud and a failure; the other, a driven woman who thought herself a genius who hadn't achieved her destiny. I read again the hundreds of impassioned letters they wrote each other—accusing and pleading, defiant and adoring, wretched and ecstatic—and I wonder. What is the relationship between them and my own life of emotional turmoil, and where is the key to an understanding of myself to be found? Do any of us ever discover the real answer?

Once, before she met Daddy, Mother wrote of herself, "I was always seeking in the crowd the face of the one who would release me." At the beginning, I know, she thought she had found the one. Daddy would help her fulfill her promise as a writer. She, in return, would inspire him to still greater heights in the theater. Ecstatically they honeymooned on the Lido, in Venice, then returned to White Plains, New York, to a charming little farmhouse surrounded by a white picket fence, which Daddy gave Mother as a wedding present. Waiting for me, Mother, being Mother, spent her time writing a romantic play for Daddy entitled *Clair de Lune*. "Pure magic!" he cried, and enthusiastically set to work designing his own costumes and arranging for a Broadway production of the play. Even more, he promised to persuade his sister, my Aunt Ethel, to act in it with him.

In the midst of this excited preparation I arrived. We moved to a large brownstone in East 97th Street, New York, where my half-brothers, Leonard, ten, and Robin, six, and their governess joined us. I was to be named, Mother had announced, Joan Strange Blythe: Joan, for Joan of Arc, whom she admired above all women; Strange, after her pen name; and Blythe, the original—and legal—name of the Barrymores.

But in the cab en route to St. Ignatius Church where Uncle Lionel and his wife Doris waited for the christening, Mother changed her mind. She suddenly turned to Daddy. "I'm not naming her Joan," she said unexpectedly. "It sounds too much like John. This child must be an individual, not an echo of her father."

Daddy bristled. "It may sound like John in that bastard British accent they use in Newport," he retorted. "But it doesn't sound like John to me. What name *are* you giving her?"

For one of the few times in her life Mother turned the other cheek. She closed her eyes for a trancelike moment and chose my name as she had her nom de plume—from thin air.

"We shall call her Diana," she announced. "Diana." She tried it again and liked it.

Daddy looked at her grandly. "Very well, Fig. She shall be Diana to you. But to me"—he cocked an eyebrow upward, thinking—"she will be Treepeewee."

Mother stared. "Treepeewee? Really, Jack! It's outlandish. Wherever does it come from?"

"That," Daddy said mysteriously, "will remain a secret. Between Treepeewee and me."

And Treepeewee—Treepee for short—a nonsense name he invented on the spot, was his pet name for me through the years. On my birth certificate, where Mother wrote it the day I was born, and in the *Social Register* before I was dropped from its chic pages, my name still reads: Joan Strange Blythe.

In the theater Daddy may have had the greatest stage presence of his time, but in my nursery he was a frightened, awkward father. He would tiptoe in, night after night, softly draw up a chair next to my crib, and sit there in a kind of marveling silence, staring at me as if I were the eighth wonder of the world. "Isn't she beautiful?" he would say. He invented new names for me. "My funniest little Treacle," or "my own silly Dringle." But he refused to touch me.

"Now, Mr. Barrymore," Mary Dempsey, my nurse, recalls chiding him, "she's your daughter. Why don't you pick her up and hold her in your arms? That's the way to enjoy her."

Daddy would draw back in alarm. "Oh, no! She's too fragile! I'd break her!"

Once Mary was cuddling me when a bell tinkled twice— Mother's signal from her room down the hall that she wanted Mary, and instantly.

"Hold out your arms, Mr. Barrymore," Mary ordered. Daddy put out his arms automatically. Mary deposited me in them and hurried off.

When she returned a few minutes later, she was astonished to find him standing exactly where she had left him, literally rooted to the floor, holding me stiffly in his outstretched arms. His face was white as a sheet.

"Good God, never do that again!" he exclaimed as she rescued me. He took a deep breath. "I might have dropped her!"

Uncle Lionel, on the other hand, who had lost his own

two children in infancy, often came into the nursery to hold and cuddle me.

It wasn't long before the violent clashes of temperament between Mother and Daddy turned the 97th Street house into something out of a Russian novel. One moment soaring off in a communion of body and soul that left them both humble, the next they were screaming at each other. Their intense egos galled them: they were in competition with each other as artists, as lovers, as parents; each insisted on being the only focus of attention in the home, on the street, at parties; each had an uncontrollable temper—madly theatrical, they could explode in a rage at the turn of a word. Both seethed with jealousy; it was no secret that women shamelessly pursued Daddy or that there was hardly a gentleman acquaintance of Mother's who hadn't felt impelled to try his charms on her.

Strange stories circulated below stairs. Martha, the cook, awakened at 2:00 A.M. to look out the window on a chilling sight—Mother, her pink nightgown streaming behind her, rushing headlong down 97th Street toward Madison Avenue, screaming into the quiet night, "I'll throw myself under the first streetcar!" Often furniture in their bedroom was discovered the next morning smashed and disarranged, expensive china shattered against the wall. Once, after a row that kept the servants up most of the night, Bridget, the chambermaid, found Daddy's pajamas ripped and shredded until there wasn't a whole piece an inch square. And once when Mother came into the nursery to say good night to me, her arm was in a sling, her right eye bruised and swollen. She was quite grand about it.

"I stumbled over a champagne case in the dark," she told Mary haughtily. This was believable because my parents' quarters and mine were separated by two large dressing rooms, each piled almost shoulder high with cases of champagne.

Mary Dempsey had her own domestic barometer. As Daddy grew more confident with me, he took me into his arms now and then. But when he hurried into the nursery and asked Mary, "May I have Treepeewee for a little while?" and vanished swiftly with me in the direction of Mother's room, Mary knew. Daddy had taken me as a peace offering. When he returned, bubbling over with good humor, to place me tenderly in my crib and kiss me good night, she knew all was well—for a little while at least.

Years later when I was living through a hell of my own, my mother said, "Your father and I should have met when we were two years old. Maybe then we might have become used to each other."

An overwhelming restlessness drove Mother. She fought a demon she could not vanquish. Although she was reared in the grand European tradition, which held that ladies and gentlemen were a caste apart, she alternately rebelled against this for herself and championed it for me. She never let me forget that the Oelrichs were one of the distinguished families of society, here and abroad.

Mother's mother—my beloved Grandma Tibi—was born in Vienna, the daughter of Chevalier Charles F. de Loosey, a diplomat who was later sent to the United States as Royal Consul General of Austria-Hungary. Grandma Tibi grew up at the court of Emperor Franz Joseph. As a child, my grandmother played duets with Franz Liszt; she was taken to her first ball by Prince Henri Liechtenstein, and to her last days wore a bracelet given her by an admirer, the Archduke Ludwig Victor, youngest brother of the Emperor.

When Tibi was twenty, in 1878, she came to the United States, where she married Charles May Oelrichs of Baltimore. The Oelrichs, American agents for the North German Lloyd Steamship Lines, had emigrated to this country in 1780. On his mother's side, Grandpa Charles belonged to the famed Mays of Maryland, a pre-Revolutionary family whose men were noted for their enormous vitality and good looks, and who invariably turned out to be admirals or statesmen. My grandfather, however, turned out to be neither; after a try at cattle ranching in Oelrichs, South Dakota, which was named for the family, he bought a seat on the New York Stock Exchange and for years, before retiring to Newport, headed his own brokerage firm. The 1890 depression didn't leave him too well off as wealth was measured in Newport, then the richest, most exclusive colony in America. Sometimes the press would confuse Grandpa Charles with his older brother, Hermann, and my grandfather would roar, laughing, "Oh, you don't want me, my dear fellow. You want the rich Oelrichs!" Grandpa Charles and Grandma Tibi lived in a lovely yellow frame house on one of Newport's less fashionable streets; but Hermann's home, an enormous white marble palace called "Rosecliff," where his wife Tessie presided with queenly magnificence, was one of the showplaces and partying places of society. Reputed to be worth more than two million dollars, it had twenty-two bedrooms each with private bath! Nonetheless, there was wealth enough in Mother's home to allow her a background of personal maids and butlers. Her coming-out party in 1908 was an event of the New York season. Impetuous, strikingly beautiful, willful, even outrageous—she was expelled from Brearley School for pouring whisky in her teacher's soup—she was the belle of Newport, courted by a prince's dozen of dukes, barons, and lesser nobility.

A few weeks after her début Mother went to Paris to visit her sister Lily. Like Mother, my Aunt Lily was a great beauty. In addition, she bore a title. She was the Duchess of Mecklenburg, having married into a collateral branch of the Hohenzollern family. Aunt Lily had plans for Mother. She gave a party to which she invited, as Mother's dinner partner, one of Europe's most eligible bachelors, the Marquess of Anglesey. But the Marquess' car broke down, he never arrived at the party, and Mother found herself sitting next to

Leonard Thomas of Philadelphia, liaison officer with the American Embassy in Paris. Thomas, then in his thirties, urbane, intelligent, enormously wealthy, wooed her with poetry, drove her at breath-taking speed through the French countryside in his Panhard racing car, escorted her to the opera, ballet, and theater—and won her. They were married that year.

As young Mrs. Thomas, Mother lived regally. A black and gold Rolls Royce was always at her call. She attended parties for the Prince of Wales. She was dined by the Grand Duke Alexander of Russia. Her portrait was painted by the French artist, Paul Helleu, who called her "the most beautiful woman in America." She followed the seasons—New York, Southampton, Palm Beach, the Continent.

But after Leonard and Robin were born, Mother's demon took over. Society was all very well, the noble names that filled her salon were gratifying, but she was bored. "Oh, if I could only get my teeth into something with a real core!" she confided to a friend. Matters weren't helped when Leonard Thomas, with the outbreak of World War I, left for the front.

Blanche Oelrichs Thomas vanished—and Michael Strange appeared. She bobbed her hair. She strolled through the streets of Newport smoking a cigarette, unheard of for a lady. She dressed in men's trousers and men's hats—wide, floppy sombreros. She began to write free verse and plays, to frequent Bohemian literary cellars in Greenwich Village. She threw herself into the Suffragette movement. Dressed all in white, she marched bareheaded up Fifth Avenue, waving a banner at the head of hundreds of women chanting, "We want the vote!" Before Mother finished with her revolt, she tried half a dozen careers—poet, playwright, actress, author, lecturer, and politician.

When Daddy met her at the Theatre Guild party, he too had reached a blank wall. His first marriage, to Katherine Harris, had ended in divorce after seven years. His stage successes left him empty: it was a painter, not an actor, that he'd always wanted to be. Years later he confessed to me, "I die a little each time I paint my face and posture in public like a scented jackass!" He had studied art in London, tried painting theatrical posters in New York, even worked as a cartoonist for Arthur Brisbane, the great Hearst editor, on the New York *Evening Journal.*

But the family tradition was overpowering. For four generations in England and America there had been actors in the family. His sister Ethel, his brother Lionel, his uncle John Drew—all were in the theater. Actually, he did not set foot on the stage until he was twenty-one. A bit actor playing with Aunt Ethel in the Philadelphia run of *Captain Jinks of the Horse Marines* was called away by death in his family. Ethel wired Daddy to take the first train from New York. Since he had been fired by Brisbane for failing to get over his hang-overs by noon, and needed the money, he went to Philadelphia.

Two years later his father, my grandfather Maurice Barrymore, in his time the matinee idol of America, a man of enormous wit and zest for life, died in a mental institution. After the funeral Daddy joined Ethel in the play, *Sunday.* Daniel Frohman, the producer, almost fired him, again for drinking. Ethel helped him pull himself together and literally forced him to join her in Ibsen's *Doll's House.* The critics began noticing him. From then on his career through *Peter Ibbetson, The Jest, Redemption, Richard III,* and finally *Hamlet* made theatrical history.

Mother and Daddy had to wait nearly three years before they could marry. When Leonard Thomas returned after the war, Mother, who detested sham and evasion, told him on their first night that she loved Jack Barrymore. Shocked, unbelieving, convinced it was only an infatuation, Thomas sent her to California to forget. Daddy followed her there. Then Thomas spirited Mother abroad on a second honeymoon, in hope of saving the marriage for the sake of the two boys. That failed too. Grandpa Charles took over. To marry Jack Barrymore, he thundered, was to plunge into disaster. The fellow was brilliant, of course, but irresponsible, footloose, and extravagant, involved with women and liquor, openly contemptuous of the rigid social caste she represented. Above all, he was an actor.

Grandpa Charles may have been an iron man, but Mother could be steel. "Nothing you can do or say will stop me," she said. Finally Thomas gave her a divorce, adding, "You'll come back to me, Michael." He was nearly proved right. While Mother was getting her decree in France, one of the Oelrichs felt duty-bound to write her that John Barrymore, recuperating from what the newspapers termed "nervous exhaustion," had been seen weaving, drunk, down the street.

When for five days Daddy heard nothing from Mother, he began cabling frantically:

> Oh, my baby, what in the name of God could make you cold to me? . . . I have been so wretched I have written you letters that were like the last wail of the damned in the valley of the dead, and torn them up . . .

Still she was silent. He had sworn he would not drink, and he had lied to her. He knew liquor had been his father's curse. She could not forgive him.

Daddy prostrated himself.

> Oh, my beloved, my dearest beloved, I have waited and longed and prayed and cursed for you all my life like a marooned soul on a deserted coast . . . Please, for the love of heaven, believe that your future is strewn with little pieces of my heart for your feet to walk on so they need not touch the earth . . . I love you, I love you, I love you . . .

Had I been Mother, I could not have withstood it. Nor could she. She yielded, she forgave, she became Mrs. John Barrymore.

CHAPTER TWO

THE FIRST YEARS of my life are a patchwork quilt of faces and places—a bewildering design made by the comings and goings of my parents as they raged their way through their marriage, alternately fleeing from each other and fleeing back to each other. Before the age of five everything is blurred. But in my search for the girl I was, I have managed to piece together those years, and, like a stage setting created by a mad artist, the picture takes shape for me.

I was only a few months old that summer of 1921 when Uncle Lionel escorted Mother to the Empire Theatre for the première of her play, *Clair de Lune,* costarring John and Ethel Barrymore. The demand for tickets sent front seats as high as seventy-five dollars a pair. Aunt Ethel—so Mother liked to think—forgot her lines and it took all Uncle Lionel's diplomacy to stave off a family feud almost before the first curtain fell.

Whatever the case, the play, written in Mother's free verse, was laughed off Broadway. One critic headed his notice, "For the Love of Mike." Another wrote, "The language . . . beat on the eardrums with increasing incoherence as the evening went on." Mother was outraged. "Those idiots!" she cried. Daddy dashed off a furious letter to the newspapers denouncing the critics—and then both went to Europe to forget it. In Paris they quarreled violently. It ended with Mother fleeing to Spain and Daddy stomping off to Switzerland to climb Mont Blanc.

He joined her in Venice two weeks later to find a handsome young poet in her wake. Daddy seethed, but they had agreed not to interfere with each other's lives. Nonetheless, his hour would come at dusk each night, when he met Mother at a rendezvous in the shadow of the Bridge of Sighs. He enfolded her in his arms and they forgot their jealousies.

Later, in Biarritz, where Daddy brought us all, another monumental row broke out. The noise awoke Leonard, then eleven. Years later he told me he never forgot that night. I lay sleeping in my crib. Robin, six, and Miss Gerdes, our governess, were sound asleep. It was after midnight and Leonard, who desperately missed his father, lay listening in bed, remembering. When Daddy courted Mother, Leonard had overheard the maids' disapproving gossip backstairs: "That fine Mr. Thomas gone off to war, and she carrying on with that Mr. Barrymore . . ." He knew something was wrong. Daddy had tried vainly to win him over. He gave him toy soldiers (Leonard threw them into an ashcan), he took him fishing and baited his hook (Leonard pulled the worm off at first chance). Now, disgusted with the shouting voices in the next room, Leonard rose, dressed, tied his bedsheets together, and let himself out the first-story window to the ground. Most of that night he wandered the dark, lonely streets of Biarritz in tears. When he returned later and climbed up to our room, all was silent. My parents slept like lovebirds. Robin and I slumbered peacefully. No one had missed him. He cried a little more then.

In Paris, Mother and Daddy astonished the international colony by the way they dressed. They appeared in twin costumes of silk and velvet, Daddy in black velvet trousers, Mother, black velvet skirts; they wore the same black, widebrimmed hats, cocked at the same angle, the same long-pointed collars, designed by Daddy—known since as the Barrymore collar—and identical flowing black ties. Sometimes Mother showed up in a tailored velvet dinner coat, a velvet skirt, and her famous rope of pearls. Her make-up could be astounding, her dark eyebrows extended like swallow's wings almost to her temples.

Daddy's jealousy gave him no peace. Dancing with Mother one night, he suddenly whirled on an unsuspecting man who smiled at her, and cried, "Is he your lover? Tell me! Is he the one?" Utterly distraught, she left him again, sending a farewell wire:

> My only beloved, goodbye. I know at last you are tortured by unrealities beyond human power to put straight nor can I make you understand your cruelty because you are in such pain yourself.

Daddy raged about their empty apartment, wrote her impassioned letters: "Oh, my darling, believe me when I say I lie outside your bedroom door and drink the poison of the tears I have made you shed." She rushed back to him.

Their spectacular quarrels continued. Once Mother, after a hysterical scene, locked herself in the bathroom, announcing that she had taken iodine. Daddy tried to butt in the door with his head. Mother emerged serenely a few minutes later, the iodine untouched on its shelf. Once Daddy rushed into the street shouting that she would find his body in the Seine. Mother, as she herself told the story, flew after him— to discover, at the end of nearly an hour's frantic search, that he had circled back to their apartment and was sound asleep.

They teased each other. If Daddy arrived late for an appointment in front of a restaurant, he would not find her there. She would be standing out of sight in a doorway across the street, secretly watching him as he waited, fumed, paced back and forth, and finally left.

"Good Chrrrist!" he would roar when she told him. "You have the soul of a sadist!"

"You deserved it," she would say. "I abhor being kept waiting."

Mother left Daddy once again, in 1924, when we were back in the States. The argument grew out of women—and drinking. Perhaps wrongly, Mother decided one day to throw out all the liquor in the apartment. Next morning she found that her cologne had vanished from her dresser. She walked into Daddy's bedroom. He was standing unsteadily in front of his bureau mirror, the bottle of cologne almost empty in his hand.

"Oh, Jack!" she exclaimed in despair. "Have you really gone this far?"

Daddy, with a grimace, drained the last drop. "Odd—but it will have to suffice," he said. He brightened. "I feel better already." And then: "Fig, you *hid* everything from me—what do you expect?"

This time Mother fled with thirteen-year-old Leonard to as inaccessible a place as she knew—to Lake Algonquin, in the wilderness of the Canadian Laurentians, five days by canoe from Quebec, the nearest point of civilization. A week later Leonard was puttering over a campfire in a clearing in the forest. He heard a voice and looked up, unbelieving: there, plunging through the underbrush, a five days' growth of beard on his face, came Daddy, bellowing, "Fig! Fig, darling! Where are you?" Mother melted. There was an ardent reconciliation under the pines, and an idyllic three days passed in hunting, fishing, and making love.

The fourth day dawned cold and wet. Mother told Leonard to wear his heavy underwear. Leonard refused. "Now, goddammit, Leonard, you put those on, or I'll wallop you!" Daddy shouted. Leonard still refused. "Leonard, you obey Jack!" Mother ordered. "No," Leonard said sullenly. Daddy walloped him on his backside, hard. Leonard's lip trembled. "You're not my father," he said bitterly. "You shouldn't hit me."

Mother, stung more deeply than she realized, turned on Daddy in fury. "How dare you touch him!" she cried. Next day two caravans of canoes silently began a separate trek back to civilization, Mother, Leonard, and their entourage of guides in one, Daddy and his in the other.

I had just turned four in 1925 when my parents, reconciled again, took me to London. We lived in the White House, once occupied by Whistler, the artist. I have a vague memory of dark doors and frighteningly high ceilings. Here Daddy and Mother joined London's most illustrious circles. Daddy drank with the Prince of Wales and with Feodor Chaliapin, the great Russian basso; he spent time with Winston Churchill. (Family gossip had it that years before, Aunt Ethel and Winston Churchill had been on the verge of announcing their engagement.) Mother found herself dining with Rudyard Kipling, taking tea with George Moore. Daddy's chief interest in London was to put on his own production of *Hamlet,* in which he had electrified New York two years before. He worked furiously; and when he opened at the Haymarket Theatre, it was before a dazzling first-night audience. George Bernard Shaw escorted Mother to the opening that night. A *Who's Who* of London's artistic life were present: John Masefield, Somerset Maugham, Arnold Bennett, Lord Dunsany, Sir Gerald du Maurier, Sir Anthony Hope.

Sitting with Mother, Shaw told her he could easily see her as a magnificent Joan in his new play, *Saint Joan.* "Learn stage technique and study," he advised her. Then both fell silent and watched Daddy in what has been described as the greatest Hamlet of all time.

On the ebb tide of that triumph my parents' marriage crashed. Mother learned that Daddy, after swearing he'd not touch a drop, had been on a binge in Paris. He denied everything. It was the last blow.

"I'm leaving you, Jack," Mother said. "I can't take the fighting and the drinking and your genius for tormenting us both. You're destroying me as a person and an artist."

He pleaded with her. She shook her head. "It's no use, Jack. You have lied to me for the last time." She stalked into her room and began to pack. Daddy followed her. "Fig, if you leave me," he threatened wildly, "I'll quit the stage for good."

She spoke with her back to him and there was cold contempt in her voice. "I don't give a Goddamn what you do," she said.

He turned on his heel and left.

Daddy—so the records show—kept his word. Never again did he set foot on the serious stage. Three weeks after *Hamlet* closed on April 28, 1925, Daddy and Mother signed a separation agreement and Daddy went to Hollywood. He was seen only in films after that. Not until fifteen years later did he again appear on a stage, and then in a burlesque of himself, *My Dear Children,* at the Selwyn Theatre, in Chicago.

The toss of the dice is strange. For I, starting on my first professional tour in *Outward Bound,* was to appear in Chicago at the very same time—during the very same week—on the stage of the Harris Theatre, immediately next door.

What influence these furious clashes, this constant uprooting, had on my development, I can only guess, for I first became really conscious of myself when I was five years old. I was in an elevator at the Madison Hotel, in New York, and I was being taken downstairs. Twice each day the twelfth-floor maid delivered me to the elevator man, who descended with me to the lobby and handed me over to the doorman, a jolly man named Louis. Louis took my hand carefully in his and walked with me once around the block. Thus aired, I was returned to the elevator man, who rose to our floor and delivered me back to the maid. I have a hazy memory of Mother, elegant and remote, seated at a desk, writing, always writing, and her invariable question, "Did you have a nice time, Catkin?" We were a cat family—Diana-cat, Robin-cat, Leonard-cat—or we all called each other Catkin.

Then—and far more vividly—I remember myself at six, living with Miss Gerdes, my governess, in Paris where I attended a French convent school. That memory is tied to an emotion. I used to wake in the morning, look in the mirror, and burst into tears. "Please, God," I prayed. "Make me beautiful like Mummy."

I was the ugliest child I knew. I looked like a Japanese doll with jaundice. My face was round, my complexion yellow, my straight black hair cut in stringy bangs to my eyebrows. I had a habit of squinting against the light—a fat little girl always in dresses too short for her. When I was introduced to grownups they usually remarked, "My, how charming!" never, "What a beautiful little girl!" I sensed there was a difference. Mother was enthralled by beauty and I knew I was not beautiful, and I was ashamed.

I was the only American girl at the convent and very much alone. Each morning Miss Gerdes, a tiny, gray-haired woman, took me to school; each afternoon she brought me back. We lived in a small English *pension* Mother chose for us before going to America to publish her latest poems. While I read my lessons, Miss Gerdes, following instructions, wrote Mother a nightly report of my activities. After that I went to bed. I had no idea that other children lived different lives.

One day in school I passed a girl's desk. On it was her prayer book, a page marked with a holy picture. It showed Jesus cradling a lamb in his arms. Suddenly I had an overwhelming desire. I glanced about: I was alone. My hand stretched out, clutched the precious picture, and hid it hastily in the front of my blue uniform. That began a curious and strangely satisfying ritual: stealing holy pictures and cards, slipping them out of prayer books, snatching them from study tables, even ransacking desks and lockers until my prayer book was full of them. Then, when I was alone or kneeling on the dank stone floor of chapel at 7:00 A.M. mass, I pored, spellbound, over them.

The glowing colors fascinated me. My imagination brought the holy figures to life. They lived, moved, spoke, and I played scenes with them. I was the lamb in Jesus' arms who had been left trembling on a ledge until He rescued him.

The Virgin spoke lovingly to me, and the angels about the Christ Child were the sisters I did not have. One elaborately designed picture entranced me. It was made like a shuttered window. I delighted in opening it and I could lose myself for hours pretending I was inside. Then I was Christ Himself, stretching out my hand to heal the lepers, the crippled, the dying . . .

One afternoon after classes, carrying my prayer book with its loot carefully held together by a strong rubber band, I ventured into the courtyard where the girls were playing hide-and-seek. *"Est-ce que je peux jouer avec vous?"* I asked timidly. It was an appeal to let me play with them. Instead, the girls giggled at my accent. *"C'est l'américaine"* they said scornfully. One picked up a stone from the gravel yard and threw it at me.

It fell short, but I was frightened. I turned to run, slipped, and fell, sprawling, on the gravel. My beloved prayer book flew out of my hand. The elastic snapped—my pictures spewed out.

I was horrified. I scrambled to pick them up, but the girls swooped down on them, screaming. Now they knew the thief. Two girls started to pummel me, and the Mother Superior hurried up. She pulled them off.

Everyone started to speak at once and point at me. I sat where I had fallen, blood trickling from my knee, too paralyzed with shame and terror to open my mouth.

"Get up, my child," the Mother told me. "Come with me."

She led me away, my knee was bandaged, and I was conducted to her office and, I thought, my doom.

The Mother Superior was a very tall woman with white skin that matched her little veil, and deep, sunken blue eyes and a perpetual smile of forgiveness. She did not become angry. "You have offended God," she told me sadly. Secretly I thought, "No, He understands. He is kind."

My penance was to say my rosary ten times.

Though I was ashamed, I was also strangely exhilarated. I

had discovered a wondrous thing no punishment could take from me. I had the power to conjure up fantasies, creating a private world of my own and escaping into it. Even when I was older it took little to open the door. Loneliness always did it; later, men—and alcohol.

No one ever sat down with me and told me who my father was. Mother refused to speak about him. She became cross, even upset, if I questioned her. "I don't want to talk about him," she'd say. "You'll meet him someday." If I persisted, her face—so expressive with its enormous dark eyes, its small, fawnlike features—would look as if a film had suddenly been thrown over it. Her lips pursed, her head was tossed back, a pulse began to beat in her jaw. "That'll do, Diana," she would say, and I didn't dare go on. Sometimes I heard mysterious snatches of conversation. "Poor Jack," Mother would say. "He's starting another motion picture, I understand. When I think what they're doing to him in that monstrous factory—what's happening to that genius in Hollywood . . ."

I never understood what "that monstrous factory" was, nor what "Hollywood" meant. In Paris, once, a chance meeting only deepened the puzzle. A tall, elegantly gowned lady bowed to Miss Gerdes as we entered our *pension*. She stopped for a moment and stared at me. *"Ah,"* she said, with a note of surprise, *"C'est la jeune fille de Monsieur Barrymore, le grand acteur?"*

Nanny was abrupt. "Yes," she said curtly and hurried me inside. I was sure she whisked me away because she was ashamed of me. The lady's words were baffling. "Is this the young daughter of Mr. Barrymore, the great actor?" It was all very confusing. Robin and Leonard, my half-brothers, were Robin Thomas and Leonard Thomas. I was Diana Blythe. It took some time before I understood.

I began daydreaming about my father. He became a shadowy figure, half-God, half-man. One day I stumbled on a thin book Nanny had packed away. It was *Confessions of an Actor,*

by John Barrymore. I opened it to the frontispiece, a photograph of a handsome man cradling in his arms a wide-eyed
baby dressed in flowing white. I thought, just like Jesus and
the lamb. Under it I laboriously spelled out, "John Barrymore and Daughter."

I ran to Nanny with the book. "Nanny—is this my daddy
and me?"

She looked at it, picked me up, and kissed me. I was sur-
prised to see her eyes were wet. "Yes, my darling, it is, it is!"
And she used the same unsatisfying phrase Mother used.
"Some day you will meet him."

I could not know then that the newspapers were full of
reports that Daddy had fallen in love with a new leading
lady, Dolores Costello, in his latest film, *The Sea Beast*. Or
that Mother, just before bringing me back to the United
States, had asked Daddy for a divorce.

The only warm memory that comes to me from my childhood
is made up of my visits to my grandparents in Newport.
Grandma Tibi and Grandpa Charles lived in the same yellow, old-fashioned house in which Mother had been born.
They loved me very much and in their eyes I could do no
wrong. Each morning I awakened happily in an enormous
four-poster bed and hurried into Grandma's room to say my
prayers and breakfast with her. A plump, motherly woman
with gray hair piled in high curls above her forehead and a
wonderfully tender smile, she would be sitting erect, wearing
a pink peignoir and supported by masses of lacy pillows almost concealing the huge headboard painted with pink
rosettes. Her voice carried only a trace of her Viennese up-
bringing. I knelt by her bed and repeated after her, "Our
Father, Who art in Heaven . . ." Then breakfast came on a
silver tray. I watched, fascinated, as Grandma, lying back,
took the tray from the maid and placed it on her capacious
bosom. And there it perched, precarious yet apparently safe,
with its two boiled eggs, croissants, brioches, pancakes, bacon

and coffee with whipped cream. I trembled for her, but the tray never slipped.

Toward evening, after spending the day at his club where most of the members seemed related to him, being either Oelrichs, Havemeyers, Mays, or Tiffanys, Grandpa Charles appeared. Tall, ruddy-faced, blue-eyed, he was impeccable in wing collar, pearl stickpin in his gray ascot tie, gray suit with piping, and heavy gold chain across his waistcoat. He was a striking figure, and strong-willed. He had refused to attend Mother's wedding when she married Daddy, and spoke to her only months later. Each evening after dinner he took me past the liquor cabinets with their gold-monogrammed glasses, past Grandma's famous collection of Meissen china, to his study. Here, before the fire, I snuggled into his lap for my bedtime story, listening dreamily to the tale of a mouse with a monocle named Colonel MacPherson. When bedtime arrived, Grandma Tibi, her approach heralded by her high-buttoned shoes that always seemed to squeak, came in and took me upstairs. I knelt and said my prayers, asking God to bless us all—Mummy in Paris; Daddy in far-off, mysterious Hollywood; and Robin and Leonard away at St. Paul's School, where Grandpa himself had gone. Then, a final prayer to God to keep me a good girl, and I was tucked into bed.

At Grandma Tibi's I met other Oelrichs—Mother's brothers, Uncle Harry Oelrichs, who let me play with his silver brandy flask, which always gurgled delightfully, and Uncle Charles, whose daughter, my cousin Marjorie Oelrichs, who later married Eddie Duchin, the bandleader, and died tragically in childbirth. At Grandma Tibi's I had a sense of family that I had nowhere else.

Only the knowledge of my grandparents' love could have made me bold enough to do what I did one Christmas week. All that day I sat on the porch watching the pretty little girls walking by, looking like Christmas cards come alive in their bright red velvet coats and white muffs, with gay ribbons in

their hair. I could think only of my ugly bangs. Grandma
Tibi was in her rocker in the sunroom, Grandpa was away
at the club. I stole upstairs, sneaked Grandma's scissors out
of her bedside sewing kit, hurried downstairs and, standing
before a large Venetian mirror, snipped off my bangs. I cut
them straight across my forehead.

I held the tufts of hair. Where to hide them? I spied the
Christmas tree, already decorated with colorful bells and
fluffy angel's-hair. I pushed my bangs under the angel's-hair
when suddenly I heard the telltale squeak of Grandma Tibi's
shoes.

I fled behind the tree.

"Are you in there, Googie?" came Grandma's voice, using
her pet nickname for me.

I dared not answer. Perhaps she would go away. But the
door swung open, and I had to step out from behind the tree.

She looked at me, horrified. "Whatever have you done to
your bangs, baby?"

I burst into tears and ran to her. "Oh, Grandma, I cut
them off, I hate them so!" She bent down and put her arms
around me. "My poor little Googie, you shouldn't have done
that." Then, as I tried to control my sobs: "Now, now,
Mummy won't be back from Europe for a month, and they'll
almost be grown back by then."

I looked up at her, terrified. "You won't tell her,
Grandma?"

She shook her head. "We'll keep it a secret—just us three,
Grandpa, you, and me."

I stuck out a fistful of hair. What was I to do with this?
Where was the rest of it, she asked. I told her I hid it under
the angel's-hair.

She looked at me. "But, Googie, why did you do that?"

I spoke sheepishly. "Because I knew I was being bad and
my hair would be devil's-hair."

For a moment my grandmother said nothing. When she
spoke, her voice was soft. "We'll play a little game, baby, and

see who can take it off the tree fastest." And when we were finished she took me into the kitchen and made a special treat for me, hot milk with a teaspoon of coffee, topped with whipped cream.

That night as usual Grandpa told me my bedtime story before the fire, but when Grandma appeared to take me off to bed, he rose too, and both of them came up to my room with me. Grandma Tibi helped me undress, listened to my prayers, and tucked me in. I snuggled into the pillow. I looked up a minute later: Grandma and Grandpa were both standing there, looking down at me. Grandpa suddenly bent down and kissed me. "Googie," he said, "you look so pretty. Sleep tight, baby."

A feeling of warmth spread all through my body, and I think I was asleep, in utter contentment, before the door closed behind them.

Because I loved it so much there, I couldn't wait until I was deposited with my grandparents. "Is Mummy going away?" I would ask Miss Gerdes when there was much bustling about. If Mother stayed away, I might be taken to Newport. "She's leaving on a lecture tour, but she'll be back soon," Miss Gerdes usually replied. On one occasion, however, she said, "Mother isn't going away—she's rehearsing for a new play. Maybe I can take you to see her."

One snowy afternoon the promise came true. Gerdes bundled me up and took me to the theater. Mummy, she told me, was in a play called *L'Aiglon,* about the son of a great French king named Napoleon. Spellbound by the splendor about me, I sat bolt upright in the box. Then, to my astonishment, I saw Mother walk onto the stage, looking not at all like my mother—for usually she was in a trailing robe or an evening gown—but like a young boy!

"That's my Mummy!" I piped up excitedly and was promptly shushed by Gerdes, while faces below turned up and stared at me. I gazed at my mother, fascinated. She wore a boy's white felt suit, white jacket with red collar, white pants, and long, knee-length black patent leather boots. Only her voice was familiar, and the way she tossed her head when she was annoyed.

In one scene she suddenly became very angry. She seized a candlestick and smashed it into a mirror with a shattering noise. I was terrified. This was really Mummy. Then, just before the curtain fell, she sank to the floor. She lay there without moving. I became panic-stricken. In the absolute silence of the theater I screamed, "Oh, Mummy's dead!" and burst into tears. An embarrassed Gerdes had to lead me out, sobbing. She tried to comfort me.

"It's only a play, darling," she repeated again and again. "It's only make-believe. You'll see Mummy right away and she'll talk to you and kiss you. She isn't dead at all." And Mummy was there a few minutes later, smelling of something that was to become so familiar to me in later years—grease paint and powder—and she was hugging me close, with many murmurs of, "Oh, my little Catkin, I didn't want you to be frightened. My little Catkin!"

I clung to her. I didn't know in words what I wanted to say to her, I knew it only in my heart.

CHAPTER THREE

I LEARNED THAT I was a lady at seven. That was when Mother returned from France and we moved into a three-story graystone on East End Avenue overlooking the East River. It had a charming little garden to play in and I was delighted—until Mother made it clear that I was to have nothing to do with neighborhood children. "They're common, Catkin," she explained. "They're not as well brought up as you. I don't wish you going to their homes or bringing them here." I obeyed.

I was enrolled in Miss Hewitt's Classes, a select private school for girls, and perhaps Mother thought I'd choose playmates from among the chic little ladies there, although she considered few of them really ladies either. But I was shy, the girls were already banded into cliques—the Astors and Vanderbilts always voted for each other in class elections—and I felt out of it. My schoolmates included Gloria Caruso, the dark, pretty daughter of the great tenor; Brenda Frazier, a chubby little girl with huge black eyes and the whitest skin I'd ever seen; gay, roly-poly Rosemary Warburton, stepdaughter of William K. Vanderbilt; Tucky French, who was to marry John Jacob Astor; Edith Gould, Jay Gould's granddaughter, both quiet and studious; and a lovely little blonde, my distant cousin, Cobina Wright, Jr., whom I envied so much because she was everything I was not—slender, fair, straight-legged, beautiful.

41

Years later her mother, Cobina Wright, Sr., told me how she had brought Cobina to visit Mother and me at Grandma Tibi's, in Newport. We children had never met. "You were swinging away so solemnly in the back yard," Cobina Wright, Sr., told me. "The moment you saw Cobina, you jumped out of the swing, ran to her, and threw your arms around her in a bear hug, crying, 'Oh, I love you, I love you, you're so pretty, so pretty!' " Cobina, startled, struggled to free herself, but I hung on so passionately that she began to cry and her mother had to rescue her.

I have little memory of this, but it fits into the picture of myself as a child. I was affectionate. Instinctively I sought affection from my mother, but she was too imperious, too remote. She was like a great lady out of a story book. She seemed always to breast forward against the wind, like a magnificent figurehead on the prow of an old pirate ship. She never walked, she strode; she never appeared, she made an appearance; she never spoke, she declaimed in a hauntingly melodious voice said to be one of the four or five finest speaking voices in the world. There was an electric quality about her. She carried herself like a little general, her back rigid, her chin up, her dark eyes flashing—a figure so full of vitality, so striking, that when she entered a room she extinguished everyone else in it. People invariably exclaimed, "Who *is* that woman?"

Most of the time I wasn't allowed to see her. Because for hours each day she was a recluse, writing pages of poetry behind the locked door of her room. She called it "The Captain's Cabin." On the top floor, it had portholes instead of windows; it was lit by ship's lanterns hanging from the ceiling; and her bed was a wooden bunk suspended by whitewashed chains. I wasn't permitted to enter unless she summoned me by a little bell. Margaret and Sarah, the two maids, and Gerdes herself made that clear. "Miss Strange is never to be disturbed when she is working," they warned me. Another rule was that I could only introduce her as "My Mother, Miss Strange"—never as just "Mother."

She rang her bell for breakfast usually about noon and took it in bed, a tray brought her by Sarah. She flew into a rage if the mail that came up on her tray carried disconcerting news about Robin and Leonard at school, or a clipping sent by a friend reporting the latest gossip about Daddy.

One Saturday I heard her roar, "Get out of here! Bring that tea back when it's hot!" I dashed out to see Sarah running down the long, booklined hall, holding the spurned breakfast tray before her in both hands, exclaiming under her breath, "Hail Mary! O Mother of God, preserve us!" That is one of my most vivid early recollections: Sarah, distraught, forever running in and out with Mother's tray; Sarah praying up and down the hall.

When I ventured, always with my heart beating a little faster, to knock on Mother's door—my private signal was two quick, two slow thumps—I never knew if I would hear, "Come in," or an imperious, "Stay out! Stay out! I can't talk to you now." If it was "Come in," I pushed open the door. Mother usually lay languidly in her bunk, in a blue quilted robe, her left hand trailing on the floor, a pad of white paper in her lap, a pencil in her right hand, and crumpled snowballs of paper all about her. The room would be in disarray: skirts, blouses, scarves draped over chairs; shoes on the floor; a confusion of lipsticks, lotions, letters, telegrams, keys, and money on the dressing table. Mother never picked up after herself.

She would look at me vaguely, her mind far away. "What is it, Catkin?"

"Oh, Mummy, we're having a musicale at school and Gloria Caruso is going to sing and Miss Hewitt wants me to stand up and recite in front of everybody."

Mother impatiently ripped a sheet of paper from her pad, crumpled it, and tossed it away. "No, I don't think so, Catkin." She was already writing on the clean page. "She can exploit that Caruso child, but she won't exploit you." Her pencil paused and she looked directly at me. I always felt a little frightened when Mother looked directly at me. "The only reason she chose you is because she knows your name is Barrymore. We won't have any of that! Tell her thank you, but say your mother doesn't wish you to be the center of attraction. Now, go along and let me work, Catkin."

"Yes, Mummy." I slipped out, making sure to close the door silently behind me.

Now legally separated from Daddy, Mother loved to surround herself with attractive and accomplished ladies and gentlemen, and she selected her friends with great care. Since my brothers were away, I found myself pressed into service to entertain celebrities in the sitting room until Mother, always late for appointments, was ready to come down and receive them. Some were suitors, some part of her literary circle. I was never able to separate them in my mind. But there were always visitors in the late afternoon.

Martha opened the front door and relieved the guest of his hat and coat. That was my signal to appear, like a little usher, dressed in my accordion-pleated party frock reaching to two inches above my knees. I curtsied as Mother had taught me, and enunciated clearly, "Miss Strange is expecting you. She will be down in a few moments. Won't you come this way, please?" and led Mother's gentleman caller into the parlor. Then I smoothed out my skirts and sat primly in a chair. Sometimes the visitor simply stood and looked curiously at me, sometimes he sat down and asked me polite questions about school. The moment Mother appeared, sweeping into the room with her hand outstretched, I rose, curtsied, and excused myself. I had been taught that too.

Usually the names meant nothing to me. A Mr. Cole Porter and a Mr. Alexander Woollcott and a Mr. Clarence Mackay and a Mr. Harrison Tweed and a Mr. Noel Coward, and a Mr. Averell Harriman who took Mother dancing (so Martha whispered to me). A Mr. Thornton Wilder, a soft-spoken man who wrote, a Mr. Eugene O'Neill, a very silent man who also wrote, a Mr. Louis Bromfield, a hearty, chuckling man who wrote, too, and a Mr. Sinclair Lewis, whose face was mottled and red, and whose hair was red, and who had an explosive laugh, and who also wrote.

Once the name did mean something. I knew it was a special occasion because Mother called me into her room. "Catkin," she said, "you're going to meet a genius this afternoon. Charlie Chaplin is coming to tea. I want you to go downstairs and wait for him. I'll be down right away."

"Charlie Chaplin!" I was wide-eyed.

"Yes," she said. "He'll be here any minute. Now, you go."

I tripped happily downstairs. There had been gaiety about the house, because Robin was home on vacation. Leonard had gone to spend his holiday with his father. Mother was always less irritable when Robin was with her. She adored him.

I waited in the hall with Martha. I heard a car grind to a stop outside. I rushed to the window and pressed my nose against the pane. The first thing I saw was a crowd of nearly twenty children who almost engulfed a quick-moving little man dismounting from a large black car. I watched, puzzled, as he pushed his way through them to our steps. They were all stretching their hands out, and he was distributing little slips of paper—movie passes. Somewhere in the rear of the excited crowd I saw Robin, a satisfied smile on his face.

I'd seen Charlie Chaplin only on the screen in his tramp costume, and when Martha opened the door I didn't recognize the handsome, blue-eyed man in blue overcoat and Homburg who advanced on me. I stared at him, feeling cheated.

"Of course you're Diana," he said to me as he gave his coat and hat to Martha. He smiled, a boyish smile that lit up his face. "Did you set all your friends on me?"

I came to with a start. "Oh, no, Mr. Chaplin. I don't know anything about that." Then I remembered my manners. "Miss Strange will be down in a few minutes——"

He laughed, put his arm around my shoulder, and we walked into the parlor just as Mother, in time for once, made her entrance. Mr. Chaplin greeted her warmly. They spoke for a moment and then Mother looked at me. I curtsied prettily and said, "I have to go now, Mr. Chaplin. Good-by. It was so nice to have met you."

Minutes later Robin strolled by me backstairs. "Oh, Robin," I exclaimed, "doesn't he look different without his mustache and funny pants and cane?"

Robin smiled loftily and jingled his right hand in his pocket. "Money," he said. "Lots." He pulled his hand out and it was full of change. "I charged everyone a quarter for the privilege of meeting our guest," he said. He looked at me. "You're lucky I didn't make you pay."

"Oh," I said, outraged. "Really, Robin!" I used Mother's most devastating word. "Sometimes you're so *common!*"

Robin was to have a tragic life. He was born three centuries too late. He should have lived in the days of Louis XIV, a courtier in lace cuffs and powdered wig. Robin was Dorian Gray come to life. He was elegant and exquisite, and he loved the elegant and exquisite. His face was angelically beautiful. His eyes were startlingly blue, his features small and perfect, his pale skin so translucent that I felt if I were to push my finger against his cheek, I would touch not soft flesh but the finest Dresden china.

If I was shy, Robin was the opposite. My first memory of him was of a tall boy—he was then twelve—with a shock of ash-blond hair sitting at dinner with Gerdes and me and demanding that she break a raw egg into his tomato soup. Gerdes did as she was told. I watched, appalled.

"Ooooh, Robin," I exclaimed, wrinkling my nose in distaste. "How can you eat that? It makes me sick just to look at it."

Robin glanced disdainfully at me. "Diana, you're such a little peasant!" he said witheringly and applied himself to his soup. He enjoyed rare, exotic foods and sauces, and expensive, elaborate clothes. Until he was nearly eight, Mother kept him in long, golden curls; he could have posed for a portrait of a princeling of any royal house of Europe.

My brother Leonard, then seventeen, was tall and slender, with Mother's brown eyes and his father's air of reserve. I saw little of him during my childhood. As Robin was happiest with Mother, so Leonard got along best with his father and was either away at school, in France, or living with him in Palm Beach.

When Robin was home, he had two rooms to himself—a bedroom and a playroom, the latter a wonderland of mechanical toys from F. A. O. Schwarz, complete to a movie projector. I was not permitted in his playroom, and I resented it. Once, hearing the whirring of the machine, I knocked timidly at his door. "Robin, you're showing something I very much want to see—won't you please let me in?"

"Oh, go away," came his voice. "You're much too young."

I wandered into his closet and tried on some of his clothes.

If I were only a boy, I thought, I wouldn't be kept out of that room and I could see all the wonderful pictures . . .

Robin came in unexpectedly. Instead of becoming angry, he laughed. "Let's go to your room," he said. He rummaged about my closet and found a yellow satin pleated dress I wore for dancing lessons. As I watched, he put it on. He gazed at himself in the mirror, front and side.

"Look at me and look at you," he said. "Really, I should have been the girl instead of you because I'm so much prettier."

I thought of my crooked teeth and my little mouth and my off-center nose. "I know, Robin," I said humbly. He stepped out of the dress and tossed it back to me. "You do have pretty eyes—what you can see of them under those frightful bangs."

He teased me unmercifully. Among his possessions was a mechanical tiger as large as a cat. He knew I was afraid of it. One night I awakened suddenly with a sense of panic. There was an animal in my room, growling. I felt the weight of something alive on my legs. I managed to switch on the light. A few feet from my nose, Robin's tiger, terrifyingly lifelike, was poised on my blanket. It snarled, jumped half a foot toward me, snarled, and drew itself up to leap again. I scrambled wildly out of bed and rushed into the hall, shrieking, "Margaret! Sarah!"

Mother was in the Captain's Cabin, a flight above. She hurried out on the landing. "What is it? What is it?"

I was shaking, no longer with fear, but with fury. "Come into my room, Mother—you see what Robin did!"

She came in, trailing her long robe. Then, "Oh, Diana," she said. "He really didn't mean to frighten you. He was just playing a little game."

"A game, Mummy?" I followed on her heels into Robin's room. He was in bed, reading. "Now, Robin-cat," Mother said. "Did you mean to scare Diana?"

Robin was all innocence. "Oh, Mother, no. I meant it just as a joke."

"Well, of course you did, Catkin," Mother said. "I *knew* that's all you meant." She turned to me. "You know it's only a toy, Diana. You needn't have become so hysterical." She kissed us both and was gone in an eddy of the lemony perfume she always wore. I was left standing, looking at Robin.

His eyes met mine in a smug little look, as if to say, "Aha, you see? I can do anything I want to you, and Mother's never going to say a word to me."

I knew he was right. When Robin and I screamed profanity at each other, it was I who had my mouth washed out with soap; and when we fought and Robin tore my hair and I scratched his face, it was Robin whom Mother took to the Captain's Cabin for comforting, and I who was locked in my room without supper to ponder my disgraceful temper.

There was never any doubt of it. I knew my mother loved him best.

CHAPTER FOUR

THEN, SUDDENLY, my parents were divorced. I wasn't told about it, but one night Mother came into my room and sat on the edge of my bed. She began to talk to me. How were my studies? I was surprised for she hardly ever asked about my school work. Was I quarreling with Robin? She was happy to learn from Gerdes that I was finishing my breakfast each morning. Maybe I would stop gorging myself on bonbons all day. Then, unexpectedly, "Catkin, you like Harry Tweed, don't you?"

"Harry Tweed, Mummy?" For a moment I wasn't sure which one of her many callers Mr. Tweed was.

She described him, and I knew. He was the tall, slow-smiling man who let me climb up on his shoulders and then carried me about the room so I could pull out books from the topmost shelves. "Oh, yes, Mummy, he's nice, he plays with me."

"Would you like it if he became your stepfather?" she asked. "If I married him and he lived with us?"

All that passed through my mind was what fun I'd have climbing all over him. Then a sudden thought struck me. "I'll still have my real Daddy, won't I?"

Mother's voice, when she wished, could be a caress. "Of course you will, Catkin." She bent down and kissed me, and I was engulfed in lemony fragrance. "You know, he lives far away and he's married again, and that's why you don't see him."

That summer of 1929 in London, six months after Daddy married Dolores Costello in Hollywood, Mother married Harrison Tweed, a distinguished attorney of impeccable social background who was later president of the New York Bar Association. I was their flower girl. When we returned to New York the following year, it was to a luxurious new apartment at 10 Gracie Square, with a balcony overlooking the East River. Here, save for summers abroad or spent at Harry's country estate at Montauk Point, Long Island, I was to live from my ninth to my twenty-first year.

Directly across the street from 10 Gracie Square was the Brearley School, where Mother had gone. Because it was so convenient, I was transferred there from Miss Hewitt's Classes that autumn. I was not a good student, nor was my record anything to be proud of in the half-dozen other schools I attended later. I was never expelled, as Mother had been; sometimes, at the end of the year, I was requested not to return. In the early grades I was withdrawn and stubborn. Then I developed a brashness, an impatience, which never let me sit still or remain silent if I wanted to speak out. I took a secret pleasure in breaking rules. I hid food in my desk. I never took assignments seriously. Although I was really bright and quick, everything bored me, except art and English. I drew well—mostly grotesque dwarfs, misshapen houses, wraithlike trees. If I eked out a C in history, it was despite the fact that my schoolbook hid a copy of D. H. Lawrence's *Lady Chatterley's Lover*. It was forbidden reading, so I read it, feeling very sinful yet fascinated by the taboo world of sex it opened to me. Time and again a teacher marched down the aisle to seize my contraband literature.

I had already learned, at Miss Hewitt's, where babies came from. (I didn't dare ask Mother.) Brenda Frazier and Cobina Wright and I whispered about the mystery after watching a pregnant woman walk down the street. Brenda and I suspected that we knew the answer, but we weren't sure. "Why don't you ask your mother?" I told Cobina. I knew she talked everything over with her. "I will," she said. "I'll ask her when I get home from school today."

Next morning in the girls' room she told us. She had taken her mother into the bathroom, locked the door, and demanded, "Mommy, Brenda Frazier and Diana Blythe said that when a woman has a big stomach it means she's going to have a baby. Is that true?"

"Yes, that's right," her mother said. God planted a seed that grew like a lovely flower into a beautiful little baby.

I looked at Brenda. "Yes," I said. "But how does the seed get there?"

Cobina hadn't thought of that. "I'll ask my mother," she said promptly. Next morning she reported back. Her mother had told her that God gave fathers the power to plant the seed, that when she was older she would understand it all. Neither Brenda nor I could comprehend this miracle now because we were too young and didn't know enough.

But for someone who had read *Lady Chatterley's Lover,* it wasn't so hard to understand.

At 10 Gracie Square Mother knocked a wall out to make an enormous sitting room suitable for her literary soirées, and decorated a bright new study in which to write and prepare her lectures, "The Stage as an Actress Sees It." On occasional Saturdays she took me walking along the East River while she composed poems aloud. I trailed after her as she strode along swiftly, bareheaded, with her walking stick, a blue cape flowing behind her, the wind whipping her long bobbed hair. She practiced voice exercises. "O wiiild wessst winnnnd, thou breath of Au-tumn's beee-ing." She would turn and wait for me to catch up, then start off again. "Repeat after me, Diana," she would order, and hurrying along, trying to keep up with her long strides, I would do my best. "You have a nasal voice, just like your father," she said once. "I'm going to start giving you voice lessons." When we returned to the apartment, she instructed me at the piano, running up and down the scales, making me intone vowels after her, teaching me how to hum like a bee to clear my nasal passages.

We had been at Gracie Square only a few months when I came home from school to find her waiting impatiently. "Catkin, your father is in town. He'll be over in a few minutes. Get out of that uniform and into your blue dress. Be quick about it."

She didn't need to urge me. My father! I flew up to my room and dressed, all thumbs. I'd never met my father! I had a picture of him in *The Sea Beast,* which he'd sent me when I was eight, and I had hung it on my wall in the place of honor over my bed. But that wasn't like meeting him. Then I was downstairs, waiting tensely with Mother.

He came in the door—a tall, slender man in gray, head held a little to one side as if he were questioning someone. "Hello, Fig," he said to Mother. They shook hands but did not kiss. He turned and held out both hands to me. "Hello, Treepee," he said softly. I walked over to him and he knelt down and held me close for a moment. There was a smell of after-shave lotion about him, tangy, like peppermint. He drew back and looked at me.

"Who does she take after, Fig?" he asked.

Mother shook her head. Her voice was subdued. "I don't know, Jack. I think she has my eyes, but there's something of you in the expression about the mouth——"

"You know, Treepee," Daddy said to me, "you look a little like your Aunt Ethel. I think you really do."

Mother said, "I'll be back in a minute, Jack," and was out of the room, leaving me alone with my father.

He sat down cross-legged on the floor. "Why don't you sit in that chair, Treepee," he said. I took the chair and sat, ill at ease. "I understand you like to paint," he said. He drew out a cigarette, lit it, and looked around the room. There was a Daumier at one end and, over the fireplace, Monet's painting of the Houses of Parliament in London. He pointed to it. "Do you like that?"

"Oh, yes, Daddy." Then I was silent. All I could think was, *he doesn't have a nasal voice!*

"Michael says you draw very well," he went on. "She showed me one you made of the castle of Ludwig of Bavaria. I thought it ver-ry good. That's what I used to do."

I said, "Yes, Daddy, I know." I remembered having been told that.

"Would you like to be an artist? I wanted to be once."

"I think so, Daddy," I said. I was silent again. There was so much I wanted to say and I didn't know what to say. He continued to talk about painting, and how Monet managed to get the effect of reflected moonlight on the windows in his painting. "That's a very great art," he said.

Then Mother was in the room. "Catkin, your father and I want to talk. He's got to make a train very soon. Say good-by to him."

I kissed him and almost ran from the room. I'd hardly had a chance to talk to my own father! Somehow I hadn't expected it to be that way.

Harry Tweed had news for me at breakfast a few days later: Mother was writing a play about Lord Byron, the poet. "It makes Michael very nervous, writing," he went on. "Just remember that if she seems short with you, old top."

Mother worked furiously, locking herself in her room all day. Every rule was doubly invoked. Any kind of noise—a conversation outside her door, a clattering of dishes in the pantry, a dropped book—threw her into a frenzy, so that all of us, from Harry to cook, spoke in hushed tones.

Toward evening she made her appearance—elegant, perfectly groomed, exquisitely controlled—looking at all the world and the people in it as though they existed on a level slightly under her nose. Everyone, I came to realize as I grew older, treated Mother as she expected to be treated, as though she required a red carpet spread before her. Even now a scene comes vividly to me of her grandness and my fear. Mother was to take me and three classmates to the operetta, *Roberta*. It was an occasion for me. I had begged for guests because I had so few friends: maybe this would make me more popular. I dressed with great care in my room. I had spent the summer with Grandma Tibi, who was given to European laces and trinkets and furbelows, and she had chosen most of my wardrobe.

I looked pretty, I thought, as I hurried downstairs where Mother waited with my guests.

Mother took one look at me. Her eyebrows arched, her back stiffened, she became tense. Her right hand flew to her hip, to the sword side—so she had stood in *L'Aiglon*—and her eyes flashed.

"Diana! Where on earth did you get that frightful dress?"

I stood transfixed. Mother could fly into a maniacal rage in the blink of an eyelash.

"Grandma Tibi bought it for me," I ventured, praying she would not humiliate me before my friends.

"And that hideous beaded bag?"

Tears were springing to my eyes. "Grandma Tibi," I managed to whisper.

"Diana!" Her voice rang out through the room. The girls seemed turned to stone. "Diana, you look like a clown riding to a circus! I will not take you to the theater like that. Take off those garish trappings instantly and put on your white tulle. You might at least try to look like a civilized member of society!"

I turned and rushed blindly up the stairs. *I hate her! I hate her! I hate her!* I wept to myself. *How could she!*

Her sudden changes of mood, the lightninglike flashes of anger that shook her, bewildered me. Once, months later, I begged for a pair of red slippers to wear to a party. "No," she said. "You wear your patent leathers."

"But Mother," I protested, "everybody's wearing red."

"You are not everybody and you never will be," she retorted. "You're a lady and you'll dress like a lady."

I dared to talk back. "I don't care," I shouted. "I want to wear red!"

She slapped me stingingly across the mouth. I fell back, startled. Then she exploded. "You'll wear what I tell you to wear, my girl, and there'll be no nonsense about it!" Her voice rose to a scream and she took a step forward. "Goddamn it! I'm an artist! I can't be bothered with all these stupid——" Words failed her. She whirled around, strode out of the room, and slammed the door.

I stood, trembling, on the verge of screeching at the top of my lungs against the monstrous injustice of it all.

A moment later there was a rush of footsteps in the hall outside and Mother burst into the room. She threw herself on her knees beside me, hugged me to her and cried tearfully, "Oh, my Catkin, how can I be so harsh to you! Will you forgive me, Catkin! We must never fight again! I love you more than anything in the world!" I melted, flung my arms around her, and wept with her. "I know, Mother, it was my fault, I won't do it again, I promise, Mother." And we rubbed away each other's tears and forgave each other.

It was always to be like that. The only time I received a show of affection from Mother was immediately after she hurt me. It was always the slap—and then the kiss.

Even when she was calm, Mother was unpredictable. She could be utterly charming to my friends—and amazingly rude. We would be chatting happily, all of us, Mother included, when she would suddenly become silent, a strange reserve fallen upon her. If she spoke, it was only to make a caustic remark. After a few moments she would stand up and, without another word, walk out.

I'd excuse myself and hurry after her. "But, Mummy, why——"

"Oh," she'd say, "those terribly common friends of yours! Why *must* you bring them here?"

I was never prepared for anything Mother might do.

Nor was I ever sure how she would react to my attempts to confide in her. Most of the time she seemed impatient or abstracted; at other times her expression was such that I froze up. It wasn't that she told me not to tell her anything. She was disinterested. She was bored. And something in me died if I thought I bored her.

Yet, secretly, I was proud of my mother. She was so beautiful, so brilliant, so talented. One day a girl brought to class a clipping from the New York *Times*. "Isn't this your mother?" she asked. It read:

MICHAEL STRANGE ACTS IN OWN PLAY

The very exotic and versatile figure of the American stage and literature, Michael Strange—known in society as Mrs. Harrison Tweed—upheld her reputation tonight at the Westchester Playhouse by playing in a superb manner the two most important roles in her new theatre vehicle, "The Byrons" . . . She reached splendid heights of dramatic presentation . . .

I never told Mother about the girl and the clipping. But I carried the notice around until it was dog-eared.

Harry Tweed, lean, blond, and imperturbable, took all this in his stride. He was involved in major legal cases, I knew— he was attorney for the Rockefeller interests—but he always found time to exchange a few words with me. Ours was a mad household, what with Mother's tantrums, her quarrels with Harry (she scorned his Union Club friends as dull, he thought hers Bohemian), her rows with me and with the servants ("Harry!" I heard her shout. "Will you tell them I am *not* to be called Mrs. Tweed? I know you're bloody important in Wall Street, but I *have* my own name and I want to be called *Miss Strange!* Will you make them understand!"), Robin's temperamental outbursts (when he was home) against the tawdriness of life in general and my stupidity in particular. Sometimes I felt the only certainty I knew was Harry's breakfast, unvaried for the twelve years I lived at 10 Gracie Square: two three-minute soft-boiled eggs, a bowl of Kellogg's Corn Flakes, toast, and coffee. I used to think to myself, everything's all mixed up like *Alice in Wonderland,* but here's something I can always count on: Harry's pleasant, "Good morning, Diana," and those reassuring soft-boiled eggs and Corn Flakes.

"Now, let's forget it, old top," he'd say when I met him as he returned from the office and he knew I'd gone through a scene with Mother. He'd kiss me on the cheek. "Tell me how school went today."

As a matter of fact, school was not going too badly at that time. I'd gained some little fame because of Mother. Now, overnight, a rumor spread that John Barrymore, the great star of *The Sea Beast,* the lover of Greta Garbo in *Grand Hotel,* was my father. I knew nothing about it until two classmates, who until then treated me as though I were invisible, rushed up to me. They wanted to settle an argument. The taller one said, "John Barrymore is really your father, isn't he?" The other interrupted, "I said that's not true. Your name is Blythe, so how can he be your father?"

"Of course he's my father," I said airily. "Blythe was our name way back, that's all."

The second girl wasn't convinced. "But he's in Hollywood—you never see him."

I couldn't let that pass. I couldn't let anyone know that I'd met my father only once, and then but for a few minutes. "Why, I go to see him all the time. I saw him in Hollywood only last summer."

That began it. I started to make up stories and to embroider on them. I described in detail Daddy's 250,000-dollar yacht, the *Infanta,* in which he and Dolores Costello were

cruising to South America. The newspapers told me all I
needed to know. I described his fabulous house on Tower
Road, the most spectacular in Hollywood. I'd met my famous
Uncle Lionel and Aunt Ethel, and Daddy had taken me to
the home of Clark Gable and I'd actually talked with Fredric March and Greta Garbo and Joan Crawford and Ronald
Colman. After supper I would pore over the entertainment
section of Harry's *Times* and in my room thumb over the
movie magazines I secretly bought (Mother thought them
trash) to see who was in Hollywood, and what pictures they
were making. I jotted the names down in my exercise book
and memorized them. Never had I studied a classroom subject so intensely. Of course, I told the girls, my father wrote
me the latest Hollywood gossip. Each day I met a barrage of
new questions and managed to answer them. Gloria Caruso
had been the celebrity at Miss Hewitt's: now I was one. I
loved it.

I became fascinated with my family history. In the Brearley
library I devoured everything I could find on the Barrymores. I read how Daddy's father, my grandfather Maurice
Barrymore—"attractive, witty, magnetic"—played with Madame Modjeska, Lily Langtry, Olga Nethersole, and Mrs.
Fiske, leaving a trail of broken hearts across the country. I
lingered over descriptions of Daddy's mother, my grandmother Georgie Drew Barrymore, who died in 1893 when
Daddy was only eleven. Critics wrote about her wit, her
vivacity, her "way of saying anything that came into her
head." Maybe *I* took after her, I thought. I read about my
great-grandmother, Mrs. John Drew, one of the greatest ladies of the American stage. Why, she alone made Philadelphia the theatrical capital of the United States nearly a
hundred years ago, when she managed the famous Arch
Street Theatre. I read about my great-great-grandparents,
Thomas and Eliza Trentner Lane, who earned their living
as actors in London in the reign of King George III . . .

I was impressed. Diana, I thought, really, what a family on your father's side too!

"Diana, child," Minnie Bell, the housekeeper, whispered to me. "Mrs. Tweed—I mean Miss Strange—wants to see you, right away." She nodded toward Mother's room meaningfully. I hurried down the hall, thinking, now what? Mother was resting in her chaise lounge.

"Sit down, Diana," she began, in her no-nonsense voice. "I was at a dinner party last night with Willie K's wife." (Although Mother was fond of William K. Vanderbilt, who had been a Newport beau, she was cool to Mrs. Vanderbilt, always referring to her as "Willie K's wife.") "She said to me, 'Michael, I didn't know Diana visited Jack in Hollywood this summer. How did you happen to let her go?'"

Mother looked at me. "I felt like a perfect fool. Now, Diana, where do you suppose she got that cock-and-bull story?"

I didn't know which way to turn. I tried to brazen it out. "I don't know, Mummy. Maybe she read it in one of those silly columns."

"I'll bet you don't!" she retorted. "Now it's a lie to top a lie! You've been telling that story all around school—Rosemary told her!" Mother was angry, and the more she thought about it, the angrier she became. "You know how I detest lies! You're just like your father! You're a congenital liar! He couldn't tell the truth if his life depended on it, and neither can you. If he took a walk and nothing happened, he'd come back and tell me the most fantastic story . . ." She ran her hand wildly through her hair. "Oh, Christ, am I going to have it all over again with you? Get out! Get out!"

I got out, fast. But I wasn't remorseful. I secretly admired Daddy for being so intelligent as to make up something interesting if nothing happened. Mother never knew how much I lied. Perhaps lied is not the right word. I *invented*. As once I'd made the Holy Family come to life, now I transformed 10 Gracie Square into a special world of my own. One entire floor of the building was unfinished, a series of empty cement rooms. There had been plans to build a squash court, a swimming pool, and other recreational facilities. But the depression halted these. Time and again I went down to the skeleton court and waved my wand. I was the champion playing a match. I won the gold cup, charmingly I congratulated my challenger on his valiant—but utterly vain—struggle. I moved on to the next room. It became a ballroom, with huge mirrors and glittering costumes, all of the period of Marie Antoinette, because I vaguely remembered being taken through Versailles by Nanny. And I was Marie Antoinette myself, regal and gracious, bowing to the lovely ladies and gentlemen who curtsied to me, averting their eyes as they did so lest they be blinded by my awful radiance . . .

As if to prove my stories could come true, Mother received a letter from Dolores Costello. "Would you consider sending Diana to us for a little while this summer?" she asked. "We have plenty of room and we'd love to have her. She really ought to become acquainted with her father and the rest of the family."

I'm not sure how I learned of the letter, but I did; I wanted desperately to visit Daddy. If Dolores wrote such a letter, he must want to see me! And there was Uncle Lionel, and a little half-sister, Deedee, two years old, and my new little half-brother, John, Jr.

Mother refused. I pleaded, but she was adamant. There was no reason for me to become emotionally involved with my father now. I was too impressionable, and in any event I was too young to go to California alone.

I threw a tantrum. I rushed into my bedroom screaming, "I'll kill myself!" I made for a window, seven stories above the East River, not sure whether I'd jump or not. Horrified, Mother grabbed me.

That night there were iron bars on my windows. Mother

explained, "I knew you were only play-acting, Catkin. You really wouldn't have jumped. But you might miss your footing and you *might* go out."

Staring at those bars, night after night, I made up my mind. If Mother was keeping me prisoner, like the Count of Monte Cristo, I'd escape. I'd run away to Daddy in Hollywood. I confided in Marjorie Willer, who was my age. Marjorie thought running away from home would be fun. I gathered up some of the money Mother always left about loose, packed three dresses, two of my drawings I thought Daddy would like, a bathing suit, and sunglasses, and stole out of the apartment just before dusk. Mother was incommunicado in her room and Harry hadn't returned from the office.

We went by way of Central Park, the two of us, bound for the bus station near Times Square, each with our little suitcases and great determination in our hearts. A half-hour later, trudging along in the growing darkness, we looked up to find two policemen planted before us. It was the end of our adventure.

And it led to my being sent to see Dr. Florence Powdermaker, the psychiatrist at Brearley.

CHAPTER FIVE

MOTHER WAS IN A RAGE. She strode back and forth, boiling. "How dare you tell her you have an unhappy home life! You've got everything in the world. Look at your closet —it's full of dresses. You go to the best schools. You go to Europe in the summer. No child is better off than you. My childhood wasn't half as happy as yours!"

Harry Tweed sat, silent, puffing his pipe, looking up now and then from the financial page of the *Times*. "Michael," he said. "Simmer down. If that's what the child told her, that's what she feels."

Mother turned on Harry. "Do you know *all* she told her?"

I *had* told Dr. Powdermaker a great deal. She had been kind and reassuring. For the first time an adult was interested in me and listened to me. She drew more from me than I dreamed I could reveal to a stranger. I told her my mother and stepfather quarreled, that I saw little of my mother and I wasn't allowed to see my father, and that my brothers were away at school and my governess lived outside the apartment and I had no one to talk to. Mother disapproved of nearly every girl in the neighborhood, so I couldn't play with them. I had one friend, Innes James, who lived next door, of whom Mother did approve, but Innes always had things to do with her own family. I told Dr. Powdermaker I hated the clothes I had to wear—I wanted longer dresses and higher heels and a permanent because I detested my straight hair, and Mother said no to everything. I couldn't stand wearing Mother's velvet dresses, which she insisted on having made over for me, and I couldn't stand the bathroom full of steam as Minnie tried to get the shine out of them. I told Dr. Powdermaker my daily routine: breakfast with Harry, then school, and after school, my bath and study in my room and no one seeing anyone else until the dinner bell. If Mother was giving a dinner party, I remained in my room and my dinner came in on a tray. Sometimes I was brought down to be introduced to Miss Gertrude Stein or Mr. Michael Arlen or Miss Tallulah Bankhead or the Duke of Alba. I stayed ten minutes, learning to be a lady. Then I was sent back to my room. I told Dr. Powdermaker of the long, silent evenings when Mother remained behind her locked door and Harry sat in the living room going over his legal briefs and the two maids entertained policemen friends in the kitchen and there was nothing for me to do.

"What do you do then?" Dr. Powdermaker asked.

"Oh, I go up to my room and study." It wasn't true. I lied to her. I was ashamed to tell her what I really did. I stood before the mirror and tried on dresses and attempted to curl my hair with spit and pretended I was Madame du Barry being wooed by handsome lovers—I had so many, they were like a deck of cards, I just shuffled and chose the most beautiful and fell into his arms, swooning . . .

"Thank you, dear," said Dr. Powdermaker. She telephoned Mother. I obviously had problems that needed discussing. Would she come to school and talk with her? And now Mother was livid. "All right," she said to me. "Go to your room. I think you put on a perfectly disgraceful performance! Harry," she said. "You go talk to that absurd woman. I won't."

She sat down abruptly and looked at me. I was astonished to see tears in her eyes. "The trouble I have with my children——" She rose suddenly and ran from the room.

"Michael!" Harry, a look of concern on his face, hurried after her. I slowly made my way to my room. I could not know that only a few weeks before, Robin and a classmate at school in Colorado Springs had entered a suicide pact. Robin swallowed his overdose of sleeping pills, but at the last moment his friend panicked and rushed for help and doctors had to pump Robin's stomach, and there had been a scandal.

I don't know what Harry was told by Dr. Powdermaker, or what he told her. But one day I was summoned to Mother's room to be informed that she and Harry had decided I was to go to a boarding school. I had been too much with adults and too much alone. I needed to be kept busy and to be surrounded by girls of my own age and background. They were sending me to Garrison Forest School, outside Baltimore. It was small, proper, exclusive, and there'd be no lack of activities—riding, tennis, swimming, dancing, music— to keep me busy. "Yes, Mummy," I said dutifully. Any change would be for the better. "I think I'd like that."

I was thirteen, going on fourteen, and I tried to buckle down at Garrison Forest, but I had a hard time adjusting to boarding school. I carried out Mother's orders to send her every month a list of books I had read, for her approval. The list I headed, "Books I Have Read, November, 1934," included twenty titles, among them *Ivanhoe, Never the Twain Shall Meet,* and Maxim Gorki's *Mother*—the last so sad that I wept.

With it I sent a note (proving I was a harsh dramatic critic): "Last Friday I saw the movie *Spitfire.* I thought it was awful, and Katharine Hepburn overacts so much! She has the most awful voice I have ever heard—she sounds like a little boy! And the plot was awful!" I added, "I hope you will be pleased to know that I buy only two movie magazines every two weeks now."

I did not write Mother that I had seen Katharine Hepburn before. I didn't tell her because the picture was *A Bill of Divorcement,* and Daddy played in it. I watched it with a mixture of emotions I could hardly express, less understand. In the film Daddy was an insane man who after fifteen years returns, cured, to his family, and meets his eighteen-year-old daughter for the first time. Katharine Hepburn played Daddy's daughter. *I* could have been Miss Hepburn, I thought. I really *was* his daughter . . . She was going up the stairs when he entered unexpectedly: she watched him as he stood there uncertainly, looking about trying to recall the room as it had been. Then she slowly came down the stairs to meet him, face to face. I had the strangest feeling when they met. Playing his make-believe daughter, Miss Hepburn couldn't have looked more searchingly into his face than I, sitting tensely in my seat in the movie. He was *handsome,* my father, more handsome than I had remembered him the brief few moments we'd been together at our only meeting. On the screen his eyes were dark, like Mother's, and when he grew angry and for a moment pretended he was going mad again, it was like Mother in one of her rages.

It's only a movie, I told myself. It's only a picture. In the film Miss Hepburn learned for the first time that there was insanity in her family. But Daddy's father, my grandfather Maurice Barrymore, really died in a mental institution . . . What a romantic idea, I thought! Insanity in the family!

When I came home for Christmas vacation, I found a surprise. Aunt Ethel was to be our dinner guest Christmas Eve and join us for midnight mass at St. Patrick's. Mother took me aside. "Catkin, when Aunt Ethel comes, let's all be charming. We don't like each other particularly, but, after all, it's Christmas."

Mother didn't explain any further what she meant, but I had always understood—as children know such things—that Mother and Aunt Ethel were distant, not only over the *Clair de Lune* episode, but also because Aunt Ethel, fiercely loyal to Daddy, felt he had gotten the worst of it with Mother. Now I said only, "Yes, Mother." I was eager to see my famous aunt: she'd visited us before, when I was too young to remember.

Aunt Ethel appeared, a tall, imperial lady in gray who swept into the room to be greeted by everyone, and then extended her hand, palm down, for me to take. There was something so regal about Aunt Ethel that people automatically rose when she entered. It was an indescribable quality —her bearing, her lovely, patrician face, her enormous eyes that held you . . . Overawed, I took her hand and curtsied. It was like being received by royalty. "Diana," she said. "How you've grown! You're lovely." Before I could utter a humble "Thank you," she had turned and was gazing raptly out our huge picture window. "Isn't that the most divine view!" she exclaimed, in her magnificently throaty voice. She couldn't take her eyes from it.

At dinner, after martinis in the drawing room, Harry sat at the head of the table, Mother at the foot, and Aunt Ethel at Harry's right. I divided my time between the turkey and Aunt Ethel, stealing glances at her from where I sat next to Mother. Hadn't Daddy said I looked like my Aunt? She was beautiful! I was flattered, but I could see no resemblance. As dinner progressed, Aunt Ethel turned repeatedly to the window. "Isn't that the most divine view!" she repeated. You saw the dark expanse of the East River, the garland of lights over Welfare Island, and the black tracery of the bridges spanning the river. It was beautiful. At dessert Aunt Ethel turned again and, for the fourth or fifth time, exclaimed, "Isn't that the most divine view!"

"My God, I wish she'd take it with her!" Mother muttered under her breath. I could hardly believe my ears. I stole a glance at Aunt Ethel, but apparently she hadn't heard.

There had been considerable wine during dinner, and brandy after dinner. Presently it was time for us to leave for mass. Aunt Ethel rose in her chair, stood unsteadily for a moment, then sat down abruptly. "Oh, dear," she said. Harry gave her his arm. She rose again, pushed the chair back, ventured a step, slipped, and fell.

Then several things happened simultaneously. Mother spoke up swiftly. "Oh, I'm so terribly sorry, Ethel. These floors have just been waxed and I haven't been able to do a thing with them!" Robin leaped to Harry's aid, and together they helped Aunt Ethel to her feet. She sat for a moment, her hand to her forehead. "Robin-cat," said Mother smoothly. "I don't think Aunt Ethel feels well. Do take her into my bedroom and let her rest. Perhaps you should stay with her."

Robin was only too happy. He hadn't wanted to go to midnight mass anyway. He escorted Aunt Ethel into Mother's room, and Harry, Mother, and I went off to church. "Mummy," I asked on the way, "is Aunt Ethel very sick?"

Mother dismissed it. "Oh, I shouldn't worry, Catkin. It's just a Barrymore headache." She seemed almost gay.

Next morning Aunt Ethel was gone. I'd had hardly a chance to say more than hello to her!

At boarding school, when I found myself assigned to a large room with eight beds in it, I complained to the head mistresses —Miss Offutt, small, fluttery, gentle, and Miss Marshall, mannish, broad-shouldered, tweed-suited. "I'm afraid I'll have to have my own room," I said. "I can't possibly sleep with other girls."

Miss Offutt shook her head. "Everyone has roommates here, Diana. We can't make you an exception."

I became very grand. "I am *not* everyone," I replied stiffly. "I'm sure Mother wishes me to have privacy."

When the reply was still no, I rattled about in bed, I snored, I sighed, I whistled. The other girls were beside themselves. Within three days a beaverboard partition was erected—I had my own room. It didn't make me particularly popular.

I found myself succumbing to a terrible homesickness. I dared not telephone Mother. I began to dream about her.

It was the same dream night after night. In it Mother pursued me wildly, her eyes blazing, her voice rolling and echoing, her right hand flying to her side again and again. I had no idea why she pursued me or why I ran. She raced after me and I fled before her and I tried every trick to throw her off. Suddenly I turned into a steak, and the steak into tiny pieces, and each piece was alive, and all kept running in different directions so that she could never get all of me at once . . .

I would wake, starting up in terror—then, relieved, want her desperately.

Unexpectedly a letter came from her. "Catkin, your father has just returned from a trip to India. I've given him permission to visit you on one condition—you are not to leave the grounds with him. I want that understood . . ."

I ran to Miss Marshall. Could we have Daddy to dinner? It was arranged: tea, then dinner. I could invite two guests to join us at the headmistress' table. I asked Pam Gardiner, who was seventeen and always ready for fun. I got along better with older girls; besides, Mother knew Mrs. Gardiner. Then I invited Alice Fox because Foxie's father was the famous cartoonist, Fontaine Fox, and Daddy, I reasoned, would feel at home with her.

Monday afternoon, the day of his visit, crawled. Almost my entire class crowded the front porch of the main house as time came for Daddy's arrival. We always dressed for dinner, but tonight the girls outdid themselves. Never had such a celebrity visited the school. A few months before, we'd dined Foxie's father, and while Mr. Fox and his Toonerville Trolley were known everywhere, who could compare with John Barrymore? Who could have dreamed that the screen's greatest lover, in person, would call on the girls of Garrison Forest?

"There he is!" someone exclaimed. And there was a huge black limousine entering the far gate and beginning to roll up the long, curved driveway. I became panicky. "Please, everybody, go inside," I cried. "I want to meet my father alone."

The car halted before the steps leading up to the porch. The door swung open and Daddy stepped out. He looked as though he had walked out of one of his own films. He was wearing a tan polo coat, with a gray suit, and a gray hat pulled rakishly down over one eye.

"Treepee!" he exclaimed.

I tried to be grand, because I knew the girls were watching from the windows, but I couldn't. I found myself running down the steps and into his arms. He hugged me for a moment and then kissed me. "Well," he said, "you've grown into rather a young lady!" Then he added, "I've brought you the most di-vine records from India, and a machine to play them on." The chauffeur appeared, his arms full of packages, and trailed us as we went up the steps. It was all so unreal—here I was, walking with my own father . . . I didn't know what to say, so I said hurriedly, "Daddy, don't be horrified, but all the girls are panting to be with you. They're peeking out from behind the curtains right now. You'll be so bored."

"No, no," he said, almost as though he were shocked. "Don't say that, Treepee. You're the one I've come to see and as long as I'm with you, I certainly *won't* be bored."

We walked, arm in arm, into the house. Three girls were leaning nonchalantly against the fireplace. I didn't introduce him to them. I was out to impress, and I led Daddy straight into the library where Miss Offutt and Miss Marshall, with the full faculty lined up, were waiting nervously to greet him.

The next hours passed in a whirl. We had tea and cakes: he spoke brilliantly of his trip to India; when it was time to go in to dinner, he rose and offered his arm not to Miss Offutt or Miss Marshall but to me. As I swept in with him I thought, how popular I'll be now.

Later, in my room, Daddy sat down, a little out of breath from the stairs, and watched indulgently while I opened my gifts: records, a hammered copper kettle, strange little rings and bracelets studded with odd-colored stones. "You know, your grandfather Maurice was born in India," he said. I'd read about that: how my great-grandfather Herbert Blythe was a British judge in India during a great mutiny. Maurice Blythe was born in the dungeons of the British fort at Agra, where his mother had fled for safety. Later, Grandfather was sent to England to study at Harrow and Cambridge, but instead of turning to the practice of law, to his family's horror he became an actor. Not to embarrass them, he borrowed the name of Barrymore from a theater poster, and in 1875, at the age of twenty-eight, he came to the United States. "I never got around to visiting the fort," Daddy was saying. (Years later I learned why. He never got to Agra. En route, he stopped at a brothel, became fascinated, and hired it for his exclusive use for a week.) Now Daddy was talking about me. Mother had told him our school recently put on the play, *If I Were King*. Was I in it?

"I wasn't in that, Daddy," I replied. "But I'm in a French play—*Le Voyage de M. Perrichon*. I play a man's part, in man's clothes, with pillows to make me big in front——" I gestured.

"Ah," he said, and he knitted his brows as he had done in *A Bill of Divorcement*. "They've saddled you with the Barrymore curse." He rolled the r's of Barrymore. "Pillows and false faces, like your father." He lit a cigarette. "Do you like that, Treepee? Do you enjoy standing before strangers and saying lines you've memorized?"

I wasn't sure, I said. I loved make-believe. I loved to pretend. "Miss Penrose says I have a vivid imagination and that I can make myself believe I'm anyone I want to be."

He said nothing for a moment. Then, "You were rather good in art, I seem to remember. You liked to draw. Are you doing anything with that?"

My best marks were in art class, I said. "But everything I

do is strange and ugly, like dwarfs and devils . . . I never draw pretty faces."

He smiled. "Perhaps you take after me," he said. "Do you know, Treepee, I once wished to be an artist more than anything else? Does the name of Gustave Doré mean anything to you?" I nodded. We had studied Doré's sad, even frightening drawings. "Well, when I was a young man, I wanted to do for Edgar Allan Poe what Doré did for Dante—you know, he illustrated Dante's *Inferno*. I hoped to do the same thing with Poe's poems. They haunted me. But somehow——" He paused and drew deeply on his cigarette. "I never did much with it."

He changed the subject. "Wouldn't you like to hear some of these records? I'm told they're very good—I picked them up in Bombay." We played several. They were sad, wailing compositions. "I guess I don't understand that kind of music, Daddy, but maybe I will when I get older," I said.

And then the visit was over. He had to return to his hotel in Baltimore, an hour's drive away. He'd look in on me the next day, if he had the chance, before taking the train West.

I couldn't fall asleep that night. I was too stimulated. I knew something of what was happening to Daddy. Stories appeared about him in the newspapers which came to our library, and in my movie magazines. If I missed anything, one of the girls was sure to tell me about it. So I knew he and Dolores were separated and that he had been ill. I got out of bed, put on my robe, and hurried down the hall to Miss Penrose's room. She was my English teacher, a kindly, white-haired woman who was my one friend on the faculty. For a little while we talked, until I was calm enough to go back to bed.

After breakfast Miss Marshall beckoned to me. "We're going to make a special concession, Diana. Your father has asked to take you and one classmate to dinner tonight, and we're allowing you to go into town with him. I assume you'd like to invite Pamela——"

I was enraptured. It *was* a concession, because we could go into Baltimore only every other week end. As for Mother's order, I put it aside.

"Oh," exclaimed Pamela in delight. "Won't this be something to tell around."

Daddy called for us with two friends, a heavy-set man who was a night-club entertainer, and a slender young man who was a musician. I tried to look grown up. I wore a brown dress with a white collar and a pair of brown high-heel pumps I borrowed from Foxie. Mother never permitted me anything higher than a Cuban heel. I teetered about in Foxie's shoes half the afternoon learning how to walk in them.

In the car Daddy said, "We're going to rather a di-vine place, the sort of place you'd never go to, being in school."

Excitedly, I opened my purse and took out lipstick and dabbed at my mouth. Daddy watched me. "Are you supposed to be wearing that?" he asked doubtfully. "Of course, Daddy," I replied airily. "All the girls do when they go out."

We found ourselves in a luxurious restaurant. Daddy turned to me. "I don't know, Treepee, would you like something to begin with?"

He and the two men and Pamela had ordered cocktails. I'd never had liquor, save a little wine and water as children have with their meals in France.

"A drink, Daddy? I've never really had a drink."

"Oh," he said and turned to Louis, the entertainer. "That certainly does not sound like a Barrymore, does it?" He rolled his r's and pronounced his b's, p's, t's, and all hard consonants explosively, as though they were shot from a cannon. Then, almost to himself, he added, "Come to think of it, it does not sound like an Oelrichs, either." He summoned the waiter and told him what he wanted for me.

When it arrived I looked at it dubiously. "What is it, Daddy?"

"It's exactly like a milk shake. It's a brand-y Alexand-er."

"Oh," I said. "That sounds love-ly." I found myself mimicking Daddy. I took a delicate sip. It did taste like a milk shake, but it had a spicy flavor and left a warm glow in my throat. I liked it. By the time dinner was over, I had had two.

The head waiter whispered to Daddy. Newspaper photographers were outside. They'd learned Daddy and I were here, and insisted upon taking a picture. The public had never seen one of John Barrymore and his teen-age daughter. "Daddy," I ventured. "Mummy doesn't like my picture taken for newspapers."

Daddy lowered his head and from under knitted brows fixed me with an ironic stare. "I seem to recall a picture of you and Michael arriving on some ship from Europe," he said. "She did not seem particularly displeased by the photographer's bulb." He turned to the waiter. "Show them in." Then, while he looked at me and I smiled weakly at him, the flashes went off. The photographers thanked us and were gone.

"Indeed, Treepee," said Daddy, "you evidently come by it naturally. You handled yourself extremely well. Shall we celebrate this occasion with another drink, gentlemen?"

Now Daddy and his friends were chatting animatedly over coffee. Daddy had a large brandy glass before him; he finished it, and then a second. "Well, young ladies, this is your party. What would you like to do now?"

Pamela and I looked at each other. What did two women of the world do when they were on a date with the fabulous Barrymore? I spoke for both of us. "We'd like to go to the movies," I said. "They've got Fredric March in *Les Misérables* at the Century—and he's so wonderful! I saw him in *The Sign of the Cross* three times!"

Daddy all but cackled. He rose. "I must not forget to tell him that," he said. "Let us proceed."

"Daddy!" I exclaimed. "You *know* Fredric March? Really? Will you ask him to send me his autograph?"

Pamela stepped on my foot. But Daddy only laughed

again, and the two men smiled. "It is a solemn promise, Treepee."

At the Century Daddy sat with Pamela, and I sat between his two friends in the row behind them. At my right Will, the musician, after a few minutes put his arm around my shoulder. I was terrified but tried to pretend nonchalance. Nonetheless I sat stiffly through the film looking straight ahead. Daddy sat with his arm around Pamela and, as I watched, kissed her. I thought, horrified, "Why they're smooching! How disgraceful of Pamela, even if she is nearly eighteen!"

We came out at eleven-twenty. Daddy said, "I'd like another drink. And a little music."

"But Daddy," I protested, "I promised Miss Marshall we'd be home by twelve."

Daddy cocked an eye at a clock in a jewelry window. "We have time, Treepee. Never hurry your father." He took us to a night club and ordered drinks. "Another brandy Alexander?" he asked me. I shook my head. I felt a little queasy. I didn't know whether it was the sad story of *Les Misérables* or the brandy Alexanders. "I feel more like a sarsaparilla, Daddy," I said.

Daddy's left eyebrow rose. "Sarsa-parr-illa?" he repeated in a voice of disbelief. "Good God, do they permit it? Did that not go out with Prohibition? Why, Treepee, don't you know that sarsa-parrr-illa erodes your kidneys, gives you pyloric spasms, and turns your liver the color of ochre? The greatest savants of India have told me so." He turned to Louis. "Lou, have you not heard that, too?" Louis nodded solemnly, and not until Pamela giggled was I sure that Daddy was pulling my leg. "Waiter!" he called. When the waiter came he pulled him down, glanced surreptitiously to the right and left, and whispered in his ear, "For my daughter—no noise now—one sarsa-parrr-illa. Keep this to yourself, will you, like a good fellow?" The waiter was about to go. Daddy tugged him down again. "Would you bring me a double brandy?" he

asked. "And for this lovely vision"—he indicated Pamela—
"the same?" Pamela shook her head, but Daddy insisted.

After his two friends left, Daddy took Pamela and me
home by cab. He sat between us and his arm was around
Pamela. I dozed off, to wake with a start at the sound of
gravel crunching under our tires as we turned into the school
driveway. It was nearly one o'clock. Daddy and Pamela were
both asleep, leaning on each other's shoulders. As the cab
pulled up before the main house, the porchlight fell on
Daddy's face. It was smeared with lipstick. I wiped it off with
my handkerchief. He did not wake. I tried to rouse him, but
he was sound asleep. Pamela woke after a shake or two. I
kissed my father on the cheek. "Good night, Daddy," I said.
Then I turned to the driver. "Please take him home," I said
grandly.

The driver cleared his throat. "Miss, I hate to tell you
this, but your father is passed out. I can't drive him back to
town this way. He can't tell me what hotel he's staying at."

I'd never heard the phrase "passed out." But I gathered
that Daddy was drunk. I felt embarrassed and helpless. Pamela was standing at my side, drooping. There was nothing to
do but go inside and get help. A light glowed on the first
floor. I took Pamela by the arm and we trudged up the steps
and into the house. Miss Marshall was waiting up for us.

"Pamela, please go to your room at once," she commanded.
"You're older, you should have known better. Diana, go to
your room too."

"It wasn't her fault, Miss Marshall," I spoke up. "We both
tried to get home on time."

"Go upstairs, please."

"But Daddy's in the car and we can't wake him and the
driver doesn't know what hotel to take him to."

Miss Marshall, always competent, rose. "That's all right,
dear. You go up to bed. I'll take care of your father."

I was so sleepy. I fell into bed and awakened once—when
I heard the motor start and the grind of tires as Daddy's car

pulled away. Miss Marshall had brewed a pot of hot coffee, poured two cups into Daddy, and sent him back to Baltimore.

Next afternoon, just before dinner, Miss Offutt took me aside. She looked distracted. The New York newspapers had printed the picture of Daddy and me. Ten Gracie Square had had her on the telephone. "Your mother is so very angry because we let you go out with your father," she said unhappily. "We thought it perfectly proper—after all, we sent you with another girl who was known to her." Miss Offutt's hands fluttered a little helplessly. "I do hope when you see Miss Strange you will explain the circumstances."

Mother was not amused. "There's no excuse," she retorted when I told her. "They were monsters to permit it." The following year I was transferred to another boarding school— Fermata School for Girls, in Aiken, South Carolina. It was to mark the end of my formal education.

Daddy kept his promise. I received a letter from Fredric March in Hollywood. Daddy had informed him that I wanted an autographed photograph from *The Sign of the Cross*. He was delighted to send me one under separate cover. Then, in the next week, I was amazed to receive signed photographs from other top stars. Daddy obviously had asked, for me! They came from Joan Crawford and Charles Laughton and Marie Dressler. From Leslie Howard, whose gentleness made him one of my secret crushes: "To Diana Barrymore, in distant admiration." I all but swooned. From Phillips Holmes, whose sweetness tore at my heart too: "For Diana Barrymore—a princess in every right. May your kingdom always be happy and blessed."

I decorated my room with them. Daddy's photograph in *The Sea Beast* held the place of honor above my bed; a photograph of mad King Ludwig of Bavaria, which Robin had given me because he admired him so much, peered at me from the opposite wall; and arranged about Daddy were his famous friends, all wishing me the most wonderful things, looking down at me as I went to sleep each night and rose each morning.

CHAPTER SIX

THE DOCTORS SAID Daddy was recovering from influenza, but Mother sniffed. "I never heard it called *that* before!" She, Harry, and I were paying a visit to Daddy in New York Hospital. The time was April, 1935.

Daddy sat in his robe, looking pale but eager. "I'll be out of this place in twenty-four hours," he said. "Then I know pre-cise-ly what I need. I need to take Treepee with me on a cruise." He looked at Mother, who was beginning to show storm signals. "I mean it, Fig. It will be my salvation. It's time I knew my own daughter. The *Infanta* is anchored down at Miami. Let me take Treepee with any friend she wishes. I'll have my doctor and nurse along. We'll soak up sun and fish for barracuda."

"Please, Mummy?" I begged. I would have Easter vacation then and I'd ask Innes James, next door, as my guest.

Mother agreed reluctantly, on one condition—that Harry Tweed went along. "Capital!" cried Daddy. Harry thought it a good idea too. Mother took him aside. "But only if Jack doesn't drink. You'll have to watch him, Harry." To me Mother explained crisply that Harry was coming along as chaperone. After Baltimore she knew she couldn't trust me to Daddy alone.

When we reached Miami, Daddy said, "Treepee, you'll need casual clothes. You'd better buy yourself slacks, tennis shoes, and the like." He pulled a bill out of his pocket and stuck it into my hand. I stared: it was one hundred dollars! I'd never seen so much money before. My allowance from Mother was two dollars and seventy-five cents a week. Innes and I scooted off to Flagler Road, Miami's Fifth Avenue, for a wild shopping spree. The yacht seemed almost as large as an ocean liner, complete to its own fishing launch. "You and Innes will have my cabin," Daddy announced, escorting us into a magnificently furnished suite. (He and Dolores had spent their honeymoon aboard the *Infanta*.) The master bedroom had a gold and mahogany bed with a hand-painted Italian landscape on the mirrored headboard walls, thick carpets on the floor—it was like the chamber of some Indian potentate. Adjoining was a smaller cabin with a child's crib of inlaid rosewood and satinwood that might have been made for a little prince. "I had that built for your sister Deedee when she was born," Daddy said. He looked about the sumptuous rooms for a moment and led the way out silently. Then he was gaily introducing us to the captain and crew of ten men.

The cruise, as it turned out, was no cruise at all. When we reached a point five miles off Bimini, Daddy anchored the *Infanta*. Each morning Daddy, Harry, and Daddy's physician set out in the launch to fish for barracuda, leaving Innes and me in charge of the nurse. They returned each night in time for late dinner.

During the day Innes spent her time lounging in the sun, but I was in the throes of my first crush—over Eddie, the cabin boy. He was tall and slim, he had dark, liquid eyes, he sang beautifully; and when of an evening, dressed in his white mess jacket, he serenaded me with his guitar, leaning languidly against the ship's rail, silhouetted against the velvety tropical sky, he was romance itself. When we returned to New York, Innes had a lovely tan, but I came back chalk-white. I'd been too busy trailing Eddie about the ship, puppy fashion, to see much of the sun.

Mother questioned me about Daddy. "What did you and Jack talk about?"

I tried to remember. We had really said very little to each other. In fact, except for good morning and good night—and a daily warning not to swim in the ocean—nothing. "We didn't talk much about anything, Mummy," I said. "Daddy was always out fishing with Harry."

"I see," Mother said as only she could say it. "His salvation!"

There *had* been one day when Daddy talked to me—a day when he'd talked and cursed happily at everyone. He was drunk. Where he found the liquor was a mystery. Harry and the doctor had gone over the entire ship before Daddy came aboard, and gotten rid of every ounce. The liquor cabinets stood open, empty; the bar had only soft drinks. Each crew member had been sworn into the conspiracy to keep Daddy sober. Yet, on the fifth day, Daddy, sober at breakfast, appeared not long afterward, roaring drunk.

"It's uncanny," Harry said. Later, while Daddy slept it off, the *Infanta* was turned topsy-turvy in a search for his private stock. Nothing was found. Then an alert member of the crew recalled having seen Daddy snooping about the engine room. The mystery was solved. He had syphoned off nearly a pint of alcohol from the engine-cooling system. A guard was placed on duty. Next time Daddy sauntered down, he turned around and came right up. He never referred to the episode and I thought it just as wise to say nothing about it.

A few days after the yacht trip, Mother greeted me, happy as a child. "Robin's here," she said. "He's unpacking now."

"He is?" I was excited. Robin had been acting in Chicago. I rushed up to his room. "Robina!" It was my pet name for him. We hugged each other. As we grew older, we became greater friends. We adored each other.

He was bubbling over. "Cat, I'm doing what I really want. Finally!" He had been hired by a family friend, Mrs. Bror Dahlberg, wife of the Celotex king, who out of sheer boredom backed numerous plays. Robin was appearing in her stock company's production of *The Green Bay Tree*. Robin, now twenty, had tried his hand at many things, writing, painting, studying music in Vienna, publishing an *avant-garde* magazine in London, but nothing had satisfied him.

He was burrowing into his luggage. "Ah, here it is!" He brought out a photograph and placed it on his bed table.

I looked at it. It seemed all eyes at first. Then I saw a beautiful young man with enormous black eyes and incredibly long lashes that actually cast shadows on his cheeks gazing dreamily out at me. I knew of whom he reminded me— Mother had a bust of Apollo in the sitting room. This was it come to life.

"My God, Cat, who is that?"

Robin looked at the photograph admiringly. "Isn't he divine, Diana? It's Tyrone Power, Jr. His grandfather was the great Irish actor." Tyrone was in Mrs. Dahlberg's company, too, and Robin had invited him to stay with us when he came East to look for a job after the season ended.

I couldn't get over Tyrone Power. I sighed and dreamed. He belonged on my wall. I mustered up courage to write him:

> Dear Mr. Power:
>
> I'm so delighted you're coming to stay with us. Robin showed me your photograph and I must say you look like a Greek God. I do hope you'll bring me a signed photograph of yourself. I'm waiting in great anticipation to meet you in person.

Tyrone's reply came:

> My dear Diana:
>
> Thank you so much for your very sweet letter. But I must also say, to save you any disillusionment when I arrive in New York, I am in no way a God, much less a Greek one. But we will have plenty of time to settle that question. I

sincerely hope you will be home when I arrive. You go
away to school or something, don't you . . . ?

The last line took me down a bit, but I didn't care. He'd
promised to bring me his picture and autograph it in my
presence.

Suddenly, back at school, the newspapers were full of
Daddy and a nineteen-year-old Hunter College student
named Elaine Jacobs who had changed her name to Barrie,
because it sounded like Barrymore. Daddy had taken her on
a cruise aboard the *Infanta!* Dolores asked Daddy for a divorce, and Miss Barrie was following Daddy all the way to
Hollywood, because she wanted to be Mrs. Barrymore. "I
call him Caliban and he calls me Ariel," I read in the Baltimore *Sun,* which was well thumbed in the Garrison Forest
library. I knew who Caliban and Ariel were—they were in
Shakespeare's play, *The Tempest.* But Caliban was ugly, and
Daddy wasn't ugly . . . I couldn't understand it. I thought,
suppose Daddy and Miss Barrie get married? How strange
it will be for me to have a stepmother who's only twenty—
hardly older than Pamela Gardiner!

At Thanksgiving Dinner at 10 Gracie Square, I innocently
brought up the subject. Mother froze in the act of serving the
soufflé. When she spoke, it was with suppressed fury. "That
woman's name is never to be mentioned in this house again!
Never again!" she said. It never was.

Christmas vacation I came down to breakfast to find an extra
plate, and Harry already at the table with his paper. "Is
Mother getting up this morning?" I asked, surprised.

Harry looked up. "No, Robin's friend's arrived."

Oh! It's that divine Tyrone Power, I thought. I sat down
and waited breathlessly. Robin, apparently, was due on a
later train. I heard footsteps, and then Tyrone, in person, in
a dark, striped suit, walked in. "Good morning, Mr. Tweed,"

he said, and they shook hands. He put out his hand to me. I sat, too overwhelmed to extend my own. "You're Diana, aren't you?"

I found my voice. "You lied in your letter," I blurted out. "You're even more beautiful than your picture."

Tyrone reddened and sat down. Harry salted his three-minute eggs. He said drily, "Diana, don't embarrass our guest," and engaged him in conversation.

That night I found Tyrone standing before the fireplace, studying the Daumier over it. He *was* handsome. "Did you get your job?" I ventured. He turned to me and shook his head. "No luck today," he said with a rather forlorn smile. "You know, there's a depression still on. It isn't easy. I don't expect to find one right away."

Days passed, and Tyrone found nothing. Robin introduced Tyrone to Ted Peckham, a friend, then operating his famous Escort Service, which provided Yale, Harvard, and Princeton men as escorts, at so much an hour, for any lady who wished one. Perhaps Ted could use him. But Ty, it seemed, hadn't graduated from the required school. Ted reluctantly had to say no.

One day I found Tyrone gone. He'd gotten a job with Katharine Cornell in her new production, *Saint Joan.* For Tyrone it was the first step up. From there he was signed by 20th Century-Fox for the film, *Lloyds of London,* in which he became a star overnight.

Many years later, in Hollywood, I spoke to Tyrone under circumstances I couldn't have dreamed of.

CHAPTER SEVEN

It's HARD TO PINPOINT the moment you feel grown up. I know I began to blossom out as an individual in my sixteenth and seventeenth years. Not until then did I fully realize how appalling was the result of Mother's insistence that I wear her made-over clothes. I remember a borrowed red satin dress—and a European trip. Both played a part.

On the eve of my sixteenth birthday I went to a dinner party at the home of Eileen Herrick, who lived not far away from us. She was raven-haired, vivacious, and beautiful and had a sophisticated wardrobe that made me despair when I thought of my own. That night I wore low-heeled patent leather pumps and one of Mother's made-over three-quarter-length black velvet dresses with puffed sleeves. All of Minnie Bell's steaming hadn't been able to remove the streaks.

Eileen greeted me at the door. We looked at each other. She was stunning in a full-length black taffeta gown, with gold evening slippers peeping out. The contrast was startling. "I look like something out of *Heidi*," I said bitterly. Eileen laughed. "Don't be silly," she said, slipping her arm around me. "Come in—it's really charming."

I returned home furious. "Mother," I said. "I was never so humiliated in my life! Everyone looked at me and giggled—everyone with any clothes sense at all! No permanent, no lipstick, this tired old velvet you've been wearing since you

were twenty—why, at fourteen they were all wearing lipstick
and high heels and evening dresses to the ground!"

Mother fell back on her stock answer. "They're not ladies,
Diana. They're not as well brought up as you."

"The Astors and Vanderbilts and all those people aren't
ladies?"

"Well, I assure you, perhaps their parents were, but they
aren't." She ran her hand through her hair in her favorite
gesture. "If you think that when you see them, you're seeing
ladies—you're quite wrong!"

Mother was more irritable than usual. Daddy had finally
eloped with Elaine Barrie, and wherever she turned the news
stared at her from the papers.

A few nights later Charlie Curtis of Boston invited me to
the Groton-St. Marks dance at Groton, Massachusetts—one of
the smartest junior events of the year. Mother outdid herself.
She always shopped by telephone, usually from ads in the
New York *Times*. She had Henri Bendel send out a new
dress for me, a pink taffeta with the ever-present puffed
sleeves and a neck cut around the collar bone. It would
have looked perfect on Mary Miles Minter.

That settled it. I packed the dress in my week-end case. On
the way to the train I stopped at Eileen's. "Look," I said.
I showed her Mother's frightful choice. "This is what she
expects me to wear."

Eileen was all sympathy. "You go into my closet and take
anything you like," she said. I chose the most daring frock I
could find—a lurid red satin made to order for Sadie Thompson, with a plunging neckline and hardly any back. I also
borrowed a pair of high-heel pumps.

Never had I been so popular with boys. But the Reverend
Mr. Peabody, headmaster of Groton, contentedly surveying
the dance floor crowded with young ladies and gentlemen
from America's best families, flinched when he saw me. I
was whirling about madly, being cut in on from all sides,
and having the time of my life. I was the belle of the ball.

Mr. Peabody hurriedly looked around for young Mr. Curtis, standing a little disconsolately on the sidelines. He took him in a corner and spoke to him, man to man. "Do you suppose you might ask your date to change her dress? I'm afraid it's rather—well—extreme for this occasion."

Charlie cut in and whispered in my ear. He was equally diplomatic. "Diana, I think your dress is sensational, but do you have another you can get into? Dr. Peabody's worried about it."

I accepted the inevitable. I vanished for a few minutes and reappeared in my demure little pink taffeta.

The report came back to Mother. We quarreled. "To think of it!" she cried. "Making a cheap spectacle of yourself like that!"

"Goddamn it, I don't care!" I shouted back. "You've embarrassed me in front of people, you won't let me do what other people do, and I had to borrow a dress from someone else so I wouldn't be ashamed to go to a big dance! And I'm going to do it again if I have to!"

Mother's face turned white. She did not slap me. "It's that Barrymore streak in you," she said, almost between clenched teeth. "Now look, my girl, don't *you* put on any airs! You're only *half* a lady! Remember that!" She stormed out of the room.

Eileen's dress—and my popularity—taught me a lesson. I didn't need to be so miserable about myself. I didn't need to be an ugly duckling. How I'd suffered with those bangs as a little girl! I didn't have to! I told myself, the first chance I'd get, I'd get out from under Mother's thumb. I'd *be* like other girls—I'd play the game and get the boys and be popular too. I was tired of being Newport, 1910!

My year at Fermata School only emphasized my discontent. Fermata, in the heart of the South Carolina trotting race and drag-hunt country, where life centered on gentlemen and horses, had been Mother's idea. I was bored. I had my fill of horsy talk. The subject came to a head when Mother and I began discussing my official presentation to society. I would have to come out soon. For the first time it seemed to me Mother talked to me as someone not altogether a child.

"Mother," I told her, "somehow this kind of life isn't what I want. I thought Fermata was awfully dull. The world those girls live in isn't for me. I'd like to look into acting. What else is there? The only other thing I can do is draw, but I don't want to be an artist. At least part of the family's in the theater—it would be exciting. I'd love to try it."

Mother considered that. "Now look, Catkin," she said, "you are not your father's daughter, you are mine. I want you to come out. I insist upon it. After all, you may find you have no talent and I want you to know society first. It's most important."

I didn't know if society would be so important to me, I said. After all, she gave it up. She was brought up socially, she had married a rich man in society—but then she made her own life. When she married Daddy her name had been dropped from the *Social Register*. She had been reinstated only when she became Mrs. Harrison Tweed.

Oh, it wasn't the same thing, Mother said impatiently. Whatever the case, I must come out first. And so it was settled. I would be formally presented at a dinner dance late in 1938. In preparation I would carry through all the preliminaries for a début: attend the Holiday, Dolphin, and Miss Owens' dances, required of every predeb; appear at all other approved social functions with approved young gentlemen. Mother would see to it that the proper persons wrote letters of recommendation for me to the heads of the important social committees: Mrs. Junius Morgan, Mrs. Frederick Longfellow, and Mrs. Lytle Hull, the former Mrs. Vincent Astor. Without their endorsement no début really counted.

Meanwhile, just in case, Mother would allow me to study drama at the American Academy of Dramatic Art in New

York. "I don't want you ever to say I didn't give you a chance," she said.

"Your mother tells me she wishes you to be known here as Diana Blythe," Emil Deitsel, Academy codirector, greeted me when I enrolled for the fall-spring term of 1937-38. "Good idea, I think." He took me on a tour of the school. I gaped at the photographs of its graduates: Spencer Tracy, Jane Cowl, Joseph Schildkraut, Edward G. Robinson. "Oh, Mother," I said that night. "I can hardly wait for school to begin. I was interviewed by Mr. Deitsel, and he——"

"I've seen him," interrupted Mother. "God, he has so many teeth!"

"Really, Mother!" I burst out. "The things you say! He's perfectly charming and this is the school I want. At least I'll graduate from this one. You see if I don't."

A few students stole sideways glances at me when I answered to Diana Blythe in my first class. Ooooh, I thought, they know my name is Barrymore. I ought to use it too. Daddy and Uncle Lionel and Aunt Ethel and Grandfather Maurice made it famous. Why shouldn't I use it?

"Catkin, don't use the name," Mother warned. "Do it on your own."

But within a week the entire school knew. I invited Morris Klein, a talented boy who ushered at the Roxy Theatre, to 10 Gracie Square to rehearse since Mother refused to let me go to anyone else's home. "Ask for Mr. Tweed's apartment," I told him. "If they want to know who you want to see, say Diana Barrymore—ooh, I mean, Blythe." I was the picture of pretty confusion.

He laughed. "I knew it all the time. It's no secret."

"Mother," I said. "They all know who I am. It's ludicrous to keep up this pretense."

"*How* do they know?"

"They've seen my pictures in the paper. And anyway,

Blythe is all right in society, but not in the theater. If I ever do get a part on Broadway, it won't say Diana Blythe—it will say Diana Barrymore."

Mother had to yield. "All right, tell Mr. Deitsel."

Next morning Mr. Deitsel made an announcement. "Well, do you know whom we've had in our midst? She changed her name because she didn't want to trade on it. This is Miss Diana Barrymore."

There wasn't a ripple from the class. They all knew.

The announcement marked a milestone. From then on I was no longer Diana Blythe. I *was* Diana Barrymore.

At the Academy we were taught to read lines, given instruction in voice and diction; we sat around in a circle and criticized each other's work. I learned how not to be frightened in front of people. In the spring I even had the experience of playing Miss Hepburn's part in a scene from *A Bill of Divorcement,* with a young man in crepe hair taking Daddy's part. Mother was in the audience. "Well, of course, you don't know how to use your hands and your voice is strident," she said. "But thank God you have personality."

I was not always an agreeable student. I could become impatient, even rude, to anyone I thought dull or stupid. In class I was asked to pretend I was a gorilla (I did gorillas well) a lonely tree, a wilting flower, and finally a scrambled egg. That did it. "I really don't think I'll be called upon to play a scrambled egg on Broadway," I said haughtily and refused.

I might be dreaming about the theater, but Mother wouldn't say die on my social training. Two weeks were left of the spring semester when she told me she was sending me to Europe for the summer, where I would find myself in a proper milieu. I was to board with Countess Hortense de Guitaut, in La Baule, on the Brittany coast of France. Countess Guitaut, a widow, belonged to that large group of impoverished aristocracy who each season accepted a paying

American guest, of appropriate social standing, to help bolster their finances.

I was also to visit Paris and chose my coming-out wardrobe at Captain Edward Molyneux's salon. "Eddie will know what I like," said Mother. "But I warn you, Diana." She traced a horizontal line across my chest with her finger. "Whatever it is, see that it isn't open below this line. If it is, I'll have it taken up." Leonard, who had married a French girl, was living in Paris and would help look out for me there. And Mother had written some friends—Baroness de la Grange and Mrs. William Astor Chanler—to introduce me to the right people.

Mother had forgotten nothing. I'd need a chaperone, of course. She had already reduced the applicants to three women. I made the final selection, choosing the least formidable—a tall, gaunt, and pious French-born spinster of thirty-five, Mademoiselle Eloise Vittele, who reminded me vaguely of the wooden saints who used to look sufferingly down at me at the convent. Mother approved. "She seems more a lady than the others," she said. I was to foot the bill for the trip and pay Mademoiselle's one-hundred-and-fifty-dollar-a-month salary out of the five-hundred-dollar-a-month allowance she had been receiving for me from Daddy.

"Mother, I think it's fabulous!" I exclaimed. "I'm so excited!" I meant it. To get away, at last, and be practically on my own!

CHAPTER EIGHT

THE WONDERFUL THINGS began happening almost the moment I came aboard the SS *Normandie,* the luxurious new flagship of the French line. Mademoiselle and I had been in our cabin only a few minutes when the purser approached. Would we be happier in the bridal suite? It was far more luxurious. And it would cost us no more.

I was stunned. Why did I rate such treatment? The ship was crowded with celebrities; I'd read about them in the newspapers. Artur Rubinstein, the pianist, Jules S. Bache, the financier, Brian Ahern, David Niven, Danielle Darrieux, a score of others. Why me?

The purser only murmured, "It is our pleasure, Miss Barrymore." The bridal suite atmosphere clung to me throughout the trip and in the weeks that followed. If the Barrymore name had done it, what magic that name carried!

Countess Guitaut turned out to be a sweet, middle-aged woman whose rose-and-white villa overlooked the Bay of Biscay. There was a beach, tennis courts, bicycle and riding paths. I dug tunnels in the sand with the countess' four children, nine to fifteen. I met her friends: the Countess de la Pérouse and a trio of handsome young French boys, Count Chavaceau Marsalis, Claude Gaudin, and Count Edouard d'Avignon. They were charming, attractive, devotedly mine. I had never been so popular. I flirted, I dramatized myself, I bid for attention. I loved it. For the first time Mother wasn't looking over my shoulder.

Mademoiselle, to be sure, stuck to me like a shadow. She became "Bunny"—she always seemed frightened, like a rabbit, her ears up to hear something else I'd done that Mother certainly would have disapproved of. But Bunny was gentle and long-suffering, and I knew I could always handle her.

Now that three thousand miles of ocean separated us, Mother's maternal instinct spilled over in her letters to me, and I had to reply:

Dear Catkin:

I am having a fine time. I will now answer all your questions respectively:

1. I like the Countess very much and she has introduced me to a great many counts, countesses, princes, etc.

2. I am only drinking Evian water and white wine.

3. Yes, I am keeping my bowels open with rhubarb and soda.

4. I am speaking French constantly as there is no other alternative unless I want to appear a half-wit. Last night Count de Bresac talked to me about Hitler, Roosevelt and Mussolini for an hour after dinner, and all in French. I am the only American girl who speaks French with a French accent.

5. Mademoiselle is fine, making me feel very saintly and taking me to church to pray and burn candles for you . . .

I should have written Mother about Count Edouard. He was tall and dark with Mephisto-like eyebrows and eyes the color of coal and exquisite manners. His eyes opened wide when he learned my name. "Are you a part of the Barri-more family?" He joined Bunny and the children and me in bicycle trips through the lovely Brittany countryside. We swam together and lay in the sun together.

At one Sunday afternoon picnic, in the midst of laughing at some silly thing I'd said, we looked at each other and knew we were in love. I'd flirted madly with all the boys, but there was something sweet and appealing about Edouard. I wanted to mother him and love him. After a swim, sandwiches were spread out, and wine. Edouard and I disappeared for a small walk in the forest. He kissed me, he sang French songs to me, and between us we drank a quart of warm wine.

Back with the group, we prepared to bicycle the three miles to La Baule. I had trouble walking. I began to giggle. Daddy's brandy Alexanders in Baltimore had made me sleepy. I wasn't sleepy now—I was gay and reckless. I mounted my bicycle, pushed Edouard away, and rode directly onto the highway. I was drunk for the first time in my life.

I began swooping down on the tiny French cars buzzing toward me. I played a game to see how near I could come to them, to force them to swerve, their drivers leaning out and swearing at me. I swore back merrily. Edouard ran, shouting, after me. Bunny was beside herself.

Then it happened. I rode into the side of an automobile and crashed to the pavement. A white-hot pain shot through my left ankle.

Edouard put me on his handle bars and rode me home. On the way we had to stop while he carried me to the side of the road and I threw up, to my intense embarrassment. I was put in bed with a badly sprained and bruised ankle, the Countess applied poultices and Bunny wrung her hands. "*Ma petite,* you could have killed yourself! And how could I have faced your mother!"

News came from Mother. My coming-out party would be held December 3, 1938. I would be presented jointly with my cousin Eleanor. Her mother, Cecilia vom Rath, and Mother would be in the receiving line with us. With the two of us there'd be twice as many guests—five hundred—for the dinner dance, which would make us each feel better. "Oh, Cat," I wrote, "it's an excellent idea. I'd be so nervous all alone—

it would be like a first night. Get out all the Oelrichs, Vom Raths, Mays and the rest—it will be wonderful!"

Before I left for my visit to Paris, Edouard asked me to marry him. I was seventeen, he was eighteen. "Oh," I said, "I'm much too young to be married, but I'd adore being a countess. Would everybody kiss my hand, Edouard?"

He laughed. "Of course they would, my little crazy one." He kissed my fingers.

"Very well, I'll marry you," I said. "Never mind about my being too young." I kissed him. "Anything to be a countess. And you are frightfully good-looking. When I get back to New York I'll tell Mother we're engaged. You will have to come to America and ask for my hand on bended knee. Mother is old-fashioned."

He promised. When I left La Baule it was a tearful scene. I leaned out the train window and Edouard kissed me fervently while Mademoiselle looked on in acute disapproval. "My Countess!" he exclaimed. "Oh, Edouard!" I sighed. "How will I bear it away from you."

In Paris my grief was tempered by Leonard's warm greeting, and word that Cobina and her mother were also in town. Leonard's wife, Yvonne, a pretty, petite blonde from Nice, expected her baby any day. She remained secluded in their Hotel Crillon suite, so my brother gallantly escorted me about town. We visited my favorite museums. We sipped *apéritifs* at the Café Dôme in the Latin Quarter, where Mother and Daddy once experimented with absinthe and even heroin. We paid our respects to Baroness de la Grange and Mrs. William Astor Chanler. I wrote Mother: "Cat, you're so right about this milieu! The manners and charm of these people! I feel culture seeping into my veins by the hour."

Captain Molyneux, when we visited his salon, turned out to be charming and enormously helpful. "I think we can meet Blanche's requirements," he said with a smile. He

helped me choose a magnificent off-the shoulder white creation with a Marie Antoinette fichu collar and tier upon tier
of pleated tulle. Before I left I said shamelessly, "Darling,
please give me a lot of those lovely pieces of white satin with
that black thing saying 'Molyneux' on it. I'm going to sew
them in all my clothes." Captain Molyneux lifted his eyebrows, but acquiesced.

I looked well, I felt wonderful. My little flirtations at La
Baule, Edouard's flattering attentions, all gave me confidence. Leonard, not one for idle compliments, also helped.
"Catkin," he exclaimed when he saw me, "really, you're a
damned attractive girl." I thought, the Ugly Duckling seems
to have turned out into something not bad-looking. The
smart London *Sketch* helped even more by printing my snap-
shot with the caption, "The season's belle at La Baule." It
added: "Her pictures have been kept from the public by
her author-mother, Michael Strange."

One night Leonard took me to *Le Boeuf sur le Toit,* atop
Hotel George V, then, as now, a rendezvous for celebrities. I
stared. There, seated a few feet away, were Marlene Dietrich
and Dorothy Parker! I yearned for their autographs but dared
not make the attempt. Leonard would have withered me with
a glance.

"Diana, will you excuse me?" he said. "I want to phone
Yvonne and see how she feels." Left alone, I considered
whether to accost Miss Dietrich, decided against it, and
craned my neck to see who else important was there. I turned
to my right and froze: the man next to me was Jean Pierre
Aumont, the film star! Mademoiselle and I had sighed over
him in a movie only that afternoon. I gathered my courage
and leaned toward him, and suddenly there flashed into my
mind how Herbert Bayard Swope, the famous editor, who'd
attended Mother's salons, once described her voice as "low,
slightly husky, as if induced by the pressure of sexual appe-
tites." I dropped my voice into my diaphragm and whispered
hoarsely to Mr. Aumont in what I hoped were sex-drenched

accents, "I beg your pardon, Monsieur." I spoke in French.

He turned to me politely. "Mademoiselle?" He was breath-takingly handsome.

I said hollowly, "I am Diana Barrymore."

He rose and bowed. "How do you do?" He seemed puzzled. "Miss Ethel Barrymore is your mother?"

I said, "No, she is my aunt. My father is John Barrymore." I added in my choicest Countess Guitaut accent: "Monsieur Aumont, I witnessed you this afternoon in a motion picture. I thought you were truly magnificent. You belong in Hollywood. I shall be going there when I return to the United States. I have a contract with Monsieur Selznick." Selznick was one Hollywood name I felt sure he'd recognize. "When I arrive in Hollywood, I shall myself mention you with warmth to Monsieur Selznick. You would do splendidly in our country, I know." I was incredibly grand.

Mr. Aumont smiled endearingly and said, "Oui, Mademoiselle," and, "Mais non, Mademoiselle," as I gushed on happily. I had to impress him before Leonard returned, because Leonard knew very well I wasn't going to Hollywood. Leonard knew I was just going to my coming-out party in December, and that was that.

When I paused for breath, Mr. Aumont fixed me with his enormous blue eyes and said, "May I escort you home?"

For a moment I hated Leonard. I wanted him to fall through the floor of the telephone booth. When he returned, I introduced him. Then I literally hissed in his ear, "If you want me ever to speak to you again, get lost, quick! Go back to Yvonne. Mr. Aumont has asked to take me home."

Leonard, always proper, looked doubtful. "I suppose it's all right if Mademoiselle is waiting for you at the hotel. She is, isn't she?"

"Yes, yes, of course." I had no intention of going directly home. I wanted to do Paris with one of Europe's handsomest leading men.

After Leonard made his apologies and left, Aumont said,

"Mademoiselle, I understand that Americans are impatient and do not like to remain long in one place. Would you not prefer me to accompany you elsewhere?"

This is what I'd been waiting for. I'd heard of a night club, the Scheherazade, where the lights were low, one sipped champagne reclining on red plush divans, and everything was made for romance.

Jean Pierre took me there; we danced; there was the small pressure of the hand on my back, and the knee against the thigh, and I was in bliss. Edouard and La Baule were far away. "Mademoiselle Barrymore," Mr. Aumont's deep voice was close to my ear. "I must, alas, awake early tomorrow to work on a picture. I will take you home now, yes?"

I would have happily danced all night. I was being terribly woman-of-the-world, though. I replied airily, "Ah, of course, I completely understand. We have the same unfortunate hours in Hollywood."

Outside the elevator in the lobby of my hotel, he kissed me on the cheek. "Good night, chérie," he said caressingly, his eyes a promise. I rode up the elevator as though it were a cloud.

Next day Cobina Wright, Jr., telephoned me. "Cobina!" I cried. "Wait until you see the new crush I've got!" Cobina had returned from London a few days before. "Well," she said, "wait until you see mine!"

That afternoon I steered her into the movie house where I'd been with Mademoiselle. When Jean Pierre appeared on the screen, I clutched Cobina's arm. "There he is!" I almost squealed. "Isn't he the most beautiful thing you ever saw?"

Cobina was surprisingly cool. "Darling, he's adorable. But if you'll wait until the newsreel comes on," she added mysteriously, "you'll see mine."

Jean Pierre's picture ended. The newsreel flickered on. Il Duce addressed an enormous crowd from his balcony. Hitler harangued thousands of Nazis in Berlin. We sat through a shot of Czech troops massing on the Sudeten border. Then a meeting of European royalty in London. Cobina clutched my arm. "There he is!" she said excitedly. "He" was Prince Philip of Greece. I stared at the slim, handsome young man destined to become Duke of Edinburgh. "Oh, Cobina!" I gasped. "Really?"

Cobina giggled. "We're in love," she whispered. "I'm going back to London with Mother to stay at Bea Lillie's, and Philip is picking me up at the station." She sighed. "Isn't he the dreamiest boy you ever saw?"

Jean Pierre Aumont never called me. I had little time to suffer: two days later Mother was on the telephone from New York. "Come home immediately!" she ordered. Her voice rose and fell over the transatlantic cable. "Louis Bromfield just telephoned me to get you out of Europe—he's sure there's going to be a war and the Germans will take Paris. Come home at once, Diana. If you can't get passage, hire a battleship, but come home!"

"Oh, Cat!" I cried into the phone. "How absurd can you be! We'll manage to get on a boat!" We flew about, finally obtaining reservations on the SS *Champlain,* leaving later in the week. A telephone call to La Baule canceled our stay there, and brought Edouard, ardent and desolate, to my hotel the following evening. Mademoiselle refused to let me go out alone with him. He could call on me in the hotel. When she wanted to remain in the room while Edouard pleaded his suit, I exploded. "Now, Bunny! At least let me see him here alone. I'll guard my virtue!"

Bunny blushed and retreated.

The scene at the boat train was a repetition of La Baule— kisses, farewells, fervent promises, with Bunny standing by unhappily. Edouard was masterful. "Now, it is all arranged," he said. "There will be a letter awaiting you when you arrive in America. I shall write you every day. And darling, you write me."

I said, "Yes, darling, of course I will."

"Oh, *ma petite,* what will Miss Strange say!" Bunny worried all the way across the Atlantic.

In New York, in the cab taking us to 10 Gracie Square, Mother dismissed Edouard—and my summer love affair—with an impatient wave of her hand. "Oh, this is crazy, Diana. You're much too young. You must come out, plans are all made, and I want you to meet some nice young men, American men." She lit a cigarette. "I wouldn't let you marry a European, Catkin. They make impossible husbands. That count of yours would be sleeping with the chambermaid the day after you were married!"

CHAPTER NINE

I BECAME A DEBUTANTE in the lush, zany prewar days of 1938-39. They were giddy days of high living and full wallets, when Café Society came into its own. The depression was over and forgotten: World War II had yet to come. December, 1938, the month I made my official bow to society, ushered in a holiday season that the New York *Journal-American* described as "the biggest, wettest, craziest and merriest New Year's Eve since the caviar days of 1929." Money was plentiful, people were happy-go-lucky, out for a good time. And no one more than I.

From a wallflower, dressed by Mother like a character out of *Little Women,* I became one of the most popular debutantes in New York, awarded Cholly Knickerbocker's precious accolade, "Personality Debutante of the Year."

Cholly was really Maury H. B. Paul, of a distinguished social family, who knew exactly where old-line society ended and Café Society began, and everyone in the *Social Register* turned to his column before they looked at the front page.

That winter of 1938-39 he chose Brenda Frazier as "glamour debutante" of the year. Brenda, chubby little Brenda of Miss Hewitt's Classes, had grown into a stunning beauty, with alabaster skin, enormous black eyes, a red gash of a mouth, and a classic loveliness about her. I had the "most personality" and was a close runner-up in the glamour department—so Cholly said.

How wonderful! I loved being told that—the irrepressible, madcap daughter of madcap Jack Barrymore and gifted, unpredictable Michael Strange.

I lived up to my billing. If other girls appeared with one escort, I showed up with four. Perhaps as many as six boys from Ivy League schools invited me to a dance. I accepted them all. I wanted to be sure of arriving with a small army of swains. A few days before the dance I telephoned to two or three of the boys to say, sadly, I had changed my mind. Since it was too late for them to find someone else, they'd turn up stag or with a less popular deb, which meant no competition for me. When the gentlemen I hadn't notified called for me, each arriving separately at 10 Gracie Square, complete with corsage, they stared in dismay as the next one showed up, and the next. But they all finally laughed with the gag, linked arms, and took me to the dance. I went happily. It assured my popularity, made possible the columnists' admiring comments: "She's surrounded by men wherever she goes."

I was supercharged. Weren't all the Oelrichs? Weren't all the Barrymores? It was expected of me. I let no one down. I went to three, four parties an evening. I never tired. I feared only to be left behind—or to be bored—or to bore. The word "dull" was the most crushing epithet I knew.

There seemed to be nothing I couldn't get away with if I treated it as a lark. I drank soup through a straw at the Plaza, wore a waiter's tuxedo to "The Colony," fired a cap pistol at Féfé's Monte Carlo. Men, I had discovered, were really bored with the staid and the proper. Girls, I had also discovered, would always be jealous of me because I flirted outrageously. I loved being the center of attraction. I thought that people rather expected me to be, and I knew I expected myself to be. There was a name, and a tradition, and even an eccentricity that I was privileged to uphold.

Between Cholly and Walter Winchell and Dixie Tighe, who reported society highjinks in the New York *Post*, my clippings grew. I thought it rather clever when I read, "There are two schools of thought about Diana. One says she is the kind of girl who kicks her hostess in the shins and announces she's bored; the other maintains she's a sweet, uninhibited child who just loves life." I didn't mind particularly. I took the brickbats with the compliments. It was a crazy, carefree time. Everyone was out to have fun.

I considered myself sophisticated. Few things astonished me. Only now and then I was horrified. One evening I was invited to a dinner party at the home of a distinguished gentleman jeweler. Raoul, which is not his name, had invited me before, but I had always refused. He had a reputation with young girls. "Well, maybe you'll come this time," he said. "I'm having———." He mentioned the name of a famous motion-picture actor I'd met as a child.

I was intrigued, and Mother said I might go. She knew the guest of honor.

Enchanting as ever, Raoul greeted me and introduced me to a slender, gray-haired, extraordinarily personable man. Cordie, which is not his name either, was charm itself. How was Michael, he wanted to know? He knew Daddy too. Had I seen him recently? The doorbell interrupted us. A strikingly beautiful blonde and a petite brunette equally lovely, entered. The chitchat was gay, the cocktails perfectly mixed, the dinner exquisitely served. Cordie was a masterful raconteur: he kept us all completely in his spell. Afterward he went to the piano and plunged into Manuel de Falla's exciting "Ritual Fire Dance." I sipped champagne and listened, awed. Here, I thought, was a superbly accomplished man who possessed every grace, who could do everything brilliantly. From where I sat, I saw only his head as he played. He seemed lost in the music. Suddenly his hands came down in a mighty finale, he jumped up like a marionette—and he was naked! He had been playing with one hand while shedding his clothes with the other!

I gasped. I couldn't believe my eyes. As I stared, he pranced over to the little brunette and the two did an impromptu ballet up the stairs, the brunette tossing off her clothes with every step. Out of the corner of my eye I saw Raoul, already divested of his tuxedo, disappearing down the hall with the blonde, who had little to remove in the first place. I sat, frozen, with my goblet of champagne. Everyone had vanished. I was alone. "Really!" I thought. After a moment I said aloud, to nobody in particular, "I need to get my coat. I'm going home."

I went up the stairs, still unbelieving. There, on the landing, were Cordie and the brunette. "Excuse me," I said icily, as I stepped over them to reach the closet and retrieved my coat. I left. No one stopped me.

I was all but speechless when I told Mother. She flew into a rage frightening to see. "I'll have them flogged!" she screamed. "I'll drive them both out of the United States!"

Next morning a delivery boy from the jeweler's was at our door with a package for me from Raoul. It was a magnificent jeweled watch and bracelet. "Send them back, Diana," Mother ordered. I was going to anyway. The gift went back to the sender with a note from me: "No bribery!"

I turned to Mother. "And you think it's not proper for me to go to night clubs!"

I really had been outraged. I liked to shock people by saying, casually, "Oh, I bet he's marvelous in bed." But I knew little about such matters, even at eighteen, and I secretly envied Mother. As a great beauty who lived by her own standards, I knew she was supposed to have had many lovers, and everyone knew Daddy's reputation. I yearned to be a woman of the world, but the abandon I had seen the night before horrified me. I'd always dreamed of lovers and admirers in the great tradition of Madame du Barry and Eleonora Duse.

Mother had made it clear that a young lady never slept with a young gentleman unless it was understood that she would marry him. This was protocol, and I followed it. The boys who took me out were "nice" boys. They smooched and

necked, but most of them were too frightened to attempt
seduction. Their sex experience, what they had had of it,
was usually limited to a few uncomfortable visits to Polly
Adler's establishment in midtown Manhattan. Like me, they
sounded far more sophisticated than they actually were.

Looking back at El Morocco and the Stork Club, the Sert
Room, Le Coq Rouge, all the glitter spots we whirled
through, I realize that my good time consisted less in enjoying myself, more in not being bored. I had no close girl
friends. I judged my success by my dance programs and the
chic names on them. I looked through my clippings—hardly a
day passed without a mention. "Jim Clark, Jr., cousin of
the Vanderbilts, and Diana Barrymore are that way . . ."
"Francis Kellogg, the Princeton lad, is wooing John Barrymore's little girl, Diana . . ." "The favorite companion of
young Diana Barrymore is Sir William Becher, English
baronet . . ."

I was engaged, that season and the next, to half a dozen
of society's most eligible bachelors. At one point I had an
understanding with both Sir William and James Shewan of
Southhampton, New York. I couldn't decide. One night
Billy took me out, the next night, Jimmy. I didn't want to
lose either. Jimmy appealed to my love of the theatrical by
calling for me one evening dressed in kilts instead of a
tuxedo.

"What are you dressed up for?" I gasped. "Are we going
skirling? And where are the bagpipes?"

"Never mind," he said. "Do you like this?" He proudly
showed me his family crest embroidered on the edge of his
kilt. Sir William's coat-of-arms, Jimmy knew, was to be found
in the *Almanach de Gotha*.

"Oh, divine!" I cried, and off we went to the Stork Club,
wondering if Jimmy would make it. The guardian of the red
rope smiled and bowed us in. Rules, after all, were made to
be broken. A photographer snapped us dancing—and there
was one more item for the "madcap" Diana legend.

Billy Becher did propose to me. He invited me to visit him
in his ancestral home in Sussex. He was debonair and handsome, he spent most of his time pleasantly hunting and playing cricket, and he assured me that I'd love the South Downs.
"Lady Becher," he said. "It has a nice ring to it."

I laughed. "Darling, I could have become a French countess last summer, and that has a nice ring to it, too. But,
Billy, I can't think of anything drearier than wandering
about the moors in a tired old raincoat, hunting guinea hen
or whatever you hunt. And I'm too young to be married."

Billy went back to England but not before he told reporters that he expected to return a year later. To make me Lady
Becher. "She is the best-looking debutante I've met in America," he said gallantly. "She has more zip, vitality, and anima-
tion than any of the others."

The week I denied I'd plighted my troth to Billy, I had
dated Julian Gerard, Jr., Johnny Galliher, Jimmy Clark, Jr.,
George Ehret, Francis Kellogg—and, for the first time, Tony
Duke. But only Tony—Anthony Drexel Duke—became important.

It was Julian who had brought a dark-haired Princeton classmate to my table at the Stork Club a few weeks before my
début. "This," said Julian, "is Tony Duke. You two ought
to know each other."

Julian went off to the dance floor and Tony slipped into
his chair next to me. Tony was lithe and handsome, his hair
crew-cut, his eyes dark with hidden glints of humor in them.
Many young men about town had a kind of softness about
them verging almost on femininity. In contrast Tony was
masculine and magnetic. There was something about him
both vital and rugged and yet relaxed. We got along famously
from the start.

When the party was about to break up, I found him by
my side again. He had come with another girl. In the columns their names had been linked together for some time.

"Look," he said conspiratorially, "let's both get out of here and meet some place else. Anywhere—where we can be alone."

I looked around. Julian was happily dancing with Tony's date. "All right," I said. "We'll both make our apologies tomorrow."

Ten minutes later we were at a quiet table in the Maisonette Russe at the St. Regis Hotel. It had soft lights and red divans like the Scheherazade in Paris, and it was made for romance too.

That began it. Next night Tony took me out. We dined at the Colony, we drank champagne, and we fell in love. It was as simple as that.

Night after night we dated, usually ending our evening at the Stork Club, because we had first met there. We had our own table, reserved for us each night. I was Tony's week-end guest at the Princeton-Yale game. He escorted me to the supper dance Mr. and Mrs. William K. Vanderbilt gave for Rosemary Warburton. Tony was my dancing partner at the Junior Assembly Ball. He took me to the opening of the Metropolitan Opera. We were everywhere together. Walter Winchell made it official: "Tony Duke and Diana Barrymore, John's daughter, are ahem . . . !"

Mother approved of Tony. The morning after the night I had met him, I had walked into her room looking like the Cheshire Cat. "Well," she asked, "what happened to *you* last night? Where did you go after the dance?"

"To the Stork Club," I said smugly.

"You know I don't like you to go to night clubs," she said.

"Well, Mother, you'll be delighted I went to this one when I tell you who I spent most of the evening with."

"But you went with Julian, didn't you?"

"Yes, but I didn't leave with him."

She looked annoyed. "Now, Diana——"

"I met this extremely charming young man called Anthony Drexel Duke."

"Oh?" Mother showed interest. "Really? What's he like? Is he like his father? Is he like his cousin?" She called the roll of the Drexels and Dukes.

"Mother, I've never met any of them but he's divine, and he's asked me out again to meet his mother and stepfather."

"Well," said Mother, "I must say this is a step in the right direction, Cat. From everything I've heard, Tony is a sensible young man. I'd like to meet him."

But she made our courtship difficult by insisting that I be home by midnight. I protested, "Mother, after the kind of life you've led . . ."

She brought me up short. "Yes, but I was reared extremely strictly as a young woman. Later, if it wasn't so strict, after all, you know I was married and had a child by the time I was eighteen. I will not allow you to go around after midnight with anyone, I don't care how chic they are. Otherwise, you take a chaperone."

We kept to Mother's timetable, although a few weeks later I was allowed to remain out with Tony after midnight. It made little difference, for Tony didn't enjoy pub-crawling. I met his mother, Cordelia Drexel Biddle, enchanting and amazingly youthful, and his stepfather, T. Markoe Robertson, who'd been a student at St. Paul's with Leonard Thomas, Sr. I spent week end after week end at their Westbury, Long Island, home. We took long drives through the countryside, Tony and I, and I listened while he spoke enthusiastically of his plans. He wanted to devote his time to something more constructive than sports and travel. He had already sponsored a club for underprivileged boys. He was sane, balanced, yet ready for fun—so much more level-headed than many of the beaux who'd squired me about here and abroad. And when we were in town, Tony and I did simple things. We rode a Fifth Avenue bus down to Greenwich Village and wandered through the winding streets and stared into shop windows, hand in hand. In the cold moonlight we sat on a wharf on the Hudson, watching the boats pass and following the dancing patterns made in the dark, oily waters by the lights from the New Jersey shore. We sat close and content and felt we were made for each other. In the spring we thought we'd announce our engagement. My life would take on direction then.

As for the theater—who knew whether I really wanted the theater? As Diana Barrymore, my life would be empty without a stage career—or, at least, a career—and the theater was the only one indicated for me. As Mrs. Anthony Drexel Duke, however, with the distinct social and family obligations that entailed, the theater could only be a dilletante thing, at most, a gesture.

But I always left tomorrow's problems for tomorrow. I adored my Tony. That was enough. I tried to put some of my feeling in my letters to Mother, in Palm Beach, where she'd gone to recuperate from a back injury she suffered shortly after I met Tony:

> Cat, I'm so happy—Tony is too marvellous—and so good for me and my morale. Whenever I have the desire to do something I shouldn't do, he is there in my mind—I think of his sweetness and kindness and then all temptation disappears. He adores me with an affection too sweet for words. Cat, it's too wonderful, this being in love. It is a state of mind and body quite unequalled by anything! It's really getting quite hard to say 'Goodnight' . . . So I imagine maybe this spring we will announce our engagement . . .

I made plans:

> Cat, try and find out if I'm in a newsreel, because the other day Mrs. Roland Harriman asked me to come to the Boys' Club of New York and judge a baby contest. The club is where Tony gets the boys for his camp. A lot of pictures were taken . . . You wrote that you were glad I liked Tony's friends. I'm so glad I do, because it is so important to like them, since of course when we are married they will be coming out for weekends. Thank God, they all like me. You have

no idea how completely happy we are together, in *everything* we do . . .

Perhaps Mother understood what I meant by underlining the word *everything*. Tony and I had become very close. There had been a winter week end in Tuxedo Park, at the home of his brother, Angier Biddle Duke, with scores of guests. I shared a room with another deb, Joan Wetmore. After dinner everyone dashed off to another party, but Tony said, "Let's stay here, Diana . . ." In a little while we were alone.

"Darling—" I whispered. We were very much in love. Tony was to be my husband . . .

Mother's back took longer to heal than expected. She could not return North until the spring. "You'll just have to come out without me, Catkin," she wrote. "I've written Cecilia and she and Harry will take care of everything."

It was a hectic period for me. Unexpectedly I received a letter from David Selznick—Jean Pierre would have been impressed!—inviting me to take a screen test. He was planning to film Margaret Mitchell's sensational novel, *Gone With the Wind,* and was searching for a new personality to play Scarlett O'Hara. The test was scheduled for 8:00 A.M., November 29—five days before my début. To complicate matters I was also to pose that week for a Woodbury Facial Soap endorsement.

I scarcely had time to study my lines, I was so busy dating Tony. But when I dashed into the old Paramount Studios at Astoria, Long Island, a few minutes before 8:00 A.M., though my eyes were slightly red-rimmed from the night before, I knew my part. I found myself in a huge room with nearly fifty other Scarlett O'Hara's walking about in crinolines and hoop skirts, murmuring their lines to themselves. I was to read with a young actor, Richard Carlson, who took the role of Ashley Wilkes.

I was rushed through make-up, dressed, brought before a camera, introduced to Mr. Carlson, and launched into my scene, a dramatic one. I still remember the last lines:

Scarlett: You're afraid to marry me! You'd rather live with a stupid little fool who can't open her mouth except to say yes and no and raise a passel of mealy-mouthed brats just like her!

Ashley: You mustn't say those things about Melanie!

Scarlett: I "mustn't" be damned to you! Who are you to tell me I mustn't! You made me believe you wanted to marry me!

Ashley: Now, Scarlett, be fair! I never at any time . . .

Scarlett: It's true! You did! And I shall hate you till the day I die! And I can't think of any name bad enough to call you! [I slap his face—he bows and walks out. Fury possesses me.]
Oh! Oh! Oh!

I did my best. But when it was over and they thanked me and said good-by, and I began walking in the cold daylight looking for a cab, I knew I was never going to play Scarlett O'Hara. I knew I wouldn't get the part. There was a leaden feeling in the pit of my stomach. I hadn't been at all good. I thought, suddenly, I'm glad I'm coming out.

My début was a brilliant success. Cholly Knickerbocker heralded it for days: "No debutante party of the season has occasioned more interest than the dinner dance which marks Diana Blythe's official Mayfair début . . ." The place was the River Club, the guest list of five hundred was a combination of the *Social Register* and the *Almanac de Gotha,* and the New York *Journal-American* headline read: DIANA BLYTHE, PERSONALITY GIRL, IN BOW . . . I stood in the receiving line with Eleanor and Cousin Cecilia, who wore a diamond tiara, greeting our guests and stealing glances at myself in the mirror. Dinner had been set for eight o'clock; there was so much visiting about that the guests were not seated until nearly ten, when Harry Tweed gave his arm to Mrs. Cornelius Vanderbilt, his dinner partner in Mother's absence, and escorted her to their table. Mrs. Vanderbilt had lingered in the receiving line to press my hand. "My dear," she said, "when I came in and saw you standing here, for a moment I thought it was Blanche. Diana, the nicest compliment I can pay is to say that you are the living image of your mother at her own début—you look lovely, the way every girl should look when she makes her bow. Stay as you are, my dear . . ."

I sat at the head of one table of debutantes, Eleanor at the head of another. Tony was in the place of honor, seated at my right; and just before we were served, there was a chord from the orchestra, and Tony rose. The tables quieted down. He delivered a little eulogy about me. Then with an apology to Eleanor, whose swain would toast her, Tony raised his glass high: "I give you the most beautiful, the most talented, the most exciting debutante of 1938!" And everyone drank to me, and later, amid the Oelrichs and Thomases and Mays, we danced for hours—the Lambeth Walk, the Castle Walk, the Big Apple, the Samba, the Shag. Photographers' bulbs flashed and faces glowed and the enormous flower-decked room throbbed with gaiety. In the midst of it, smiling and chattering and being passed from beau to beau as I danced, I thought with a sudden pang, this is my moment of triumph, everyone is here except those I want so much to be here— Mother is in Palm Beach, Daddy is in Hollywood, Robin is in Paris, Leonard is in London, and it's all not right, somehow . . .

Two days later I went to Palm Beach to visit Mother. I had to return in three weeks for Brenda Frazier's coming-out party, and I had promised myself I would come back with the deepest suntan this side of Hawaii. It was the only way to eclipse Brenda. With her flour-white skin and onyx eyes and jet-black hair, she was incredibly striking. Everyone would look only at her. My one chance was to appear in a perfectly white dress setting off a skin as magnificently bronzed as an Ethiopian princess'. So I greeted Mother, learned her back was getting better, brought her up to date on gossip, and hurried out to lie in the sand, soaking up the hot Florida sun.

One day as I lay there someone dashed by madly and I was spattered with sand. "Damn it!" I exploded. I sat up. "Can't you look where you're going?" I snatched off my sunglasses and found myself looking up at Errol Flynn.

He pointed at me. "I know you—you're Diana Barrymore." His eyes crinkled with amusement. "I'm awfully sorry, really. I was clumsy."

I wanted to burrow down into the sand. "I'm sorry I was rude," I said. He laughed, and then I laughed. "You swim, don't you?" he asked. Swim? I'd been swimming and frolicking in the surf of Montauk Point ever since Mother married Harry. "I certainly do, Mr. Flynn."

"Okay, let's go!" He grabbed my arm, pulled me to my feet, and we raced across the sand to dive head-first into the waves. We swam straight out to sea in a fast Australian crawl, and then, exhausted, floated face up to the sun.

We discovered that Robin and Lily Damita, Flynn's first wife, were friends. We talked about them. Then about Daddy. Flynn admired him above anyone in Hollywood. He spoke about Daddy's genius as an actor, his skill as a fisherman, their mutual love of sport.

On a high wave he said, "Would you like a drink?"

"Love it," I said. "I'll race you back."

We swam furiously toward shore until we felt the sand under us, and then we ran out of the water and across the beach. My hair was cut short, I wore no bathing cap and with my wet clinging suit and wet head, I ran hand in hand with Errol all the way to the clubhouse, past all the beautiful girls sitting languidly in their beach chairs with their beautiful red fingernails showing and their faces and hair lacquered into immobility. They looked at Errol as though he were

God—he was a magnificent figure in a bathing suit—and I felt them burning because I'd snared him.

In the bar he said, "You're a society girl, but by God, you're alive! You've got blood in your veins. The rest of these dames do nothing but sit on their backsides looking beautiful and ordering another gin and tonic. They never go near the water."

This began three weeks of sunning, swimming, and good times with Errol. There was no romance. He wanted a girl to talk to and swim with and laugh with. He treated me with brotherly affection. "You say you're not pretty," he said. "You really are. But you don't do right by yourself. Don't be afraid to use lipstick. With those dark eyes it will bring your entire face up. You're alive, Diana—look alive!" I took his advice. I made up heavily, with darker lipstick, and I used eyebrow pencil and mascara for the first time. I danced, I drank champagne, I had fun.

Mother was frankly bored. Often, before a party, she and I fortified ourselves with martinis. "I can't take those dreary society people without two stiff drinks," she admitted. Cobina Wright, Sr., was in town, gay, sensible, affectionate. Mother introduced me to Atwater Kent, and Atwater Kent, Jr., and the four of us made the night spots—the Patio, and the Alibi, and the Everglades Club. Atwater, Jr., took me to Evelyn Walsh McLean's sumptuous parties, and I touched the baleful Hope Diamond because I wasn't supposed to touch it. I enjoyed myself—I shuttled between two worlds, Mother's chic Sun & Surf Beach Club, and the gayer, far more attractive circle of Errol and his friends.

One morning I came home a little woozily. It had been a big night. That afternoon Cobina searched me out on the beach. "Diana," she began, "I must talk to you. You had far too much to drink last night. You were loud, raucous, at the bar. I recognized your laugh when I was still outside. Everyone was staring at you."

Had anyone else dared lecture me, I would have become

insufferably haughty. I couldn't, with Cobina. "Darling," I protested, "I only want to have fun. I can't help how I laugh. You know I'm not the subdued type—and really, I'm doing nothing wrong."

"I know you're not, dear. But you simply must not drink like that," she said. "You know how your father drinks—it might be inherited. You should be doubly careful. It will show in your face, and you won't remain a young, beautiful girl."

"Oh, don't be silly," I retorted. "I'm not drinking that much!"

Cobina was hurt. "Why would I waste my time telling you if it weren't for your own good?" she demanded severely. "I don't care if you drink yourself insensible, if that's what you want. But as an old friend I must give you this advice, Diana. Then you suit yourself. You've come out, you're old enough to know what you're doing."

I hugged her. "Oh, I know you mean well, and I love you." I gave her a big kiss and dashed into the surf.

Mother said nothing to me about drinking—then—either because she knew that Cobina had, or because she feared to make an issue of it with me. She did say, "If you think you're going to drink too much champagne, take a teaspoon of olive oil before you go out, Catkin. You won't absorb the alcohol so easily."

Tony met me at the train in New York. I kissed him. "Tony," I began, "It was so fabulous! I——"

He said, "Diana, you have too much make-up on."

I was shocked and hurt. He had never said anything like that to me before. "Oh, really!" I exclaimed. But I took a Kleenex from my purse and blotted my lips.

In the cab to 10 Gracie Square, Tony seemed preoccupied. At the door to the building he stopped. "Diana, I'm not coming up."

"Why not, Tony?" I asked. "Why on earth not? What's the matter with you?"

He said, "Well, I think we've made a mistake. I just don't think we should see each other any more."

I was stunned. I almost burst into tears, standing there. But I had too much pride. I was dreadfully hurt. I said, controlling my voice, "All right, Tony. Good night." I left him standing there and went into the building and up the elevator.

My mind was in a whirl. Had he received reports from Palm Beach? Was it too much Errol Flynn and partying and champagne? And what if it were? I hadn't done anything wrong!

In my room I closed the door and leaned against it and looked around. Everywhere, on the walls, pictures of Tony —Tony at his brother's wedding, Tony at my coming-out party, Tony with me at the Stork Club, Tony with me at the . . .

I became hysterical. I threw myself on the bed and cried like a baby. I had lost Tony, I knew. I had lost him.

And what would Mother say?

As if to underscore my misery, I read in a column:

It now appears that members of Tony Drexel Duke's family are quietly doing their utmost to upset his romance with attractive and talented Diana Blythe Barrymore . . . Tony is a cousin of Doris Duke Cromwell and his mother was Cordelia Drexel Biddle of Philadelphia. Tony, an undergraduate at Princeton, is decidedly one of THE catches of Gotham, and Diana, just back from Palm Beach with a glorious suntan, appears to have caught him. But she won't meet the Duke heir at the altar without plenty of opposition from his family.

Mother returned. She came into my room and looked around in surprise. "Where are Tony's pictures? You've taken them all down. Have you two had a fight?"

I told her the truth. "Not a fight, Mother. It's over."

She looked at me. "What did you do?"

"I didn't do anything." I told her what had happened.

Mother sat down and thought it over for a moment. "Well," she said, and her voice was fresh and strong, "you know who it was, of course. His mother. That woman never approved of you in the first place. All those invitations for week ends to throw you two together so much he'd get bored with you." She tossed her head. "Perhaps it's just as well. Who else have you been seeing?"

I wanted to kiss her.

"Oh, all sorts of chic boys, Mother, Hershel Williams, Jimmy Clark, Francis Kellogg, Stephen Rhoades . . ."

Francis Kellogg, Jr., sweet and thoughtful, took me to the Princeton dance that week end. Fran, who belonged to the same club as Tony, said, "I think you ought to know Tony will be here tonight."

For a moment a terrible sense of loss swept over me. Then I said, "That's all right, Fran. It really doesn't matter."

We danced. Beyond the dance floor was a terrace with a lawn. After a few drinks I said, "Let's go out and get some air." We moved to the terrace. There, in the shadows, were Tony and Alice Rutgers, holding hands.

"Hello, Tony," I said. Before he could reply, Fran and I were down the terrace steps and walking across the lawn.

Days later the newspapers announced the engagement of Mr. Anthony Drexel Duke, of the Duke tobacco fortune, and Miss Alice Rutgers, of the distinguished family for whom Rutgers University was named.

Then, and then only, I took Tony's pictures from my bureau drawer, where I'd hidden them, and threw them away.

CHAPTER TEN

Diana, you don't know what the Dukes, Biddles, and Drexels said about you among themselves—or what "doing their utmost" meant. You don't know why they broke it up—if they did. Probably you'll never know. But what's society that you should give two hoots in hell for it? What's it mean to you? You've been wondering for a long time. Maybe you are only half a lady—but how marvelous and exciting and incredible that other half is! Who else can add Barrymore to Oelrichs?

And let's face it—society is pretty vapid. Don't we admit it? It's a round of emptiness and snobbishness and eternal boredom, of phony values set up by high society . . . Your father is the fourth generation of the most distinguished acting family in history, and he still couldn't make the pages of The Social Register . . . What's worthwhile about your life as a debutante? A starry-eyed youngster trying to play a walk-on in some two-bit stock company—and trying with all her heart—is more to be respected than the vacuous debs you pose and pretty yourself with.

You knew what society meant to you, so far. You knew the routine by heart. You rose about 10:00 A.M., but it didn't really mean rising. It meant sitting in bed and ringing for breakfast and then gadding about town by telephone. You and your friends, all in bed, talked about the party last night,

118

and what everyone wore, and how dreamy or dreary they were. Sometimes you went methodically through your address book, from A to Z, ringing them all up, gossiping with them all. They had the time. So did you.

By noon you pulled yourself together and managed your bath. Then, decisions. Good God, what dress, what hat, what shoes to wear! when you had forty dresses (fifteen evening gowns), twenty hats, twenty pairs of shoes, ten suits, three fur coats. One system was to keep blacks, blues, and greens together; then, close your eyes, choose one, and carry through the color scheme.

Then, lunch, "Brenda Style"—which meant with the most casual acquaintances. "Hello, sweetie, who are you lunching with today? Oh, fine! I'm lunching there, too, why don't we make it a table of four? All right, Twenty-One at two o'clock." At lunch you table-hopped to chatter with everyone you'd chattered with at the dance last night, including the girls you dissected over the telephone earlier.

Lunch took an hour and a half, perhaps two. Some girls drank martinis. You always took a sherry at the beginning, unless you'd had too much champagne the night before. Then nothing set you up like a whisky sour. You grew to like whisky sours.

After lunch, your committee meeting. You sat around, dressed up like a mannequin, and discussed plans for the next ball. You screened the boys who were to be invited. That was only protocol, because you had been carefully screened yourself or you wouldn't be here, in the home of Mrs. Vincent Astor, planning the dance. If you were snobbish, the boys were even more so, more careful where they went, with whom they were seen.

If no committee meetings, you had your hairdresser. Par was three appointments a week. Or a gay afternoon shopping. Your allowance—and that of your girl friends—was generous, from three hundred to five hundred dollars a month. This for lunches, incidentals, and minor purchases. Your clothes *allowance was another matter. You never paid attention to cost. Whatever you saw and liked. "Charge it," you said. Only Harry Tweed saw the bills.*

Cocktails in the late afternoon, then dinner or a dinner dance or a party. After a party, a second party, and even a third. Your escorts drove you to Westbury or some other suburb. You sat in front of a huge fireplace at a smart inn or in someone's home, equally smart. You saw a great deal and took it in your stride. Everyone knew, in Tuxedo Park, in Southampton, in Westport, in all the chic week-end homes, that it was not unusual to see ladies and gentlemen emerging from each other's rooms at odd hours of the night or morning. And yet how society talked about the morals of people in the theater! Society's morals were shocking to anyone not in society: for what else had the ladies and gentlemen to do to escape boredom and themselves?

Yes, a merry whirl, and in the midst of this racing about, sometimes the family might register a mild protest. Mother might say to Julian or Francis or Hobey Clark—your latest escort—"Really, Diana is simply doing too much. Please get her home early tonight." Or Harry might say, "Don't you think, old top, you could manage to stay home Sunday for a few hours after lunch and calm down a bit and perhaps read the Times?" *Actually, you rarely read anything but the society pages and the columns to find the latest gossip about yourself and your friends. You might as well be living on Mars so far as anything else was concerned. Of course you knew Hitler was overrunning Europe, but generally Lowell Thomas' 6:45 P.M. broadcast took care of all other matters. Unless you were out cocktailing and didn't hear him at all.*

You enjoyed being a little flirt and a madcap and reading about yourself. But somehow it was all so vapid and so infantile! *You were your father's daughter, and Mother had never allowed herself to be held back from* anything, *and if you* really *weren't wanted . . .*

CHAPTER ELEVEN

I SET ABOUT BUILDING bridges to my father's world. I returned for my second year at the American Academy of Dramatic Art. I had a Barrymore streak in me? God, I only hoped I did!

While I carried on as chairman of the Debutante Committee for the fashionable Russian Easter Ball Benefit, I wrote David Selznick in Hollywood apologizing for my Scarlett O'Hara, and I sent out feelers in the direction of summer stock.

Mr. Selznick's reply couldn't have been kinder:

> ... the odds were several thousand to one against you as a Scarlett, but since I wanted to see a test of you, I felt that it might as well be in a scene from "Gone With the Wind"— especially since I know too little of your work to cast you accurately in a test. I think you are probably right to try the stage first. I do hope you'll keep in touch with me looking toward the day when both you and we are ready for you to start in pictures ...

But from Walter Hartwig, director of the famous Ogunquit, Maine, Playhouse, came the offer of a job in summer stock!

Like Mr. Selznick, he felt I was an unknown quantity. But he'd find parts for me. He had talked to Mother.

Of course [he wrote delicately], I would not put you in such a position that would unfortunately show up any limitations you might have. But if you are the potential actress I think you may be, I and my audience will know it before the season is over.

My salary—ten dollars a week.
I was launched in the theater.
Really, it hadn't been hard at all!

Mother decided that, if this was what her daughter wanted, it must be done in style. I arrived in Ogunquit with my chaperone, Bunny; my maid, Elsie; Moka, a rare Papillon puppy I had bought in France; and a directive from Mother to stay in neither hotel nor boardinghouse but to take my own cottage for the season. I began rehearsals for the ingénue part of Alice Sycamore in the Moss Hart-George S. Kaufman comedy, *You Can't Take It with You*.

I wrote Francis Kellogg:

Oh, Fran, it's impossible to put into words the joy I'm getting out of this work. All the people in the cast are professionals—and God, what swell people they are. Actors are the only people in the world, Fran—I mean it! I now know this is the only thing I want . . . My place is in the theatre!

Everything began to happen. Columbia Pictures wanted me to take a screen test. Paramount Pictures wired me: *What are your future plans?* 20th Century-Fox sent a man to interview me.

And one afternoon I had other callers at my cottage. I telephoned Mother about them:

"Cat, there are some gentlemen here from *Life* magazine and they want to do an article about me and take pictures and put me on the cover."

"Cover? Put you on a magazine cover? Certainly not. It's disgraceful. I don't care what magazine it is. They're just exploiting you!"

"But, Mother, it's wonderful publicity for the Playhouse. They promise they'll do it in good taste, and Mr. Hartwig thinks it would be very good for me."

Mother was adamant, but I begged and pleaded, and Mr. Hartwig came supplicatingly on the phone, and finally she yielded. Photographers swarmed about my cottage, my dressing room backstage at the Playhouse. I posed in a wicker rocking chair with Moka, making up for the stage, frolicking on the beach. Three weeks later I bought a copy of *Life* magazine for July 31, 1939, to find myself, in a bathing suit, on the cover.

I remember looking at myself, reading the story, and glancing at my photographs inside . . . and thinking absolutely nothing. It might have been someone else I was reading about.

The same curious feeling of detachment was to overcome me all through the years when I read about myself—whether the stories were good or bad. It might be someone else. It was never really me.

My two months of summer stock took me a great stride forward. The critics were kind. I was not yet an actress, but I was on my way. Eliot Norton, the distinguished Boston *Post* reviewer, wrote:

> Diana's role was a sizable one . . . That she should emerge from two years of acting school and as many semesters in New York's glittery "café Society" as another Cornell or Hayes would be too much to expect . . .

Wires poured in. One I pasted above my dressing room mirror. It was from Daddy, in Chicago, where he had opened in *My Dear Children*, his first play since *Hamlet* in London. It read:

> Dearest Diana. Just read a magnificent notice of your first performance by Norton of the Boston Post. Congratulations!

Feel very proud of you. I am ruffling my tail feathers like an old hen. Much love.

Daddy

Of course it hadn't been a "magnificent" notice. But Daddy *had* cared enough to read it—and wire me.

Then, a big leap forward. William A. Brady, the producer, sent for me. If I made good in an audition, I might go on tour in *Outward Bound,* with Laurette Taylor and Florence Reed! He sat behind an enormous desk in his 48th Street Playhouse office when I tripped in. I wore a blue pleated skirt and middy blouse left over from my Brearley days, and high heels because I thought my bowed legs looked better in them. I must have made an odd picture.

Mr. Brady, a red-faced, heavy-set man, did not rise.

"Have you read the play, Miss Barrymore?" he asked gruffly.

"Yes, sir," I said.

"Have you studied any of it?"

"No, sir," I replied truthfully. I thought for a moment. "Why study it until I know I'm going to get the part?"

The moment the words were out I knew I was insufferably brash. William Brady was one of the greatest showmen in the country. He had made dozens of stars. And he had been good enough to offer me the opportunity. But I was so young. I wasn't even nervous. The world was my oyster.

He looked at me from under shaggy brows. "Young lady," he said almost wearily, "people very big in the theater study before they read. When they're really stars, we don't ask them to read for us. But nobody knows what you can do."

I kept up my front but my confidence began to ooze away.

"In all fairness I should tell you that you're not the only one we're considering," he said. "Olin Downes' daughter is also reading for the part." I knew who Mr. Downes was: the famous music critic of the New York *Times.* Was everybody's daughter trying to be an actress?

"Come back tomorrow at two for your reading," Mr. Brady went on. "I'll see you then."

"I'll really try my best, sir," I said, a little ashamed. As I turned to go, there was a movement in one corner. A man had been sitting there in the shadows. Now he came forward. Brady introduced him. "Miss Barrymore, this is Bramwell Fletcher."

I held out my hand to a slender, blond-haired man with a pale, sensitive face. I'd heard of him, of course. He had starred in the New York production of *Outward Bound,* which had closed a few weeks ago.

"Mr. Fletcher, unfortunately, isn't going on the tour," Mr. Brady said.

I remember looking fleetingly at Mr. Fletcher and saying politely, "Oh, I'm sorry."

He smiled charmingly. "So am I. I do hope you're going to be one of us." His accent was British. "Good luck with your reading tomorrow."

As I went home I thought, how blue his eyes are. Just like Robin's.

Next afternoon I came on stage in the empty theater to find the cast there. I knew none of the actors, although I'd heard all my life of Laurette Taylor and Florence Reed. Miss Taylor was a small, mousy woman who seemed preoccupied. But my eyes didn't rest long on her. I stared, fascinated, at Florence Reed. What an extraordinary picture she made!

She was seated in a corner, wearing a pale brown hat with long orange-colored ostrich feathers protruding up and down at one side. Her eyes were enormous. Her mouth had been made up so that it appeared to be two astonishing Cupid's bows that almost reached her nostrils. She smoked a cigarette from a tortoise-shell holder almost five inches long. She wore a plaid tweed jacket with brown skirt to match. She was in platform shoes with soles so thick as to be almost grotesque— a tiny woman, under five feet, with those enormous, hypnotic eyes—yet how commanding. She came up to me. She seemed to fill the room. "Child," she said, and her voice was as striking as the rest of her: low, hoarse, sounding like a man's voice with a razor caught in his throat. "Child, I knew your father. Come over here and sit next to me and listen carefully to what's said." She touched my arm. "And don't be nervous. There's nothing to be nervous about."

I liked her instantly.

The director briefly outlined the play. *Outward Bound* is an eerie fantasy about life and death. The action takes place in the smoking room of an ocean liner. Among the passengers are a clergyman, a snobbish dowager (Miss Reed), a pompous industrialist, a little Cockney charwoman (Laurette Taylor), a drunken weakling, and two young lovers. The voyage is mysterious from the start. None of the passengers know the destination. The crew is never seen. There is only the steward—and he evades their questions. Slowly the horrifying realization dawns on them: they are all dead, outward bound to an unknown shore—heaven or hell.

Because the young lovers, Ann and Henry, died in a suicide pact, they cannot set foot in either heaven or hell, but are doomed to shuttle back and forth forever. I was to read the part of Ann.

When my turn came the director said, "You enter stage right and stand here, Miss Barrymore." He indicated a chalked X on the floor.

I waited in the wings for my cue. When it came, I entered.

Suddenly a hoarse, impatient voice rasped from the darkened auditorium. "Goddamn it, young woman, don't you even know how to cross a stage?"

It was Brady, all but invisible in the dark expanse of seats. He had stopped me on my very first entrance.

I was flustered. At the American Academy they had given us all the fundamentals—how to walk, how to kneel, how to pick something up from the floor—but I was acutely self-conscious among these professionals. At Ogunquit nobody had ever really coached me. Perhaps they had assumed that a Barrymore knew or had been taught. Or perhaps they had been afraid—literally afraid—to tell me what I was doing wrong.

I spoke up. "I'm sorry, sir. I'm scared."

"All right." His voice was a little less gruff. "Take a breather and come back and do it again, and do it better."

I went into the wings and tried again. You're just crossing the sitting room at 10 Gracie Square, I told myself. Simply walk, Diana. Brady's voice came. "Much better. Thank you." Then a pause. "Now, let's hear you read."

My lines were taken from Ann's most moving scene, in which she pleads with her lover not to die. When I finished, I sat down trembling, next to Miss Reed. She removed the cigarette holder from her mouth and looked at me. One enormous eye winked. "Good," she said. "Now go home, child, and study it."

I got the part. Salary, one hundred and fifty dollars a week. I signed my first Equity contract. I was a *professional*.

The day Mr. Brady gave me the good news he also told me that in Chicago, our longest engagement, we would play the Harris Theatre, next door to the Selwyn, where Daddy was appearing! Both had the same stage entrance!

I dashed off a letter to Daddy:

I'm looking forward so to seeing you again. My billing will be so small you probably won't even know I'm in the play, but I'll be coming there with Laurette Taylor and Florence Reed in *Outward Bound*. I'm going to be right next door to you!

Back came a wire:

Can't wait to see you. Let's share the same dressing room. Let me know arrival your train. Love. Daddy.

Wholeheartedly I took Florence Reed's advice. I not only studied my part, I wrote a careful, eight-page analysis of

Ann's character. I *became* Ann. Mother took a hand and coached me. "I helped your father in *Hamlet,* and he listened to me," she said. "Now, *you* listen to me. You don't know how to use your hands, your voice is strident, and you're too melodramatic. We're going to make you good in this part, Catkin."

Nonetheless, when we opened nearly a month later in Philadelphia, en route to Chicago, I was terrified. Though it wasn't New York—and only New York counted, I'd learned—Philadelphia was the birthplace of the Barrymores. I sweated through my dress, even through my shields. Five minutes before my call I glanced in the mirror. I was horrified. My mascara had begun to run, smearing my cheeks. I made up again in a frenzy. I'd never been this nervous in summer stock . . .

I remembered my lines. I forgot nothing. Apparently Mother's coaching helped. One critic found me "carrying on in the Barrymore tradition, with genuine acting ability." Another: "She plays the part of Ann with conviction, but hardly the polish of a seasoned Barrymore."

But Brady said, "Young woman, with work—hard work, I mean—I think one day you'll be a star." Florence Reed, whose opinion I valued above all others, said, "Child, you did that very well. I'm most pleased with you." She kissed me. "The rest is up to you."

Oh, the thrill of those curtain calls! When I heard that applause for the first time—the applause you hear only in a large, crowded theater—I said, I want to hear this the rest of my life! There is no sound like it in all the world. It echoed through my veins and moved me to the soles of my feet. I drew it to me. Oh, to float off on a sea of that wonderful, admiring sound . . .

I watched the others. When we took our curtain calls, I was in the first group of four to appear; then, finally, Florence and Laurette; then Laurette alone. I watched from the wings as she came forward on the stage, all alone, and bowed humbly to the thunderous ovation, for her alone. I said to

John Barrymore, handsome, flamboyant, the greatest actor of his day, became the romantic ideal of millions of women.

Blanche Oelrichs Thomas, of Newport society, was beautiful, talented, and temperamental. When she and John met, they were irresistibly drawn to each other, and she obtained a divorce to marry him.

Their marriage was a fantastic series of quarrels and reconciliations, laughter and tears, ecstasy and anguish. Their antics were the talk of the international set wherever they happened to be—London, Paris, the Riviera, New York.

Their only child was Diana Blythe Barrymore. John, an electrifying presence on the stage, became almost shy in the nursery. His infant daughter filled him with a tenderness and awe that was seldom revealed to others.

Under her pen name, Michael Strange, Diana's mother cut a spectacular figure as poetess and playwright. Her tragic portrayal of L'Aiglon in Rostand's play established her as an actress.

Diana and her mother, left, during one of their frequent transatlantic voyages. After the tempestuous Barrymore-Strange marriage crashed, Diana was turned over to governesses and Michael remained a remote and unpredictable figure to her child. Diana pored over movie magazines and gossip columns to learn about her famous but absent father. When he visited her at boarding school, the thirteen-year-old girl was beside herself. He took her to dinner, below, and hovering news photographers caught this touching moment.

Although born of two fiery strains, Diana as a child was quiet, withdrawn, lonely. At the exclusive Fermata School, left, she dutifully joined the group, played tennis, went riding—but she still felt alone. As Diana grew up, her mother, forever busy with her own career, began to take more interest in her. Michael Strange's dramatic touch reveals itself in this portrait of Diana, below, taken at 10 Gracie Square.

Photo by Thomas Neil Darling

Photo by H

Suddenly—almost overnight, it seemed—Diana blossomed into a beautiful young lady. Here she is, back home after a summer in Europe and ready to make her debut.

Cholly Knickerbocker named Diana "Personality Débutante of the Year" (1938). With her cousin Eleanor vom Rath, top, she made her official bow to society. Even amid the champagne and the dancing, below, Diana was not certain that the gay social whirl was all she wanted.

Photos courtesy of the Stork C[lub]

One of the brightest ornaments of New York's night clubs, Diana was seen everywhere. Above, at the Stork, squired by two of her most frequent escorts, Tony Duke (left), and Julian Gerard, Jr. Below, at cocktails with her rival for popularity, Brenda Frazier.

was society versus the theater—and the theater won. After several mall parts in summer stock, she made her Broadway début—at the ge of nineteen—in *Romantic Mr. Dickens*, before a dazzling first-ight audience.

Her mother, who had coached her, shared Diana's stage success. Critic Brooks Atkinson called it "the best Barrymore début" in years. On the heels of this triumph came Hollywood's first fantastic bids—too flattering to resist.

A tired but proud John Barrymore welcomed his glowing daughter to the film capital and a new life. It was their fifth meeting, and they had so much to learn about each other.

Hollywood excited and confused the twenty-year-old starlet. They glamorized her until she hardly recognized herself (above). Yet, irrepressible as ever, she could still clown, as she is doing below with her father and celebrated Uncle Lionel.

United Press P

Photo courtesy Ernst Studio

The career Diana chose gave her little opportunity to see her two half-brothers. Leonard Thomas, in the Navy during the war, grew closer to her when her life took a more tragic turn.

Photo courtesy of George Platt Lynes

Robin Thomas inherited Michael Strange's artistic temperament. Diana always felt protective toward Robin, who never quite found himself.

Above, Bramwell Fletcher, the actor, Diana's first husband. The marriage, seemingly successful at the beginning, failed for both of them. Her second marriage—brief but turbulent—was to tennis pro John Howard (below). Already Diana's personal problems were starting to complicate her career.

International News Photo

Robert Wilcox, Diana's third husband. "After two errors, I've finally made a home run," Diana jubilantly wrote her mother.

A thoughtful study of Diana Barrymore today.

myself, if ever I take a call alone, if ever I become a star, as long as I live I'll do it the way she does. She came out, with little, hesitant steps, as if to say, "Who, me? Are you sure it's me you want?" As if to say, in astonishment, almost in bewilderment, "What, you are applauding me? For what? For what . . . ?"

It was a consummate piece of acting. The audience loved it, I loved it. This was all make-believe, all let's-pretend, the most delightful and magical thing in life, and what else was there? This was what I wanted!

On stage Laurette was a great actress. Backstage she was an unhappy woman fighting alcohol. She had made a sensational comeback in this play after years of absence. Her notices were eulogies. But she drank. Fortunately she could play Mrs. Midget drunk or sober. Mrs. Midget was self-effacing and fearful, unconsciously funny and unconsciously pathetic, always a little confused. The part called for a fluttering of hands, a slurring of words, nervous, uncertain mannerisms. The audience suspected; it never knew.

But backstage there were doctors and Vitamin B injections and pots of black coffee and distraught stage managers, and cast members angry and bitter because they never knew what cue Laurette might throw them—or fail to throw them.

Drinking was no problem to me. I drank nothing until after the show. Then, like anyone else, a martini or two before supper, and, if a late party, a few highballs. Sometimes, in the long, boring train hops, someone in our Pullman pulled out a bottle of Old Grandad and passed around paper cups, and we all got a little high. And that was it. Though I was humble before Laurette's superb acting, I thought it disgraceful for anyone, no matter how great, to take the theater so lightly as to drink before a performance. I had spent three hard weeks rehearsing and working with Mother. I had written my thesis on Ann. I felt righteously indignant.

Laurette did not like me. She had wanted Eloise Sheldon,

a girl my age who was her secretary and protégée, to have Ann's part. During the entire tour Laurette was distant. Now and then she criticized my delivery. Once she reduced me to tears. Only Flo's reassurance helped me keep my balance.

Strangely enough, though I knew Daddy's alcoholic ad libs in *My Dear Children* were the talk of Chicago—a woman's club actually denounced him for "profanity"—I never coupled him with Laurette in my mind as two great people of the theater who had a drinking problem. I never thought of it that way.

I never thought I would have it too, one day.

En route to Chicago, I was repeatedly interviewed.

I'm crazy over the theater [I told the reporters]. I realize my name has made it easy for me to get my first chance. It's already brought me picture offers. But I want to stay on the stage and learn my trade.

I'm glad I'm out of society. It has its place but not for the girl who wants to accomplish things. All the debs do is primp, talk, smoke, strut and think of husbands and hair-dos.

I know what else you'll ask. About my father, and what do I think of Elaine Barrie, and am I going to be married. I'm sorry, I won't talk about anything personal. When I've been in this business ten years, I'll probably be standing on my head for the press, but I want to be dignified while I can.

CHAPTER TWELVE

Peering tensely out the train window as we pulled into Chicago, I glimpsed Daddy on the platform, dignified as a judge in a dark overcoat and Homburg. I got up, relieved. He was there, and he wasn't drunk. I'd read about his stage clowning, his front-page fight with Elaine Barrie, who walked out of the show because he spanked her too hard in one scene. I wasn't sure what to expect. I worried, too. What would I say to him? Would he like me better now that I was older? And when he saw me act, would he think I was any good?

Then I was off the train and facing him. I didn't know whether to kiss or shake hands. Then I didn't think any more. I threw my arms around him. "Oh, Daddy, it's so good to see you!"

He hugged me while the photographers' bulbs flashed, and police held back the crowd. Then he stood off and looked at me.

"Well," he said fondly, "isn't she lovely! I worked like hell on *Hamlet* and *Richard III,* but she's the best thing I ever produced!"

"Oh, Daddy!" I cried. I kissed him again. He was handsome and natty, but I hadn't remembered him so gray, or his eyes so tired. "Treepee," he was saying gravely. "One moment, please." He posed me so the camera would catch my profile. "You had your face hidden. My dear, you ought to know better than that." The flashbulbs flared again, and I held my father close. I wanted to bury my face in his shoulder and let the tears come, but I dared not.

"We'll go to dinner tonight at a favorite place of mine called Ricardo's," Daddy said. "Would you like to ask Laurette to join us?"

"No, I certainly would not, Daddy."

He raised an eyebrow. "Ooooh, has she been behaving bad-ly?"

"Yes, she has," I said.

"What do you do, just close up shop when she can't make the performance?"

"So far we haven't missed a performance. She gets through it somehow because she's a genius."

Daddy made no comment. After a moment he said, "I have two charming men in the company. One is Stiano Braggiotti, the other is Philip R-r-r-reed. Do you like them tall, dark, and handsome?" I laughed and he added, "Splendid. I will invite Mr. R-r-r-reed."

Daddy was living with his male nurse, Karl Steuver, in a small house outside Chicago. He had taken it because he was besieged by people when he showed himself downtown. I would stay at the Ambassador East, where Mother had reserved a suite for me and my maid, Elsie.

At dinner Daddy drank. I was too young to say, Daddy, don't. I thought Karl would handle that. And Daddy, sober, could be so theatrical that often you couldn't tell the difference. Later I learned that Ricardo watered Daddy's drinks beforehand. Besides, Mr. Philip Reed was all Daddy described him, and he and I got along beautifully.

"Can you play *boccie,* Treepee?" Daddy asked suddenly.

He explained that *boccie* was an ancient Italian game of bowls. After dinner he took me to the basement, where Ricardo had built a *boccie* court. Daddy removed his jacket, carefully rolled up his sleeves, and showed me how to play.

"Don't feel badly if you don't do well at first," he said. The object was to roll heavy wooden balls into a small target circle some thirty feet away. The trick was to knock your opponent's bowl out of the ring, using English so that yours remained in its stead. I tried my hand. By a lucky chance I knocked out one of Daddy's perfectly placed bowls. Mine remained, spinning, in the very center of the target.

Daddy scowled at me, unrolled his sleeves, put on his jacket, and silently led me upstairs. "We shall not speak of *boccie* again," he said. "Treepee, you have an opening tomorrow which is important. I want you in bed early, though actually you could play your part looking haggard because you've just killed yourself."

I thought, he really bothered to read the play to see what my part was.

Shortly before eight o'clock that opening night I hurried backstage. Loud voices emanated from Laurette Taylor's dressing room. The door was ajar.

I peeped in and gasped. There sat Laurette before her mirror, her clothes disheveled, blood trickling from an ugly gash in her forehead. One of the cast was carefully staunching the cut. Laurette was trying, unsteadily, to make up. "I will go on," she said thickly. "Nobody can tell me I'm drunk! I'm perfectly able——"

Someone closed the door.

Soon we all knew. Florence Reed had arrived a few minutes earlier to be stopped by Eloise, Laurette's secretary. Her face was white. "Laurette is drunk," she said.

"Not opening night!" Flo exclaimed. "Don't tell me!"

She hurried into Laurette's dressing room and found her sitting there, helpless. She had come to the theater weaving. Backstage, she fell and struck her head against a radiator.

Morgan Farley, who played the Steward, told the audience, "We regret that we must cancel this evening's performance. Miss Laurette Taylor has suffered a sudden stomach attack and is unable to appear." There could be no understudy for a star like Laurette.

Nor was she able to appear the next night. Our first performance of *Outward Bound* in Chicago took place at Wednesday matinee. Laurette insisted indignantly that she had suffered a heart attack on opening night. However, she missed no other performances during the remainder of our twelve-week tour.

Both *Outward Bound* and *My Dear Children* had matinee performances on Wednesday. Daddy solved the problem of how to see me by moving his matinee to Thursday our opening week. As a result he was in the audience that first Wednesday afternoon.

I came down with a bad case of nerves. Flo tried to soothe me. "Now, child, don't be frightened. It's just another person out front."

"Oh, Flo, it's bad enough to act for your father. But when your father happens to be John Barrymore . . ."

When I went on, I tried to pretend that this was like a graduation exercise: my father was in the audience to see me graduate. The cast was with me all the way: they knew what I was going through. With Daddy in the audience we all played over our heads.

The curtain rang down, and I waited. Daddy came to my dressing room. He held out his hands and took mine. His eyes were very dark. On his face was an indescribably tender yet shy expression, and one achingly familiar to me. Suddenly it flashed into my mind, in the split second he stood there without speaking, that this is how he looked when he advanced on Katharine Hepburn, that long ago, in *A Bill of Divorcement,* looking into her face for the first time. "Treepee," he said gently, "it's right, it's very right that your name is Barrymore."

I let the tears come then.

Later he said: "You have an assurance, Treepee. You treat the stage as though you belong on it. Now, work. Watch the men, watch the drinking, watch everything. I don't say live for your career—but be careful, and work. Work on other plays while you're in this one. You have excellent actors and actresses here—work with them if they'll work with you."

A few days later Daddy gave an extra performance of *My Dear Children* for me. I could scarcely believe the posters in front of the Selwyn:

SPECIAL MATINEE IN HONOR OF DIANA BARRYMORE

I sat in the third row and saw my father on the stage for the first time. Daddy's part, that of an aging matinee idol on a Swiss holiday who meets three daughters he hadn't known existed, called for him to wear an Alpine costume, with full-length German *lederhosen*. How swollen his ankles were! I knew vaguely about edema, but I failed to associate it then with excessive drinking. I thought he was brilliant in his role, his timing superb, his ad libs so wry and apt. I marveled at his quickness and skill. He was witty and sardonic. He's really playing a play within a play, I thought. He's as much a part of the audience as we. He's getting the same kick out of the raffish character he's portraying that we are. He recited "The Owl and the Pussycat," gently smelling a bouquet of red roses in his hand, giving the words the most insane emphasis—the audience fell out of its seats. He was uproariously funny.

Yet twice I was embarrassed beyond words. The first time came during a bedroom scene. Daddy said, "That couch reminds me forcibly of my little daughter. How regularly she wet the sheets! I was kept as busy as the Sorcerer's Apprentice!"

There was a shocked gasp and then a roar of laughter from the audience. I felt my face flame; I laughed, too, though I could have squirmed my way through the floor.

The second time occurred when Daddy launched into a travesty of Hamlet's "To be, or not to be." I remembered what Mother had told me before I left New York. "Diana," she said, "I knew your father when he was great. You're going to see him on the stage when he can't be good, he can't be right. Don't be disappointed, Catkin. Just remember that he was the greatest Hamlet and one of the most extraordinary men who ever lived."

"Oh, Mother," I had cried. "Please don't talk about him as though he's dead. The papers say he's wonderful in it, even if it is slapstick."

When I heard Daddy parody the speech he once delivered and made people turn hot and cold—which gave them one of the most exalted experiences of their lives—and now made them only guffaw, I knew what Mother meant. "How disgraceful!" she had said. "How common!" It *was* disgraceful and it *was* common, and he *was* my father—and yet it was *not* disgraceful, it was *not* common. He *was* brilliant, and it *was* a privilege to see him, still the greatest of them all! He's in this dreadful thing because he wants to pay his debts, and he ad-libs because he can't remember, and he clowns because he drinks, and he drinks because he's tortured as other men are not, and that's the price of genius for him, right or wrong. And suddenly, sitting there, listening to everyone laugh at my father, watching the quick, sidelong glances at me to see how I took it, I hated them all. They couldn't understand. I couldn't understand either, but I knew there was *something* that must be understood.

Later, in his dressing room, he sat, completely spent.

"Well, Treepee, what do you think of this miscarriage of a play? And of your poor old father?"

"Oh, Daddy," I said. I pressed my lips to his forehead. "I thought you were wonderful!"

Before our Chicago engagement ended, Daddy took me to a notorious night club. A tall blonde danced over to him and perched on his knee. There had been much noisy drinking. She began to kiss and caress him.

"Daddy," I said haughtily, "this is a disgraceful place! How could you bring me here? I want to leave right now!" I put on my cape and started to get up.

Daddy stretched out his arm, the girl still on his knee, and pushed me back into my seat. "Miss, sit down! You-will-leave-when-your-father-tells-you-to-leave! And not before! Don't you get grand with me, Miss Newport!" He turned back to the girl.

A few minutes later, as though suddenly penitent, he dismissed the girl, called for the check, and we ended in the Pump Room. When I kissed him good night, he looked at me. "I'm sorry, Treepee," he said. He seemed almost like a little boy. "Oh, Daddy, forget it," I said. "I need to be taken down a peg now and then."

Two months later when Daddy brought *My Dear Children* to the Belasco Theatre in New York, I had my first—and last—personal experience with Miss Elaine Barrie, my stepmother. Mother refused to go opening night—Daddy's first Broadway opening in seventeen years. "I can't bear to see Jack debase himself," she said distraitly. "I won't be able to bear it. You go, Diana. You should, but I can't."

Whether Mother knew that Miss Barrie was in town, reportedly trying her best to win Daddy back, I don't know. I made plans to keep Daddy with me. Immediately after the performance I would call for him in his dressing room; we'd go to Féfé's Monte Carlo with the Premingers and other friends, and then to Robin's apartment for supper. At 2:00 A.M. Karl would take Daddy back to his hotel.

Everything went on schedule. When the final curtain fell, I flew into Daddy's dressing room and slammed the door behind me. "Treepee," he said, surprised. "What's all the excitement?" I didn't tell him I had seen Miss Barrie in the audience.

The knock came. I opened the door two inches. There she stood in a gold mesh dress, sloe-eyed and sexy. "Go away, Miss Jacobs," I said clearly. "Just go away. Nobody wants you here."

She tried to put her foot in the door. I kicked it away. "Where are you and Jack going?" she demanded.

"Never mind," I said and slammed the door

Miss Barrie continued to pound on it until the management arrived. Daddy must decide.

I pleaded with him. "Don't let that woman in, Daddy. Please. Let's be together—just us—I've a party planned——"

Daddy refreshed himself thoughtfully from a small bottle. "Well," he said, "Treepee, I really don't know." He sounded very tired. "Perhaps we should permit her to come in and state her business."

Miss Barrie swept in and I swept out. The door closed. The corridor outside Daddy's dressing room was jammed. Lucius Beebe commented, "That dress, darling, she's dressed for battle. Watch out!" I went back to the door. Daddy and Miss Barrie were in a loud argument over Doris Dudley, who had replaced her when she left the play.

Then Julian, Robin, and I held a council of war. I was determined Daddy would not go out with her. A moment later his door opened. We entered in a flying wedge, surrounded him, and moved him swiftly out, leaving Miss Barrie in the room alone.

As we were leaving, I learned, Miss Barrie buttonholed Dixie Tighe, of the New York *Post*. "Where are they going?" she demanded. Dixie replied blandly and untruthfully, "The Stork Club." Miss Barrie, suspicious, checked up, and found we had gone to the Monte Carlo.

When we arrived there, we were almost bowled over by Miss Barrie, rushing up to kiss Daddy on the cheek. I threw myself between them and a photographer just as the camera clicked. At least Miss Barrie wouldn't have *that* picture to show around. Daddy said nothing. We escorted him to a table where I saw to it that every seat was occupied by our friends.

I looked up a moment later. Miss Barrie was standing beside us, looking down on Daddy with half-lidded eyes and half-open mouth. The huge room was silent. Everyone stared with interest at us.

"Jack," said Miss Barrie caressingly, "wouldn't you like to dance?"

Daddy looked at her as if she weren't there. "I'm terribly sorry," he said wearily. "I've broken my foot. I can't get up."

Miss Barrie's eyes melted. She leaned over him. "All I want is twenty-four hours with you, Jack," she said huskily. It was the kind of voice I tried to use on Jean Pierre Aumont. Miss Barrie was better at it. "I cannot go on without you. I don't want you for keeps, Jack, darling—just give me twenty-four hours of bliss."

"Miss Jacobs," I said, trying to keep my temper. "You will do us all a favor if you get lost. Just go away."

Daddy, however, appeared rather touched.

"Ah, but this is like the gentle rain from heaven. Please, my little Ariel, join us. Have a seat." He did not rise, however, to offer her one.

Elaine found a chair and squeezed her way to the table.

Julian, to break the tension, asked me to dance. I accepted. That was a mistake. When I returned Miss Barrie was in my seat, hanging on to Daddy's arm and looking mistily into his eyes. Daddy appeared to be thawing.

"Look, Miss Jacobs!" I burst out. "This is my father. We are Barrymores and you have nothing in common with us. Please go."

Miss Barrie turned her gaze on me. "Maybe so, but I know him a lot better than any other Barrymore. I'm staying."

I grew very grand. "Daddy, either this woman leaves or I do."

Daddy couldn't—or wouldn't—fight it. "Well, you leave, Treepee," he said pleasantly.

I fought back the tears. "Very well," I said haughtily. I left.

CHAPTER THIRTEEN

THERE WERE TWO high points in those Alice-in-Wonderland years just before I went to Hollywood on the eve of my twenty-first birthday. I fell in love with Bramwell Fletcher. And I made my Broadway début as an actress.

Mr. Fletcher fascinated me. For the first time I was courted by a mature man who knew the world, who could speak to me of the theater, poetry . . . and love. He was eighteen years older than I, yet no Yale or Princeton beau had swept me off my feet so swiftly.

One Wednesday afternoon, after seeing Clare Boothe's anti-Nazi play, *Margin for Error,* I went backstage to congratulate Otto Preminger on his great performance. As I hurried toward Otto's dressing room, Mr. Fletcher, who was also in the play, suddenly came bounding down the stairs toward me. He stopped short and flashed a charming smile. "Well," he said, "how *are* you, Miss Barrymore!" I wondered if he had seen me leave the audience to start backstage, and deliberately timed this meeting?

"How do you do," I said. I hadn't spoken to him since our first meeting months before in Mr. Brady's office. "I thought you were wonderful."

He said abruptly, "When can I see you? Let's have dinner together."

I was enchanted. No actor of his importance had invited

me out before. Vaguely I recalled having read in a column about the breakup of his marriage to Helen Chandler, the actress.

He went on impetuously. "How about tonight? After the show?"

"I'm sorry, I'm busy." I was.

"Then tomorrow night?"

"I'm busy then too."

"The night after tomorrow?"

I laughed. "It sounds incredible, but that's taken too. I won't have a free moment until Saturday afternoon."

"Fine," he said. "After the matinee?"

"After the matinee," I said, smiling. He was like a schoolboy rather than a man in his thirties.

"All right, it's a date!" He bounded up the stairs again.

That Saturday he took me to dinner between shows at an intimate little restaurant. "I've always wanted to know you better," he said. He'd seen my pictures in the papers. He talked about me. I'd made a good beginning in *Outward Bound*.

"Have you been thinking about Hollywood?" he asked. If the right offer came along, I said. Now it was the theater only. I took it seriously; my society friends didn't. "They get a kick out of saying, 'Let's go see Diana act on the stage.' They still think it's a silly stunt that won't last."

"Oh, you mustn't even say that!" he exclaimed. "You're made for the theater. The important thing is to learn your craft."

He had to leave for his performance. "Look," he said impulsively. "Could you stand seeing the play again? Then we could have supper afterward." I hesitated. "Do say yes," he said. He added, with a twinkle in his eye, almost as though I were a little girl, "You can sleep late tomorrow. It's Sunday."

The twinkle and the little-girl challenge did it.

"I'd love to," I said.

I sat in the front row at *Margin for Error* and all through
the play Bramwell looked at me with those blue English
eyes, and when he took his curtain call, it was to me he
bowed. Later we went to supper and then for a nightcap at
his apartment.

He mixed drinks. It was a lovely bachelor apartment. I
sipped my drink slowly. He brought out half a dozen thin
volumes. "Do you like poetry?" he asked. "I know your
mother is a poet. I happen to have one of her books here."

"Really!" I thought, how thoughtful of him. The book was
Selected Poems, by Michael Strange, which had been pub-
lished in 1928. "There's a poem here about you," he said. I
knew about it; it was entitled "For Diana—On her 6th Birthday." He read beautifully:

> Relation of my daughter's violently flying dark head . . .
> To those yellow tulips transfigured in pale March sun
>   on my sill . . .
> Her elfin gestures spangling the room
> Like a sudden brightness waving our poplar after the
>   rain . . .
> Her stillness pixie rush . . .
> Mobile intensity
> Of her heart-shaped pale blur of a face . . .
> Lovely gay readiness
> Of that taut swift form
> For welcoming witches or angels . . .
> So enchanting . . . enchanting . . .
> Toeing the outer edge
> Of however flung lariat of words
> Smiling pointedly beyond
> in all the weird coquetry of an immortal state
> . . . Super equipped . . .
> The heaven of the world still yours
> My wing-swift daughter Diana . . .

"My wing-swift daughter Diana," he repeated and put the
book down. "It's a lovely picture of you."

"Oh," I said, "that's Mother's poetic license. Actually I was an ugly child." I used my favorite description of myself. "I looked like a pregnant Japanese doll with jaundice, I used to cry because I was so ugly. I'd say, how did I come out this way when my father and mother are both so beautiful? I hated myself. God, I was miserable!"

"Really?" he said. He looked at me wonderingly. "I wouldn't have believed it." He refilled my drink.

He began reading Francis Thompson, Keats, and Shelley. He read beautifully. I thought, as I listened dreamily, that he looked like the things he read—gentle, sensitive, beautiful. He's Leslie Howard, and Phillips Holmes, sweet and divinely sensitive and understanding . . . He has a *soul* . . . *Diana*, I said to myself, *you're a gone gosling*.

The mood was still on me when he excused himself and returned a moment later, carrying a pair of pajamas. "Oh, I'm sorry," I said, rousing myself. "I didn't know you wished to go to bed." I started to get up.

He smiled. "These aren't for me, my dear," he said. "They're for you."

I stared at him. I felt the color rising in my face. I wasn't sure what to answer—whether to be a blushing schoolgirl or a sophisticated woman of the world. Until now I had known only one man intimately. As I hesitated, Bramwell smiled at me. "All right, my dear, if you won't tonight, you will later," he said gently.

I began seeing a great deal of Bramwell. I managed to let Mother know as little as possible about it. My heart went out to him. He'd had an unhappy marriage; he was poetic, gently wistful, and somehow very familiar. I realized of whom he reminded me. *Goodbye, Mr. Chips* was on every screen. He was like a young Mr. Chips. We took long walks in Central Park. He wore a flowing scarf, he quoted poetry by the hour, he was moved by everything that was fine in art and literature. We had our favorite boulder. He lifted me up and set me on it, and then he leaned against it and declaimed his beautiful lines. He took me to tiny, expensive restaurants with soft lights and exquisite food. I sat entranced as he talked about himself. There had been struggle in a London insurance office, and a desperate hunger for the stage, and acting in England and the United States. He'd been to Hollywood, but the theater was his work and his life. I thought, Mother is a poet, Daddy is an actor. This is absolutely right for me. I'd met older men but they were lecherous old roués—the kind Mother had warned me against. I'd met actors, but they were often gay and irresponsible, like myself . . . Bram was different. I could learn from him and respect him. Even then I realized I needed a balance wheel. Bram would be good for me. I thought, how can I compare my society swains to him? They said oh, yes, you're acting now, aren't you, and how is it? But they really didn't care. They talked about yachting races in Bermuda and who was seen with whom and where. And the girls were shallow and imitative, trying to be that year's movie star. Now they were all Veronica Lake, their hair combed to fall into their left eye . . . They, my society friends, were the people who dined at Twenty-One and straggled into the theater in the middle of Act One—the very people actors abhorred! I just didn't belong any more . . .

Each time I came home to talk excitedly about the theater and the exciting men I met there, Mother and I quarreled. I must get over my adolescent ideas about actors. No matter how charming they appeared, I must never think of them as husbands. The way she had brought me up, I could be happy only with a gentleman. "You could never stand an un-chic man," she warned me. "If you married someone like your father, it would be impossible."

"Why?" I demanded.

"Because you're a snob, Diana, even if you don't know it, and you want a gentleman."

I thought that over. "I suppose I am, but I certainly don't want any of the ones I know."

She said, "You might meet one you do want." By tacit consent neither of us mentioned Tony Duke. "But no matter what, when you marry, I want you to marry a gentleman." She paused. "As you grow older, you will learn that gentlemen wear well."

We argued back and forth. Mother fired one more shot.

"Catkin, I can never forget the eggs on your father's robe at breakfast. Do you want to wake up some morning and see that?"

"Eggs, Mother? What *are* you talking about?"

Gentlemen, Mother explained, have manners. I should not expect such behavior from actors.

"Oh, Mother," I said. "How you oversimplify! I'm nowhere near ready to marry, and when I do, it will be a gentleman only if he's amusing."

But the fact was that I was drawing further and further away from my social friends and spending more and more time in the theater. At the end of a busy season of summer stock, during which I saw Bram as much as possible, he and I went to Toronto in the same company to do Noel Coward's *Tonight at 8:30*.

In Toronto we had our first quarrel. Bram insisted upon directing. "You're an actor, not a director, Bramwell," I said. "Don't tell me how to act!" We became temperamental. We fought even on stage—once, during Bram's speech in a drawing room scene, I tossed pellets of bread into the air and caught them in my mouth. The audience kept its eyes on me and roared. Bram stalked out of the theater and locked himself in his hotel room. I pounded on his door. "I'm sorry, darling. Please open up!" He refused. I dashed down to my room, immediately below his, rang him on the telephone, and we screamed at each other. "You made me so angry, Bram! Was it so terrible what I did?"

Bram groaned. "Let me tell you something," he began.

I dropped the phone on my bed, rushed up the service stairs, and rapped on his door. I heard him speak into the telephone. "Just a minute, Diana, there's someone at my door." He opened it. I slipped in like an eel and began pulling his hair. A moment later we were in each other's arms, choking with laughter.

One of the stars of *Tonight at 8:30* was Ann Andrews, who had played Aunt Ethel in George S. Kaufman's *The Royal Family,* a hilarious take-off on the Barrymores. Ann, who knew Mother, had something of Aunt Ethel's regal air; she was completely outspoken, and never hesitated to tell me what she thought of me and my antics on stage—and later, off stage. "Really," she said, and I thought I heard Mother's accents, "You're a monster, Diana! It's disgraceful. You should be spanked!" I promised not to cut up again.

Back in New York, Bram became my political mentor. I spoke and campaigned for Bundles for Britain, but Mother, meanwhile, had gone off on one of her unpredictable tangents and joined the America First Committee. One afternoon she announced that Colonel Charles Lindbergh was to be our dinner guest at 10 Gracie Square.

"I won't be here," I said hotly. "Britain's dying on the barricades for us, and he doesn't care! I don't want to see him."

Mother tossed her head. She blamed it all on Bramwell. "You and that middle-aged, middle-class, English quince of yours!" she snapped and stalked away. She disapproved completely of Bram. She had no idea how close he and I had become or that I saw him night after night when she thought me at friends' homes or night-clubbing.

There was no doubt of it. I was in love with Bram. And he with me. At the beginning I think he was flattered by this young girl who hung so soulfully on his words. He fought the idea of marriage because of the great difference in our ages. As the weeks went on, my fascination turned to love, his kindness and affection turned to love—and there it was. Somehow I never thought of his age. It didn't matter.

And Mother's taunts only drew us closer.

Nobody made things hard for me on Broadway. I never had to look for a job. H. H. and Marguerite Harper, authors of a new play about Charles Dickens, wanted to know if I'd like the role of Caroline Bronson, a young actress who became Dickens' mistress. After a two-week tryout in Boston it would open on Broadway!

A sudden gust of fear swept me. "It's not too big a part, is it? After all, Broadway . . ."

"No, you don't even come on until the end of the second act."

I got the part in *Romantic Mr. Dickens* without even reading for it.

Mother came to Boston, saw the first performance, and confronted me backstage. "You simply can't go into New York like this!" she exclaimed. "The critics will kill you." My voice was still flat, I needed fluidity of gesture, I moved awkwardly. She must coach me.

I was frightened. Was I *that* bad? Robert Keith, my leading man, agreed to work with us. We performed at the theater each night, and we rehearsed each afternoon in Mother's suite at the Ritz until I had perfected every nuance of my role.

Two weeks later in New York I sat backstage in the star's dressing room at the 48th Street Playhouse, waiting for the curtain to rise on my Broadway opening. The newspapers played it big: another Barrymore début, another milestone in the American theater. I had a sense of absolute unreality. Wasn't it in this theater that William Brady stopped me on my very first stage entrance? And now, little more than twelve months later, my name was up in lights on Broadway!

Telegrams poured in. Bert Lytell's summed them up:

My dear Diana, go on that stage tonight and show the world that your Aunt Ethel really inherited her talent from you. You must be as good as everybody expects you to be and as I know you are.

I couldn't sit. I wandered backstage and did the unforgivable: I peeked at the audience through a hole in the curtain. There sat Harry Tweed and Mother, regal in white ermine, and next to her Elsa Maxwell, with whom she'd had dinner, then George Jean Nathan. There were Gilbert Miller, Condé Nast, Evelyn Walsh McLean, Dwight Deere Wyman, Richard Aldrich, Brooks Atkinson, John Mason Brown, John Anderson . . .

Suddenly the enormity of it struck home. *Oh, this is insane! What have I got myself into?* I heard the applause at the close of Act One. I ran into my dressing room and sat there miserably, in costume, waiting. Act Two began. Waves of panic assailed me. *My God, I don't know line one,* I thought. *I'll get out on that stage before them all and be struck dumb. I'll . . .*

Bob Keith stuck his head in. "All right, Baby, here we go."

Like a sleepwalker I followed him and waited in the wings. I was to walk in front of a window, and while still out of sight, call, "Mr. Dickens? Mr. Dickens?"

I heard myself. My voice rang out strong and clear. At the second "Mr. Dickens," even before I came into view, applause broke out, and when I appeared, the ovation was deafening. It went on and on. I stood, frozen in the scene, my hand to my mouth, waiting for it to subside. And when it did, the ham in me came out. I didn't miss a line. I remembered everything Mother told me . . .

When I came off stage at the end of the play, I was surrounded by people. They hugged and kissed me. Mother rushed backstage in tears. Harry put his arm around me. "Very good, old top." From Harry that was comparable to calling me another Bernhardt. In the cab home Mother repeated tearfully, "Catkin! Catkin!" When we got there, she made me a glass of hot Ovaltine. It was the first time, I think, Mother had ever prepared anything for me with her own hands.

We all waited nervously for the morning newspapers. We read them in bed, wide-eyed. Brooks Atkinson had written in the New York *Times*:

> As Caroline Bronson, Miss Barrymore gives a romantic performance that is surprisingly accomplished and lifts the play out of the doldrums. This is the best Barrymore debut in some time.

Burns Mantle wrote:

> The most exciting moment of the proceedings last night . . . came at the end of the second act when Diana Barrymore walked into the action . . .

John Mason Brown:

> All in all the evening was a distressing one. Its one bright feature was Diana Barrymore . . .

John Anderson wrote that all the characters were "mere stuffed costumes" with

> . . . the exception of the lovely young actress played by the newest of the Barrymores, the lady Diana in her New York debut.

"Well," said Mother, as proud as if they were her own notices—indeed, she read them aloud as if they *were*—"aren't you glad I came to Boston?"

No professional actress would have poured her heart out as I did in the thank-you note I wrote to Mr. Atkinson. His reply came, courteous, considered:

> . . . You have every reason to be encouraged. I will not pretend that I think you are a full-fledged actress yet. What you make of acting will depend on how much you put into it and how much acting means to you . . . The difference

between interesting actresses and great actresses is a matter
of mind and spirit. I mean, those that really leave their
impression on the minds of the public have some great ca-
pacities for love and pity and are interested in human beings . . . I would not presume to speak so much like the
schoolmaster if I didn't think you had real talent for the
stage and if I didn't hope that perhaps you are going to take
it seriously . . .

I vowed to myself: *I promise. You'll see! You will, indeed,
Mr. Atkinson!*

The critic's kindness to me couldn't save *Romantic Mr.
Dickens.* It closed in six days. I was promptly signed for Zoe
Akins' *The Happy Days* and, after its brief run, for the George
Kaufman-Edna Ferber comedy *The Land Is Bright.* My no-
tices were flattering. Bram wasn't there to gloat with me:
he'd gone on tour as Katharine Cornell's leading man in *The
Doctor's Dilemma.* We exchanged secret, adoring letters,
Bram writing me care of the theater because Mother, sus-
picious, was going through my mail. Hollywood offers came.
Mother said no. "Let those machines get hold of you and
they'll ruin you," she said grimly. "Look what they did to
your father!"

I argued with her. "Mother, everything's pointing to Hollywood. I'll go there when I'm twenty-one—you let both Robin
and Leonard leave the roost even before they were twenty-
one. You don't know what it will mean for me to earn my
own money and make my own decisions and have a chance
to grow up."

"Then we'll talk about it when you're twenty-one," she
retorted.

Nor did she weaken when Louis Shurr, New York's top
agent, suggested I'd get as much as a thousand dollars a week.
"No, they'll want to sign her to one of those seven-year jail
sentences. She'll never be able to get out of that dreadful
place. I won't have it. Six months, perhaps. If it's the right
money and right studio."

Mr. Shurr threw up his hands. Who would trouble to invest in a new star only to have her walk out after six months?

But during the run of *The Land Is Bright* he called me excitedly. "Walter Wanger, the producer, will be in the house tonight. Be sensational!" I knew of Walter Wanger, the star-maker: he'd given Hedy Lamarr, Claudette Colbert, and so many others their first chance in Hollywood. After the show Louis brought Walter, a handsome, stocky man, to my dressing room. Next day we discussed business. I wanted to be starred, I wanted a thousand a week. Yes, he'd star me. Yes, he'd pay a thousand a week. As for my remaining only six months: "I don't think that after six months you'll want to go back to New York," he said. When we finally agreed, I dashed home jubilantly. Mother took the news coldly. How could I be sure I wouldn't be exploited in some vulgar piece of sex and violence? Mother herself, a few years before, had turned down a five-hundred-a-week radio contract from Morton Downey because it called for her to do a three-minute commercial. I had an inspiration. I took Mother to see *The Long Voyage Home,* a beautiful, poetic film Mr. Wanger had just produced.

Two days later she signed the contract: a thousand dollars a week, with options every six months going to two thousand five hundred a week! No more than three pictures a year, and I was free to spend six months of each year in New York to do a play if I wished. Only a Garbo or a Dietrich rated a contract like that!

The Land Is Bright closed January 3, 1942, after a thirteen-week run. I left for Hollywood two weeks later.

"You understand," Mother had said. "You are not to stay with your father." I understood that. Daddy's telegram had read:

Dearest Treepee. The guest wing has been scoured and flowered and is yours for as long as you like.

Mother had opened the telegram addressed to me. I was furious, but she exhibited surprising calm. "Until you are twenty-one you will do as I say or you will stay right here. I can't trust you, Catkin, so I must do what I think right. Remember—under no circumstances are you to spend as much as one night in that house." My father was an ill man, she said, a shell of the man he had been. I would be horrified by some of the things I would see. She had reserved a suite for me at the Beverly Wilshire Hotel in Los Angeles.

"Oh, Mother," I protested. "He would have wanted me to stay with him in Chicago, and you put me into a hotel there. Now you're keeping me away from him in Hollywood. Really, he's my own father!"

Mother said somberly, "Diana, things probably go on in that house no girl should see. Besides, his place is miles from the studio and the hotel is in the center of everything. You will stay there."

Then we fought about Mother's other stipulations. She would not permit me to go to Hollywood alone. Mademoiselle must accompany me. Mother had me sign a statement:

> I solemnly pledge to take Miss Eloise Vittele with me to Hollywood and to keep and maintain her there as my companion for a minimum of six months.

Mother, being married to Harry Tweed, could be very legal. At the end of six months I would be over twenty-one and no longer under her control.

Mademoiselle, in turn, was to sign a letter promising: she would (1) never permit me to dine alone with a man; (2) accompany me to all social events and have me home by midnight; and (3) send Mother weekly reports on my activities.

I really blew up. "Mother, for good Christ's sake, I'm not going to the Junior Prom! I'm going to Hollywood! Won't it look a little ludicrous for me to be chaperoned by my French governess and be home by midnight? The producers will think it utterly ridiculous——"

"They'll think a great deal more of you," said Mother serenely. She would not be budged.

She imposed one more important condition. Mr. Wanger had to give her the following letter:

Dear Mrs. Tweed:

As an inducement for your executing the contract between your daughter, Diana Barrymore, and the Walter Wanger Productions, Inc., the undersigned agrees that whenever your name is used in any paid advertising by any producer of any picture in which your daughter, Diana Barrymore, shall appear, it will be used in a dignified manner consonant with your position as an artist and we agree to notify all persons instrumental in publishing any such publicity of this condition so that so far as we are reasonably able we will see that your name is not used in connection with publicity concerning your daughter, Diana Barrymore, and her motion pictures other than in such a dignified fashion.

We also agree to devote our best efforts to accomplish a similar result with all other publicity.

Very truly yours,
Walter Wanger Productions, Inc.
by Walter Wanger.

Although Bramwell had returned from his tour with Miss Cornell, he dared not see me off at the station. Mother had reached the point of hysteria about him. He was too old for me, above all, he was an actor. "God forgive me if I ever let you marry an actor!" she cried. "I'd be out of my mind. It will ruin you, Diana: I forbid you to see him." I saw him secretly.

Once, and once only, I faltered in my love for Bramwell. It happened when he was away. Perhaps I wanted to test myself. Perhaps, subconsciously I wanted to forget him and so please Mother after all. Perhaps I couldn't help myself.

I went to a party producer Luther Green gave after the

opening of a new play, which starred a handsome, dark-eyed actor whom I shall call Richie Merino. In the part he was sex personified. I felt a tremendous physical attraction to him.

Luther and his wife Edie waited at the door as I climbed the stairs to their apartment. I greeted them, walked in between them, and found myself face to face with Mr. Merino. The impact was like a blow. I felt the blood rush to my face.

He looked at me, and a slow smile formed on his lips. "Would you like a drink?" he asked. His dark eyes burned.

My heart pounded. *My God, Diana,* I thought, *what's happening to you?* I managed to get enough breath to say yes.

He brought it to me. We sipped our drinks silently, standing up, looking at each other. I was conscious of no one else in the room.

"That's a very lovely dress you're wearing," he said softly.

"Thank you," I said.

"It's cut pretty low," he said.

I had to say it. "Does it bother you?"

He smiled. "It won't—later." He looked at me for a moment longer and sauntered away.

A few days later he telephoned me. Would I meet him after the show? We met, we wandered into a bar, we drank beer. "Let's go home," he said casually. "We can have a drink there."

I had no will of my own. "Where is home?"

"Over next to Madison Square Garden."

"Really?" I thought he would have a lovely bachelor apartment in a fashionable hotel. "What an un-chic place to live, Mr. Merino!"

He took me there, on New York's west side, amid the rooming houses and sawdust bars. "We'll have to be quiet, other people live on this floor," he whispered as we climbed the dingy stairs. We tiptoed through a long, dark hall. The floor creaked. He opened a door and I preceded him inside. I was in a small, narrow room, lit by a single unshaded electric bulb hanging from the ceiling. The floor was uncarpeted. The room was bare—a bureau, a bed, and a chair—and above the bed, beautifully framed, the same poetic photograph of Eleonora Duse that Mother prized in her Louis XVI bedroom at 10 Gracie Square. Oh, I thought as he closed the door softly behind him, and came to me, I'm *living*. This is Life!

Later I tried to analyze it. I thought of Bram, with all his lovely gentleness . . . and I knew. It was the hint of suppressed violence in Richie, of animal vitality held in leash; as though, at any moment, a word, a gesture, and he'd explode like a suddenly freed spring. It was to this that I responded. It had nothing to do with love or with being in love. I was in love with Bram, with no one else.

When Bram proposed to me, the day before I left, I accepted him. He would join me in Hollywood as soon as he could. He gave me an amethyst ring. I kept it in my purse.

It was pleasant, sitting in the club car of the Super Chief, listening to the steady drumming of the rails. My little dog, Moka, dozed in my lap, and on the lapel of my suit I wore the bouquet of violets Bram had sent to the train. Mademoiselle was in our stateroom, preparing for the night. Two friends were aboard—Alfred Gwynne Vanderbilt and K. T. Stevens. They were in quiet conversation now. Half a dozen other passengers were reading or smoking silently, their faces vacant as only faces on trains can be, each lost in his own thoughts. It was dark outside. I thought of Hollywood, fame and fortune—and Daddy. A new world was opening for me. The newspapers beside me spoke of it. There was a full column in the New York *Daily News*: DIANA BARRYMORE GOING WEST FOR GOLD. Well, I'd said I was going there to earn money. A thousand dollars a week! I still couldn't believe it. And in another column: "K. T. Stevens and Diana Barrymore left a lot of broken hearts along Broadway when they departed for the coast . . ."

The swains were past, I said to myself. I slipped the amethyst ring on my finger. There was only Bram.

The train roared westward into the darkness. I was on my way.

BOOK TWO

CHAPTER FOURTEEN

"Good Chrrrrist!" Daddy exclaimed. "Not since Garbo arrived have I seen so many photographers! Louella had you in the papers every day." One eyebrow went up and he nudged me with a sharp elbow. "Treepee, you better be good!"

The picture of Daddy greeting me at Union Station almost shoved the day's headline off the front page of the Los Angeles *Times*: U-BOATS SEEN OFF EAST COAST.

I stepped from the train in a blinding flash of bulbs. Daddy and I posed cheek to cheek, while Moka under my arm barked excitedly. When my eyes became accustomed to the neonlike blaze, I saw what seemed to be crowds of people.

The flashlights flashed at every step. Daddy wasn't perturbed. He'd shown up jaunty in a handsome camel's-hair polo coat, a gray suit with black-and-white shoes, and with a gray fedora over one eye, a rakish feather in the band. He held me firmly by the left arm and we carried on a double conversation, whispering to each other, speaking aloud to the press. "To think that after all these years I would father a daughter who looks like Hedy Lamarr!" he said.

"Daddy, for heaven's sake, don't say that," I whispered. "I'll feel like a fool when they see my picture." Aloud I announced, "You're a dear. I want to kiss you for that. Now get that profile out of the way."

161

We kissed. He beamed. The flash bulbs blazed. He whispered, "You've certainly learned something since Chicago." Then, aloud: "I'm delighted . . . my child should come all the way across the continent to support her poor old daddy."

We struggled forward, surrounded by newspapermen asking innumerable questions, and Mademoiselle, harassed and distrait, dragging along in the rear while reporters pressed her about my plans, my love interests, what Daddy and I had said to each other . . .

It was quite an entrance into Hollywood. I wish the exit had been as auspicious.

Daddy's car awaited us and he introduced me to Karl Steuver's successor, a huge ex-boxer named George. In the car Daddy said happily, "George, let us proceed."

I put my hand on his arm. "Daddy, we have to go to the Beverly Wilshire."

He stared. "The Beverly Wilshire? And why, pray?"

I couldn't tell him the truth. Not at this moment. "Mummy reserved a suite for me there," I said hurriedly. "She thought it would be more convenient at the beginning."

"Oh, I see," said Daddy. His voice was subdued.

I tried to explain when we had checked into the hotel and Mademoiselle had gone downstairs to look after the luggage. I had no car. I couldn't even drive. I needed the services only a hotel could provide, someone to take calls . . .

He sat in a chair opposite me, listening.

"You're a good actor, my dear, which is as it should be," he said drily. "But I suspect you're telling me a little white lie. It's Michael, isn't it? She's afraid I will corrupt you."

"I had to promise her I wouldn't stay with you," I said. I didn't tell him that she had also warned me never to be alone with him. That was too monstrous.

He rubbed his cheek. "I fixed up a whole wing for you," he said. "Had it all done—flowers everywhere and your picture's on the piano, and I've been so looking forward to this——"

Later I learned that he hadn't even been to bed, he'd been so busy arranging everything for me. And I had wondered whether he would show up at all! I had had visions of him unshaven, angry, and exhausted, annoyed because he had to trek all the way from Beverly Hills to meet a daughter he hardly knew!

"Wouldn't you like to see the house even if you don't stay in it?" he asked finally. "I thought we might have lunch there."

I was deeply touched. I cried, "Yes, of course, Daddy! I've heard so much about that house. My God, Daddy," I went on, "if you knew the stories I invented about it when I was twelve and thirteen—how I visited you and you introduced me to Fredric March and Maurice Chevalier and Greta Garbo and Douglas Fairbanks . . ."

He looked at me. "You did?" he asked. "Really? I never knew that." He seemed about to say more, then, almost embarrassed, as if I had caught him unaware, looked away. He rose. "It's quite a long drive out," he said. "We'd better start."

It *was* a long drive. I waited breathlessly to see the house on Tower Road. I'd read about the additions he'd made through the years until it had become a half-million-dollar, forty-room mansion, the most fabulous residence in Hollywood, with a trophy room, an aviary, hothouse, bowling green, swimming pools, tennis courts, and jammed with odds and ends he'd collected from exotic places around the world.

We drove up a winding, zigzag road, growing narrower as it climbed. Then I saw it. First a water tower; then a grotesque totem pole painted red and yellow; then, as we rounded a bend of the hill, the house itself was spread before me. On the right was a swimming pool, then a driveway. A big Afghan dog came bounding across the lawn to meet us.

"This is Viola," Daddy said, patting her head. I looked

about me. We were on a mountaintop. The view was breath-taking. A thousand feet below, the green plains of southern California basked in the almost tropical sun.

The house was a castle out of fairyland hanging from the crest of a precipitous mountain. Actually it was a little village, a hacienda of half a dozen buildings with red-tiled roofs, iron-grilled windows, and gardens.

"How do you like it?" he asked.

"It's fabulous!"

He took my arm and chuckled. "I'll show you around later, but let's go in now and George will rustle up something to eat."

Daddy led the way through a long foyer into a small wood-paneled study. I was still in the doorway when he walked across the room and let himself down in a huge wing-back chair. He sighed. "This is the room I live in," he said.

"But Daddy, it's such a lonely little room."

"There isn't anywhere else to be in this house, Treepee," he said. "Everything else is a shell." He paused. "This is the room I sit in every night—and remember things in."

I was appalled to find that he and George were living in three rooms in the huge house that once held more than a dozen servants. The rest of it was empty. Sick at heart, I followed my father as he took me on a tour. Huge, beamed-ceiling rooms were closed off. The library, with foot-thick oak doors, looked like a dusty attic. Daddy had been forced to sell roomful after roomful of furniture—from hangings to carpets—to satisfy creditors. He was playing the buffoon even now on Rudy Vallee's program to pay off his debts: they'd put a tax lien on his very soul!

I thought of the money he had earned, the people he had held spellbound—and now he was living here, alone. His food was cooked in one of the small kitchens; George had a room; Daddy had his bedroom and his study; and there was the rarely opened living room, with its two department-store sofas and, against the dusty fireplace, a suit of armor Daddy had worn in *Richard III*. That was all, save for the room he had fixed for me. "Let me show it to you," he said and led me into a small, gay bedroom, decorated in yellow chintz. It had obviously been newly papered; he'd put flowers everywhere, and on the bed a bright chintz spread.

I looked about. "Oh, it's charming, Daddy, charming!"

We were standing, talking, when suddenly he grew pale. He sat down abruptly. He began to wheeze.

"Are you all right, Daddy?" I cried, alarmed.

He waved his hand. "A drink, Treepee, give me a drink." He pointed vaguely to the pantry. He could hardly speak. I flew into the pantry, found a bottle of vermouth, and poured him some. His hands trembled so that when he picked up the glass, I had to put my hand about his and help him bring it to his lips.

Slowly his color returned. "A corrupt drink," he said slowly. He grinned weakly. "Don't you ever water it either," he said. "Everyone does."

I was so relieved I could have hugged him, but I was embarrassed to show emotion. I'm going to take care of him, I vowed. He's lonely, he needs his daughter. I won't be intruding . . . To see him so bright and spruce when he met me, and now, suddenly, an old man. . . . He'd put on an act to greet me.

After lunch he asked, "What would you like to do tonight, your first night in Hollywood?"

"I'd love to see Uncle Lionel. Do you know, I've never met him?"

"You haven't met your Uncle Mike?" Daddy was astonished. "We'll take care of that right away."

That night Daddy took me to dinner at Romanoff's. A tall, cadaverous man with a smile that lit up his thin face came to our table. "This," said Daddy fondly, "is John Carradine, a rare friend." Carradine, with almost Victorian politeness, kissed me on the cheek. "I'm so glad you're here," he said. "Jack's been talking of nothing but you. He told everybody, my daughter is coming."

Daddy lifted his left eyebrow but said nothing.

In Carradine's ancient Packard we drove out to Uncle Lionel's ranch. I was nervous: it wasn't a girl about to meet her uncle, it was a young woman meeting a celebrity. I knew arthritis had almost crippled him and I wasn't surprised to find that he was being cared for by two women, mother and daughter. "Mr. Barrymore's in bed," they told us. We trooped upstairs. And there was Uncle Lionel, propped up with pillows. He seemed a smaller man than on the screen—and older.

As I came through the door, he spoke up, almost brusquely: "Stand there for a moment, Diana. Let me see what branch of the Barrymore family you resemble!"

I stood there, feeling like a fool, because I wanted to run to him and throw my arms around him. Then, when I did, I couldn't think what to say. Had he received us in bed because he hadn't wanted me to see him in a wheelchair? I glanced about his spacious bedroom. Several of his etchings hung on the walls. I said, "I saw one of your etchings in the Metropolitan in New York, Uncle Lionel. May I look at these?"

"Of course, of course, my dear!" He sounded like a gentle Mr. Scrooge. Like Daddy, his first love had been painting. He'd studied art in Paris as a young man. He loved music; he'd even written a symphony. But like Daddy, he couldn't fight what people expected—and he'd become an actor too. Now, old and ill, he was holed up here, like a tired, wounded lion, nursed by two women . . .

Daddy had taken a chair on the left of Uncle Lionel's bed, Carradine one next to him. We were served champagne. I sat down, ill at ease, next to Daddy.

"John, tell Mike," Daddy was cackling. "Recite that poem

—you know the one I mean." Carradine choked with laughter. He shot a glance at me, decided I didn't shock easily, and immediately launched into a long, ribald but enormously witty poem. The three men enjoyed it hugely. It went on and on, and finally Daddy said, "Mike, I guess you're tired."

Uncle Lionel said, "Well, I am, rather." He turned to me. "Come and see me again, Diana. I hope you'll be successful here. I wish you were with Metro. That's where we've all been."

"They wouldn't pay me the money I wanted, Uncle Lionel."

He smiled. "Well, money is a rather attractive commodity, but there are other values in this business, you know."

It meant so much to me, I explained. "It's divine to have some of my own without going to ask anybody. I mean, money I earn to spend as I wish." I thought how silly it was for us to talk about money when there was so much more we could talk about . . .

Where was I staying, he wanted to know. I told him. "You're not staying with Jack?" he asked, surprised.

Daddy interjected, "It's better for her to be at the hotel. She has tests every day and I'm to hell and gone from anywhere. Treepee doesn't even drive yet."

Uncle Lionel settled back in his pillows. I kissed him good-by. "I hope we'll see each other soon," I said. "I'm going to take driving lessons and as soon as I can drive, I'd love to come out and visit you again."

"Of course," he said. "You let me know when." He waved as we left.

Daddy had me driven back to the hotel. I had to be on the set early next morning. "Good night, Treepee. I guess you've had a rather full day." He kissed me, and he and Carradine went off together.

My first day in Hollywood ended. I had met my Uncle

Lionel at last. He might have played with me when I was a baby, but he'd always been a stranger. He still was.

The newspapers wanted to know why John Barrymore and his new-found daughter were living apart. Daddy and I worked out a statement for the press:

> I adore having Diana here. She's a perfect darling. She will probably spend the week ends with me. Her suite [we both chuckled over this] is awaiting her whenever she wants it. But my place is a little inaccessible and she has so much to do. I want her to be independent and live her life. I don't want in any way to restrict her.

CHAPTER FIFTEEN

When I hurried eagerly onto the Universal lot next morning, there were Walter Wanger, director Arthur Lubin, and my three leading men—John Loder, tall and impeccable, Jon Hall, the outdoor type, and Robert Stack, boyish and charming.

Eagle Squadron, my first picture, dealt with American fliers who volunteered in the R.A.F. before the United States came into the war. I played a British society girl who joined the A.T.S. and fell in love with Bobby Stack, one of the Americans.

I found myself cut down to size at once. The make-up men groaned about my face. My teeth were crooked, they'd have to be capped. My forehead was too low, my chin too heavy, my mouth too small, my nose—why, the Great Profile's daughter had no profile! I sat in a chair for an hour while I was repaired; then I was inspected by Stanley Cortez, the cameraman who had just won raves for his artistry in Orson Welles' new picture, *Citizen Kane.*

Cortez had me turn right and left repeatedly. "An extraordinary face," he finally announced. "One side has absolutely *nothing* to do with the other. Miss Barrymore, which, if any, is supposedly your best side?" He tempered his question with a smile.

I wasn't amused. I didn't know, I said stiffly. I had no

trouble being photographed in New York. My face was good enough to be on the cover of *Life* magazine not so long ago. I added a little haughtily, "I'm told, Mr. Cortez, that you photograph for effect. So you can do me mostly in darkness, which is how you will, undoubtedly, anyhow."

Cortez considered me for a moment. What he might have replied, I'll never know, because Wanger came up to ask, "How does she look?" Cortez was brief. "An interesting face, Walter, but I don't know what I'm going to do with it."

Wanger chuckled. "I didn't buy a pretty face. I bought an actress. I know she's not pretty——"

I listened, fascinated despite myself. They were talking about me as if I weren't there. As it turned out, Cortez spent a week taking tests of me before settling on a camera angle that made me look presentable. My face lacked the fine proportion, the perfect features of the typical Hollywood startlet.

I found it hard to act before the cameras. I missed an audience. Sometimes I waited three hours, until Cortez was satisfied with his lighting effects, to say one line. My first love scene with Bobby Stack took place at night, on an embankment overlooking the Thames. Cortez fussed and I grew more and more jittery. Finally Bobby and I took our places, leaning over the wall side by side, gazing dreamily into the water. I was to say, "Oh, darling," turn to him, and melt into his arms for our first kiss.

We looked into the water. Three cameras stared back at us. Lubin called, "Roll 'em!" Something went "Szzzz," a red light flashed on, and the center camera unexpectedly began rising out of the water toward me, a huge inhuman eye looming closer and closer.

I stared at it, paralyzed. I couldn't utter a word.

"Cut!" Lubin's voice came. "Well, Miss Barrymore——?"

"I—I can't speak. That monster——"

He laughed, "Forget the camera; it's your friend. If you make a mistake on the stage, you're finished—you can't do it

over again. Here you can. So take it easy. Let's try once
more."

There were at least a dozen takes before I got through the
scene. But as time passed, I handled myself better. We worked
thirteen weeks on that picture, and while everyone was kind
to me, only John Loder, I think, realized what I was going
through. He, too, began in the theater and knew what it
meant to adjust to the camera. The others had grown up in
pictures.

Yet I was thrilled. I never got over the adventure of waking
in darkness, feeling the early-morning chill on my face, and
driving down the long, dark canyons under the stars to work.

I moved into a lovely duplex Louis Shurr found for me at
the Grosvenor House, where he lived. It had beige walls
and beige carpeting and a huge living room and a tiny
kitchen, all for two hundred dollars a month! I was ecstatic.
At last I had a place of my own. I paid the bills, not Harry
Tweed. I ordered the food, not the housekeeper. My neigh-
bors across the hall were Gloria Vanderbilt and her husband,
agent Pat di Cicco. Their two dachshunds and Moka soon
became friends, though I saw little of Gloria. Daddy was my
first dinner guest. He was driven over by George, who always
carried a sleek black leather attaché case, filled with vermouth that he'd watered beforehand. He left it next to
Daddy's chair. As the meal progressed, Daddy now and then
leaned down, opened his case, and refilled his glass. He didn't
touch the dishes in front of him. "Food?" he said. "I eat only
rarely, Treepee. This"—he looked at his vermouth thoughtfully—"this is sustenance enough." I didn't know then that
people who really drink eat little.

By the end of my first few weeks I had fallen into something of a routine. Despite Mother's orders I took some
changes of clothes over to Daddy's house and stayed there
several nights a week. It made him happy—and it was so little
to ask of me. The "horrible things" Mother predicted were
nowhere to be seen. Daddy appeared once a week on the

Rudy Vallee program, which didn't tax him too much. I wrote enthusiastic letters to Mother and to Bram. I learned to drive and bought my first car, a rakish Darien Packard, from actor Preston Foster, and I visited Dolores Costello, sweet and serene, now the wife of a physician. I met her children, my half-sister Deedee—Dolores Ethel—a lovely little blonde replica of her mother, aged twelve, and my half-brother, John Jr., a mischievous boy of ten; and I began attending the Hollywood parties I'd always read about.

The first party, appropriately enough, was in my honor, given by Walter to show me off. "Oh, wonderful!" I cried. "Daddy can take me. He'll be so proud."

Walter looked uncomfortable. "I really don't see how we can ask your father, Diana," he said. "He usually gets, well, embarrassing. I hope you'll understand——"

This was my first intimation that my father was not welcome everywhere. I'd heard how he misbehaved when he drank too much, and apparently he drank too much at parties. I tried to pass it off lightly. "Yes, of course I understand, Walter. But he warned me against you too. He said, watch out for Wanger—he's a reprobate!"

Walter laughed, relieved. "I'll ask David Selznick to pick you up," he said. "After all, you almost worked for him."

I went, but over Mademoiselle's outraged protests. This, she insisted, was exactly why Mother had sent her along. She must come to the party with me. I boiled over. "Now, Bunny, let's make sense. If you go, you'll have to sit in an alcove somewhere. I just won't let you lower yourself like that. Besides, you don't really think I need protection from Mr. Selznick, do you?"

Bunny had to yield. Mr. Selznick arrived in an oversized Cadillac, a big, brusque man with a boyish smile. "Well," he said jovially. "I see you managed to get out here even if it wasn't as Scarlett."

Walter's wife, Joan Bennett, even prettier than on the

screen, welcomed us. The guests included many friends—
Jock Whitney, Alfred Vanderbilt, K. T. Stevens. At dinner
I sat at Walter's right. Soft music played in the background.

Here and at other parties I attended those first months I
realized that the art of conversation, which Mother prized
so highly, didn't exist. After dinner the men talked shop
over cigars and liqueurs, the women bitched to each other,
or everyone watched a new film in silence, or you played
gin rummy, or you flirted. There was always considerable
drinking.

The Wangers' Capehart burst into the latest song hit.
Everyone around me found it excruciatingly funny. Well,
really, I thought. Can these sophisticated people think this
awful song amusing? Is *this* Hollywood?

As the evening progressed, I watched, fascinated, as a
famous woman star whom I'd admired since my Brearley days
grew steadily more drunk. I lost sight of her for a few minutes; later I found her in the powder room at a dressing table.
I saw with astonishment that she was crying. She looked up.
"Don't mind me, Miss Barrymore," she said. She fought to
control herself and burst into tears again.

"Is there anything I can do?" I asked helplessly.

"There's nothing anyone can do," she said. "I'm in love
with a man I can't have." The man was Clark Gable. "It's no
secret, so don't be shocked," she said. She turned her tear-
stained face to me. She was very drunk. "Don't let this town
hurt you, my dear. Don't let it do to you what it's done to
me." She had always been in love with Gable. "And that's
why I drink, because I can't have him. I've married other
men but always wanted him." A fresh spasm of tears shook
her. "Sweetie, don't let Hollywood kill you as it's killed me."

I was stunned. I'd seen her in so many films. She was one of
Hollywood's most popular actresses. And here she was, pouring her heart out to me! *This* was Hollywood too! "Let's go
down," I suggested. She shook her head. "I have to pull myself together. I'm so ashamed!" When some time passed and

she still remained upstairs, I spoke to Joan, and she brought her down.

Walter wandered over to me. "Do you play gin?"

"Only schoolgirl style," I said. "Not the kind you play."

He grinned. "Let's get up a game, you might be surprised."

Walter, Joan, Jock Whitney, and I played a table. When the game was over, someone handed me nearly two hundred dollars. I couldn't believe I had won so much, but Jock insisted I had.

It was after midnight. I had to be at work early. Mr. Selznick had another party. One of Walter's important guests, a major producer whom I shall call Mr. Lawrence, offered to drive me home. "Oh, Louis Shurr's building," he said when I told him my address. "Whom do you live with?"

"Oh, nobody," I replied. What would Mr. Lawrence think if I told him I lived with my governess!

He drove me home in a long, sleek roadster. He took me to my apartment. I turned the key, opened the door, put out my hand, and said, "Good night, Mr. Lawrence. It was so sweet of you . . ." He pushed his way past me and was inside.

I followed him, not quite sure of protocol. "May I offer you a drink?" I asked uncertainly.

He said pleasantly. "No, thank you," and suddenly seized me and tripped me so that I fell on the floor. I found myself lying on my back on the carpet; Mr. Lawrence, holding me in a hammerlock with one hand, was doing his best to disrobe me with the other. I don't know how I found the aplomb but in a muffled voice I said, "Look, I'm not under contract to you. I'm under contract to Mr. Wanger. If he wants to do this, okay. But for you—no. You're not in this deal at all, sir."

Mr. Lawrence looked at me, his red face a few inches from mine. He did not present a pretty picture. "Will you please get up and go home?" I said. He got heavily to his feet and tried to help me up. I pushed him away. "No, thanks." I managed to get up and sit down on the sofa, a little disheveled but in control of myself.

He smiled, suddenly indifferent. "You're quite a girl, Miss Barrymore," he said. "I think you're miscast though. You belong in the script department. Good night."

Upstairs, looking more like a wooden saint than ever, Mademoiselle slept. She had heard nothing.

Mr. Lawrence and I met at parties after that. We smiled remotely at each other. He may have feared I would say something. I never did. I told the story often but without revealing his name. His identity, I discovered later, was fairly well known. His favorite pastime was to escort starlets home, especially if they lived alone.

I felt completely let down. First the revelation about Daddy, then Mr. Gable's tearful admirer, and now the distinguished Mr. Lawrence, who hadn't even the finesse of a Yale freshman . . . Hollywood, somehow, was less glamorous. Suddenly I missed Bram terribly. I felt like telephoning Mother, "Come and get me. You were right. This is a horrible place." Yet I knew I would manage.

At Daddy's a few nights later he said, "Treepee, I'm neglecting you. I should take you around this town, but I'm not up to it." He had two handsome young actors in mind, however —Jack La Rue and Anthony Quinn. "They know everyone and everything," he said. "I'm going to ask them to squire you about."

"Look, Daddy," I said. "There's something I ought to tell you. I don't need anyone to take me out. I'm in love."

"In *love?*" He gave the word his own inflection. "With *whom?*"

"He's an actor too, and a wonderful man—Bramwell Fletcher." Daddy lifted an incredulous eyebrow. "For Chrrrist's sake!" It was his favorite expression. "Why, he was in *Svengali* with me, I don't know how long ago. Isn't he a little *old* for you?"

"I don't care, I'm in love with him," I said firmly. "I've been for a long time, and he's good for me. It's sweet of you, Daddy, to think of getting someone to take me around, but I don't want it, I don't need it."

How had I met Bram? I told him. "So you're really in love?" He pondered it for a moment. "Well, where is the fellow now? Why isn't he out here with you?" I explained that Bram was in New York. "Mother won't let me see him. He couldn't even see me off when I left. She doesn't approve."

Daddy's eyes lit up, "She doesn't, eh? And he's in New York? What's his telephone number?"

I told him. "Bring that phone to me," he commanded. I did so. He got Bram finally. Then, as I listened, he roared into the instrument, "Listen, you Englishman, the primroses are in bloom on my hill, and so is your fiancée—and she can't wait for you. Come out, peasant! What are you waiting for?"

Then he put me on the phone. Bram *was* coming to Hollywood for a brief visit. Daddy said, "Splendid. He can stay here." He winked at me.

Bram came out, and Daddy kept his word. Bram stayed at the house on Tower Road. One night Daddy said, "I'm going to a camp on Mount Baldy for a few days. You and Bram take my room."

Sixteen hours later, before dawn, there came stumbling footsteps and a mighty pounding on the door. It was Daddy. "You monsters!" he roared. "What are you doing in there! Get out!"

"But Daddy," I said through the keyhole. "You told us to take this room."

"Get out!" he shouted. "How dare you!"

Indignant, outraged, we unlocked the door. Daddy's mouth fell open. He said sheepishly, "I forgot—I thought there were two other people in there." For all I knew, he had. You could never be sure with Daddy.

CHAPTER SIXTEEN

Looking back now, I wonder what would have happened had I come into my father's life earlier. Because this much I know—I came too late for him—and too late for me.

We never had a chance together, there, in Hollywood.

Whatever tormented my father as a young man tormented him to the end. Liquor made the pain more bearable, though liquor was his poison. He was ill—I had no idea how ill—suffering from liver and kidney ailments, a gastric ulcer, failing circulation. His hands trembled constantly. In his radio appearances his lines were written on cardboard: in his hands a sheet of paper rustled and crackled over the air. The edema I'd noticed in Chicago was much worse. Standing for any length of time was agonizing for him. He was impatient, restless, bored. The bottle was the little door he went through to escape it all.

He never complained, he never bared himself to anyone, least of all to me. He lived alone with George in that huge, deserted shell of a house with his memories. His memories went far back. He couldn't recall what happened yesterday, but he remembered how a painting hung in the Tate Gallery in London twenty years ago. I and Mother, were part of his memories. I didn't want to be only a memory. I wanted to be very real, very close to him, the daughter I'd always dreamed of being. It didn't work out that way.

177

Daddy and I were like sparring partners. If I allowed my emotions to show, he backed away. He would make a sudden quip, turn my earnest question into absurdity with a twist of a phrase, an ironic chuckle—as though he feared to have anything but a strictly-for-kicks relationship with me. Perhaps he's been hurt too much, I told myself. Perhaps he thinks, if I grow to love this girl, it won't be good. She'll use me and leave me, like everyone else. And so we shadow-boxed.

Sometimes, caught off balance by liquor, his guard came down. There was the dinner I took him to at director George Cukor's home. George, an old friend, was one of the few who still invited Daddy. And Daddy misbehaved. He insulted people. He told purple stories at the table. He called a distinguished actress an old whore. He ripped people apart like a mischievous little boy with a dockhand's command of obscenity. I squirmed. He wasn't witty, he wasn't entertaining, he was shocking. After coffee George asked me to take Daddy home. "He's had quite a bit and he'll take more if he stays," he said.

I stood on my dignity. "Yes, Mr. Cukor, I will take him home. Right away. Thank you very much for asking us." I said to my father, "Daddy, let's go. This party is a bore."

He nodded gravely and seemed almost sober when he shook hands. "Come up and stay over tonight," he said to me in the car. "I don't want to be alone, Treepee." And as we drove, he began to mumble to himself. "Oh, those bastards. Those evil bastards!"

"Daddy, no one was a bastard," I said. "You didn't behave well. You were tight."

"I-was-not-tight," he said. "Tight is a word I never use."

"All right, Daddy. You got drunk."

With the same emphasis he said, "I did not. Nobody trusts me. You'll learn that if you stay here long enough." He was silent for a moment. "I hope to Christ you don't. I hope they don't pick up your option. Go back to New York when these six months are up. You can't keep your sense of perspective out here."

When he was in his robe and slippers, and I had poured him a watery vermouth, he grew maudlin for the first time. He spoke about me, my hopes, my future, and he spoke about Mother. "Let's call Fig," he said suddenly. "Let's get her on the phone."

"Oh, I don't think we should, Daddy. It's three o'clock in New York."

"If I know her, she won't be asleep," he said stubbornly. "Anyway, I have to talk to her about you."

"About me?" I was intrigued. "What will you tell her? That we get along together? That she happened to be wrong about us? That you don't mind the way I've been brought up?"

No, he did mind. "You should have starved a little. You've had everything handed you on a platter: schools, travel, money—even Hollywood. Could Louis Shurr have peddled you out here if your name was Diana Smith?" He brooded. "If I'd had your advantages, instead of starving and trying to be a painter . . ."

Yes, but there was a difference, I said. He was a genius. I was not.

"Don't use that ridiculous word!" he said sharply. How could I know what I had in me? I replied that if I were given the right part, perhaps, I might show my ability. "All my plays on Broadway flopped, Daddy. I never really got a terribly bad notice. But the longest run I had was thirteen weeks."

"Oh," he said impatiently, "let's call Fig now." I gave him Mother's number. He placed the call. I heard him say, "Fig?" And then, "The thing is here. It is divine. It is so beautiful— it looks like you, Fig. She's everything I expected. I'm so glad she's here."

I heard Mother's voice, clear, distinct. "Well, she's not

supposed to be there, not with you, living in that house. I told her not to."

I thought, Mademoiselle's fine French hand. She'd written her. I didn't care.

"Oh, Fig, for God's sake!" Talking with Mother, he seemed suddenly sober. "I haven't known this child for so long. I'm not doing anything wrong. I will respect her. Let her stay with me."

Mother finally agreed. I was in the house anyway, she said. "But take care of her. Don't let her go around with those awful people."

"I've already suggested a couple of gentlemen," Daddy said. "She doesn't want any part of them. She's in love."

Mother sniffed. "Yes, I know. He's old enough to be her father."

"Well, she's in love with him and I've asked him to come out here."

Mother grew furious. "I don't want her to marry that man! He's too old. Really, Jack!"

They talked back and forth and then Daddy said, "Oh God, Fig, I wish you'd come out. Please come out here."

"No, Jack," she said. "No. It's impossible." There was a silence. "Put Diana on." Daddy without another word handed the phone to me. I pleaded with her. "Mummy, please come out. It's such a divine house and there's masses of room."

She refused. There was more conversation and then I put Daddy back on. "Come out, for God's sake, Fig. We have our daughter here and I promise to make it pleasant for you. Please, Fig . . ." It was no use. The conversation ended when Daddy said, "Yes, yes. I'll take the best care of her I can. Good-by, Fig."

They never spoke to each other again.

After we had hung up he was like a young man in love. He could speak only of Mother. "She was difficult, our marriage was insane, but God, she was fun!" He said, "I loved no woman as I loved your mother. She was the only one.

The only good things I did in my life, I did with her. I loved her. Treepee, you were a love child. You were a child of love."

I was afraid he would cry. I wanted to cry. I laughed instead. "All right, Daddy." I helped him out of his chair. "Come on, go to bed. I'm tired, I really am." I put him to bed.

Despite the liquor, despite the illness, he remembered my twenty-first birthday when I had forgotten it. He telephoned me at Universal: "Why don't you come up to my place for dinner, and we'll celebrate?"

"I'd love it," I said. "Who else would you spend your birthday with except your family?"

He called for me and George began driving us out Sunset Boulevard. "This isn't the way to the house," I said. "I know," Daddy replied. "We'll just drop in a minute at Decker's place."

John Decker, the artist, was one of Daddy's great friends; he looked like an aged, incredibly decrepit Adolphe Menjou. When we arrived at his house, I walked in to find a tree and a blown-up photograph of me and under it a cake with twenty-one candles! Daddy was like a little boy, so delighted with his surprise. "Well, Treepee?" he asked. "How do you like your cake?"

"Oh, Daddy," I said and cried. It was the first birthday my father had ever spent with me.

Twice in those months I acted with him, learning how magnificent he could be. We rehearsed together for a half-hour *Romeo and Juliet* excerpt—the Balcony Scene—on the Rudy Vallee program.

I tried to play Juliet à la Katharine Cornell, the languorous dying lady. Daddy stopped me, "Don't use that made-actress voice," he said sharply. On stage, with a play in hand, he seemed years younger than the tired old man I spent so many evenings with on Tower Road. "Let me tell you something about Shakespeare," he went on. "The only reason I thought I was successful at it was because I played it as if Shakespeare had written the play for me. The part had never been acted before. Now you think the same way. This isn't a classic, it's something Noel Coward wrote for you. There's no precedent to follow. The first time these lines will have been read before an audience will be when you read them on the show."

He rehearsed me painstakingly. I needed it. We both came through beautifully. When I opened *Time* magazine and found myself described as "a luminously sensitive Juliet," I hugged my father. "You did it," I said. "You gave it to me." "No," he said. "You did it, Treepee."

The response was so overwhelming that Rudy decided he'd try three Barrymores. On March 5, 1942, two days after my twenty-first birthday, Daddy, Uncle Lionel, and I appeared over the air in *Julius Caesar*—Daddy as Brutus, Uncle Lionel as Caesar, and I as Calpurnia, Caesar's wife. Uncle Lionel sat in his wheelchair to the right of the microphone, Daddy at his left with his cardboards, and I between them.

After the show we went our separate ways: I to my apartment, Daddy with George to Tower Road, Uncle Lionel in his car, fixed so he could drive it despite his crippled legs, to his home. "Good night, my dear," he said. "We all did very well."

I tried to pick up the personal thread with Daddy a few nights later. I'd been so moved and happy in our work together on the radio. Dick Aldrich had sent me Emlyn Williams' play, *The Light of Heart,* a moving story about a broken-down matinee idol forced to work as a department-store Santa Claus to support his crippled daughter. "If you can get your father to do it, and you play the daughter, you can write your own ticket," Dick had said.

I showed my father the script. He liked it too. But the theater?

I reasoned with him. "After that dreadful thing you did on Broadway, don't you want to go back and do something really good? You can do it. I saw it with *Romeo and Juliet* and *Julius Caesar*."

He wasn't sure. A half-hour on radio was one thing, a three-act play on Broadway was another. He was too tired.

"Daddy, the two of us . . ."

He mused aloud. He was seated opposite me in what was a comfortable position for him—slumped in his chair, his feet apart, his hands, those large, surprisingly inartistic-looking hands, dangling between his knees. However mobile his face, however he might mug or pretend, nothing could hide the dark, glowing somberness of his eyes. The pupils were enormous, dilated with alcohol. He was saying, "If I could go back, in the right thing . . . this is so right, it is so much me . . . I'd probably not take a drink till after the theater."

"Maybe not even then, Daddy," I said.

He thought. "But why couldn't it be a film? Then I could do it here."

I knew what went through his mind. On a film set he'd read his lines from blackboards out of camera sight. "Why not?" I asked. Anything, I prayed, to bring him back as himself, as an actor, no longer a buffoon. "It would be fabulous!"

He brightened up. "You really think so, Treepee? I'll telephone Darryl right now." The telephone was at the other corner of the room. I heard him say, "Hello, Darryl? This is Jack." There was a moment's silence. Evidently Mr. Zanuck had replied with, "Jack? Jack who?" for Daddy said, "Jack Barrymore." Another silence. Daddy said, "I have my daughter here and we've both read a magnificent play which I think would make an extraordinary picture."

Daddy listened, his back to me. Then he said almost crisply, "Oh, I see. Well, thank you, Darryl," and hung up.

He did not repeat his conversation when he turned to me. All he said was, "Treepee, they don't seem to want me."

"There are others beside Zanuck, Daddy," I said hopefully. "Why don't you try Louis B. Mayer?"

He shook his head. "No, I'll never call anybody again. You can if you wish." He lit a cigarette with his shaking hands. "I won't do the play. I just can't."

I pleaded with him. If he had a change of scene and a serious project, if he was surrounded by friends and not drunken hangers-on—I ran to him and knelt by his chair and put my head in his lap. "Oh, Daddy, do you want *My Dear Children* to be what people remember you for? Please, come back to Broadway and do a show. We can make it. I know we can. You'd help me so much, just to be on the same stage with you. It's something I've dreamed of all my life, I think, but I've never even dared say it to myself."

He looked down at me in silence for a moment. Then he rose slowly from his chair and held out both his hands. "Stand up," he said. I did, and he put his arms around me. When he spoke, his voice was low and hoarse, a voice from which all pretense had vanished. "Treepee, *you* are going on to great things. I am already dead."

I cried myself to sleep that night, the first time in Hollywood.

Yet, a week later, I left my father.

Late one night I helped him into bed. He insisted upon his vermouth. He sipped it and looked at me. Suddenly he leaned over and picked up a small notebook from a chair by his bed. "Look, Treepee," he said. "I have a number I want you to call."

There was a phone in the small pantry and one in his study but none by his bed.

"Call? At this hour? Daddy, who would you want to telephone now?"

He said, "I want a girl to come here."

"A girl?" I didn't understand. "You mean a nurse?"

He glared at me. "Not a nurse. I said a girl. Go ahead. Call that number."

I said, "Daddy, really! This is an incredible thing for you to ask me to do. I won't do it."

He became angry. "Don't be so Goddamn finishing school, Miss! Don't you give me any of Michael's airs!"

I was outraged. "Daddy, I never finished school, but I'm not going to get a call girl for my father!"

We fought back and forth. He became cutting. Finally he said, and his voice was cold as ice: "Telephone that number."

All right, I thought. I went downstairs and made the call. Then I went to my room and packed what clothes I had. I put on my coat and sat down with my bag and waited. I met the young lady at the door. She was blonde and pretty. "How do you do," I said. "Mr. Barrymore is upstairs. I presume you know the way. You've been here before?"

She said, "Yes."

"Then you obviously know where to go. Good night." I picked up my bag and walked out. She called after me. "Who are you?"

"I am Mr. Barrymore's daughter," I said and slammed the door behind me.

I drove my car away from that house, and I drove recklessly down the long, winding road, swerving from side to side, and when I came to level ground I jammed the accelerator to the floor. The car leaped forward, the trees on either side flew past me. I stared, unseeing, at the black macadam road rushing under me. How *could* he do that! How *could* he ask his own daughter! How could he!

That night turned Daddy and me into strangers again. Two weeks went by without a call from one of us to the other. Then, shortly after midnight, my phone rang. It was Decker. "Your father's here, he's asking for you."

I dressed and drove out grimly. Decker may have been a

good friend of Daddy, but I considered him just one more of Daddy's drinking companions, a group of Hollywood characters, some very well known, who caroused with him.

When I walked into Decker's the first thing I saw was two heavily made-up blondes, sitting on the other side of a table littered with paper, drawings, and liquor. Decker was leaning against the fireplace. Daddy sat, sunken almost in a stupor, on the sofa. Nobody moved.

I was boiling. "Well, I'm here. What's the trouble?" I was furious. Those girls are common as cat-meat, I thought. They said nothing. John was bleakly silent. Daddy peered at me doubtfully. "Oooh, is my keeper come to get me?"

"Come on, Daddy, it's time to go," I said shortly. He sat there. Suddenly beside myself, I shouted at him. "Goddamn it, let's go home. I've got to get up in the morning!" I turned to Decker. "You're supposed to be his friend. You know he's not to have sex or liquor. Why do you get girls for him?" I stalked over to my father and took his arm.

He looked up as though he had just seen me. "Well, as-I-live-and-breathe! If it isn't Miss Newport."

"Get up!" I said.

He got up reluctantly, heavily, like a man who had in his mind that he had to get up to make the grave. We walked out to my car without another word, and I drove him to Tower Road in silence. I was steel. Mother was right. She had said, he's not the same man, Diana. He certainly isn't, I thought.

The huge house was dark save for a single spotlight playing on the pool. He had filled the pool for me when I came out. Now it was empty again. It was symbolic. The car stopped. He got out laboriously. I tried to help him, but he shrugged me off. I was terribly hurt and, suddenly, terribly ashamed.

"Daddy," I said almost apologetically, "I think it's better we don't see each other for a little while. I'm sorry if I've disappointed you, but I guess it's the way I have been brought up. That's the way I am."

He stood for a moment looking at me. Then he lifted one hand high and let it fall limply on my shoulder. His face had a smile, a strange combination of tears, anger, desperation, helplessness, oblivion. When he spoke, his words were slurred but the mockery was there. "Aren't you coming in to check up? Maybe your old Daddy's hidden himself a young lady to diddle with."

It was like a slap in the face. "Oh, go to bed, Daddy," I said, almost in tears. "You're disgusting, really you are. You're a drunken old fool. You bore me."

He said with a woozy dignity, "You bore me as much as I bore you. Good night."

Mother was right. That was all I could think of.

I won't call him, I vowed. Let him call me.

CHAPTER SEVENTEEN

W HO CARES? I thought. I'll live my own life.

My duplex hemmed me in. I wanted room. I got it by renting one of Hollywood's showplaces, the famous Basil Rathbone house, where Basil and his wife, Ouida, used to throw some of Hollywood's most lavish parties. It was enormous. The ballroom held five hundred people. There was a garden, swimming pool, tennis court, enclosed solarium. I was just twenty-one, and I had my own butler, cook, social secretary, and French companion. I had two dogs, Moka and Cleo, a great Dane, and my Darien Packard. I really began to *live*.

Bram, who'd been in New York, came back to test for *Keys of the Kingdom*. He took an apartment.

"This is silly," I said after the first few days. "You're over here more than you are there. Why should we pay double rent?"

Bram moved in. Mademoiselle suffered, but he *was* my fiancé, and I wasn't in a mood to be lectured.

The first party I gave got me into trouble. His name was Van Heflin. I'd met him a week earlier, when Bram and I dined at the Beachcomber's. As I rose from my seat, someone rose at the table behind me: our chairs tangled. I turned to apologize and found myself looking into the warm brown eyes of Mr. Heflin. We knew each other by sight.

"I beg your pardon . . ." I began.

"I beg *your* pardon," he said. He added almost in the same breath and so only I could hear, "You can't marry that man. You're going to marry me."

I stared at him, startled. Only that morning the latest of Mother's letters had repeated the same phrase: "You can't marry that man!" Then I burst into a peal of laughter. But when I gave my housewarming party, I invited Mr. Heflin, together with Kay Francis, Jon Hall, Frances Langford, John Loder, Eddie Albert, and several others who were working in *Eagle Squadron* with me.

As the party reached its height, I looked around. I was suddenly bored. "Ahhhhh," I said. I took a martini from a tray floating by and saw Mr. Heflin, standing off in one corner, looking as he did when he played the reporter in *The Philadelphia Story* in New York not long before—sensuous, sardonic, alone. I went up to him, as a hostess does to a guest who seems detached from it all. "Darling, can I get you anything?"

"No," he said. "I want to talk to you seriously."

"Well . . . follow me, and bring your glass with you." I said. "The only place we can have privacy is my room." It was huge, with a giant fireplace and a massive double bed in which I used to lie dreamily watching the flames dance and listening to my records.

Van saw the record player. "What would you like?"

I said, "I've been on a Rachmaninoff kick. Why not put on the Number Two in C minor?"

We sat cross-legged before the fire. The logs crackled. The music swelled . . .

We talked about him. He'd sailed on tramp steamers, he'd studied drama at Yale, he'd tried his hand at many things before ending up here in Hollywood. We talked about each other's roles on the legitimate stage. I'd seen him in *The Philadelphia Story*. He'd seen me in *The Land Is Bright*. We talked about our own hopes.

He said, "I'm serious. I want to marry you."

"How can you be serious?" I asked reasonably. "You don't even know me. I'm engaged. It's been going on for two years now. I can't marry you."

He stared into the fire. "If you marry him, you'll never get anywhere." He could introduce me to important people. Wasn't I hopeful of winning the lead opposite Robert Cummings in Henry Koster's new picture, *Between Us Girls?* Everyone in town coveted it; Ginger Rogers, who'd just finished *The Major and the Minor*, Katharine Hepburn, Deanna Durbin. It was a dream acting role: an actress who portrayed in turn six different characters—Queen Victoria at eighty-two, a girl of twelve, Sadie Thompson, Joan of Arc ... Yes, I said, I was to test for it. Then, said Heflin, I must meet his friend, Joe Pasternak, Henry Koster's ex-partner. "I'll take you to meet Joe tomorrow," he said.

Suddenly there was a banging at the door and Bram's angry voice: "Diana! Are you in there?"

He came through the door like an avenging angel. He found us sitting on the floor, the fire crackling against a background of soft music. We'd been talking so long that the entire concerto was completed and the last record was replaying itself.

Bram's face was white. "You might remember you're the hostess," he said stiffly. Van leaped up and apologized. "I'm sorry!" I exclaimed, scrambling to my feet. "Of course, I should be down there."

Many guests had left. I apologized to the others. When the party broke up, Bram turned his back on me and stomped up the stairs. Van and I were left alone. "Why don't we go for a ride?" he suggested.

Bram had been impossible. "All right," I said.

When I returned home an hour later, I took a drink to fortify myself and went upstairs. Bram was sitting in my big easy chair, reading. He looked up when I walked in. "Where were you?" he demanded. "Where did you go with Heflin?"

"To the beach. We sat in the car and looked at the stars and talked." It was true.

"Really?"

"Bram, don't use that inflection." I became angry, and grew angrier as I went on. "Tomorrow he's taking me to meet Joe Pasternak, who can be important for me. And Bramwell, he's a brilliant, successful actor. I seem to be doing well too." I began to toy aloud with a fantasy. "Maybe you and I aren't right for each other. Maybe he and I . . ."

We had an emotional scene. I was insane, Bram cried. How could I let myself be moved by sudden physical attractions? I'd always be attracted to one man or another the moment I met them. But they meant nothing. We two had something far deeper . . . Bramwell was beside himself.

I melted. "Oh, darling!" I took his head on my breast. I felt like a mother, not a lover. "Of course, darling. Look, I'm not in love with him, of course it's only you and me, only us, always."

Next morning Heflin introduced me to Joseph Pasternak with the words, "This is the girl I'm going to marry."

I laughed. "I'm afraid he's a little premature, Mr. Pasternak."

Mr. Pasternak was graciousness itself. I told him I thought Henry Koster was a genius: everyone knew how marvelously he'd worked with Deanna Durbin. He could make anyone act. "I'm praying I get the part," I said. He smiled. "So are many other girls. You'll have to go by the tests."

When Van drove me home, he said, "You're going to marry Fletcher, aren't you? I can tell it from your eyes."

I nodded. "Of course. I love him and he loves me. There was never any doubt of it."

He smiled. "All right then, I'll be your next husband"— and was gone.

Sidney Skolsky, the columnist, had the story, but treated it gingerly. His column on May 14 reported that I had given a party. He added:

> When Van Heflin, an acquaintance of Diana Barrymore from the stage, arrived, Miss Barrymore left her guests and took Van Heflin upstairs to show him some photos and stories that she had collected of John Barrymore. While Van Heflin and Miss Barrymore were doing this, the guests organized their own party, left and went to a night club. The next day Diana Barrymore wrote letters of apology to the guests.
>
> Diana Barrymore, everyone will tell you, is a good kid, but she is just another Barrymore—who continues to confuse Hollywood.

I confuse Hollywood?

Two days later Van Heflin married Frances Neal, an actress. His best man was Joseph Pasternak.

Yet, Mr. Skolsky had something. It wasn't that I confused Hollywood so much as that Hollywood confused me. I rode a whirligig. Universal publicity took over: Bob Stack and I were sent bowling with photographers in tow: a wholesome real-life romance would spice our screen love affair. The columnists descended on me: Louella Parsons, Hedda Hopper, Jimmy Fidler, Harrison Carroll. I felt as though I were being dissected in public. My new face, with my capped teeth and special hairdo, stared back at me from every screen magazine under such headings as "Begins At Top." I was Jack Barrymore's "dark-eyed, storm-cloud" daughter, a witty, ultra-sophisticated, finishing-school product, talented and temperamental, "Tall and graceful, exquisitely built, with a heart-shaped face and a child's mouth, possessed of the poise of a duchess and the brain of a Barrymore, quick and sharp . . ."

Good God, I used to think in dismay. How will I ever live up to that billing? As a child I'd been around clever, cultured people, but I never felt part of them. The few times I came downstairs to meet Mother's famous literary friends,

I'd felt just as frightened and as much the impostor. They'd ask, "What have you been reading lately?" expecting me to reply, *"The Brothers Karamazov."* Since I'd really been devouring the latest I-was-raped story in *True Confessions,* I always lied and felt guilty.

Now the same sense of inadequacy swept over me. Trying to be what people expected, I reached for the quip, the Noel Coward retort, the devastating riposte. A few drinks helped things along, but now and then I had a little too much and my tongue took over. Then I'd say aloud what most people kept to themselves.

Once John Loder brought beautiful Hedy Lamarr to visit us. As a gift she gave me a copy of Philip Wylie's newest book. I'd read reviews of it. "My God, Hedy," I exclaimed. "What an extraordinary gift for you to give me. With that face of yours I didn't think you had a brain in your head."

Hedy managed to laugh.

On another occasion Bram and I were dinner guests of the Alfred Hitchcocks. I had met Mr. Hitchcock at Ouida Rathbone's, where she placed me at her star table, between Clark Gable and Mr. Hitchcock. I talked to Mr. Gable about horses and about Daddy. I told him, "Your smile is like my father's, a half-smile that somehow makes you want to cry." I got along well with Mr. Gable. Then I turned to Mr. Hitchcock. The great mystery director proved to be chillier country. I was overawed. I tried to make up for it by gushing. He must have thought me a silly young woman.

Now, at his home, I drank too much. Maybe I thought enough martinis would bring out the "rapier wit" Louella Parsons reported I had. I didn't do well. The liquor worked a different magic. My awe gave place to a kind of secret rage: how dared he be so important as to make me feel so little? I found myself standing belligerently in front of him, taunting him: "What happened to you, Mr. Hitchcock? Your last film was a bust. What's the matter with the man who directed so many great pictures?"

Mr. Hitchcock turned to Bramwell. "Take this drunken woman out of my house," he said, and started for his study. Joseph Cotten, another guest, tried to placate him. "Now, now, Hitch . . ." But Mr. Hitchcock would have none of it. "Get that drunken woman out of here!" he said and vanished into his study.

I heard myself retort, "What makes you so damn arrogant, Mr. Hitchcock? Didn't you read the notices? Don't you know how bad it was?"

Mrs. Hitchcock tried her best. "Diana, you struck him on a sensitive nerve. He was so hurt by those notices."

Bram took me by the arm. "Dear, I think we'd better go."

At home, when my wits returned, I was appalled. Bram told me to write a letter of apology. "Oh, Bram," I said miserably, "how in heaven's name do you apologize when you get drunk and insult a man of his greatness in his own home?" I wrote the letter finally. Mr. Hitchcock never answered it. The story got out.

There was the time, too, Deanna Durbin unexpectedly turned up on my set. I caught sight of her standing to one side. I stopped short in the middle of my scene. "Who is that?" I demanded, pointing. "It looks suspiciously like Deanna Durbin."

She spoke up. "Yes, it is, Miss Barrymore." Obviously she'd come to see what I looked like, now that I was talked about for the Koster role.

"Look, Miss Durbin!" I said. "This is the last scene of the picture and we're doing it over because I didn't get it right the first time. Now, would you please get out of here, because if you watch I'll be too nervous."

Miss Durbin looked at me icily, turned on her heel, and left. The story spread that I'd ordered her off my set. The *Hollywood Reporter* carried a little item, "Diana Barrymore's highhanded manner is making NO friends."

I hadn't really meant it that way.

Bram would take me sharply to task. "You're spoiled," he'd

say. "You think just because you're so much a lady, you can get away with murder. Well, you can't, and the sooner you learn it, the better!"

I'd turn on him and pour all my accumulated anger and humiliation on his head. We fought, only to make up the more passionately. In his arms I tried to explain. People in Hollywood were quicker to be offended. In New York my friends passed everything off as a joke—no one took himself or anything else too seriously. Hollywood, for all its sophistication, lacked a sense of humor.

Bram would console me. "All right, all right," he'd say. "Simmer down, my little cyclone." That broke me up, for a current magazine story about me began, "Did you ever see a cyclone walking?"

I had little chance to brood about my bad personal public relations. My tests for *Between Us Girls* came through. Koster raved about them. I not only won the part, my salary was boosted to fifteen hundred dollars a week!

Everyone agreed I had the greatest chance ever given a young actress to show her ability. *Between Us Girls* would make or break me.

I wanted to phone Daddy and let him exult with me, but my pride held me back. I waited for him to call me.

That was how things stood with Daddy and me when he died.

CHAPTER EIGHTEEN

THE NIGHT IT HAPPENED I was at the Hollywood
Pantages Theatre, attending Universal's preview of *Eagle
Squadron*. I hadn't wanted to go. I wanted to stay at the hospital, where Daddy was very ill. But Walter said it was important for me to go, and the doctors assured me I could
leave for a few hours.

They had diagnosed Daddy's sickness as pneumonia with
complications. I'd rushed off the set of *Between Us Girls* in
the middle of a scene when I got word. I tiptoed into his
room—the first time I'd seen him since that awful night I
took him home from Decker's. He lay sleeping, strangely
white. On my later visits, he was unable to recognize me.
Once he opened his eyes and saw me looking down at him.
"Daddy—" I began helplessly. There was so much I wanted
to say to him . . . "Treepee," he said clearly. He smiled, a
wondrously sweet smile, and closed his eyes again. The nurse
put her finger to her lips and led me from the room.

The night of May 29, 1942, I called to look in on Daddy,
but he was asleep: he could not be seen. I remember standing
outside his room, listening. I could hear his heavy, labored
breathing. "He's hung on for days," the doctors had said.
"He can hang on for many more days." I tiptoed away. In
the room across the corridor, Uncle Lionel sat, silent. He
had been there day after day. He scarcely lifted his haggard
face to nod recognition. Nearby some of Daddy's friends—

Decker, Gene Fowler, the writer, Alan Dinehart, the actor—
hovered. I hurried out of the hospital, leaving word where
I could be reached.

At the theater I sat nervously between Bram and Walter
in the sixteenth row—I remember because I'd told the usher
my seat number—with Universal executives all about me,
and tried to concentrate on the screen. But all I could see
was my father lying in the hospital, and Uncle Lionel, silent
and bowed, in the room across the hall. When my eyes focused
on the screen, I saw myself in my first picture. I knew instantly that I was not good. I was stiff, I was stodgy, I lacked
emotion. When I kissed Bobby Stack in the love scene we'd
repeated so often, I was wooden-faced. My A.T.S. uniform
made me look like a sack; the low heels and short skirt only
emphasized my bow legs. And under Stanley Cortez' lighting
magic, my crooked nose remained crooked but a railing
emerged as a work of art.

There was a burst of applause as the picture ended. I had
no heart for the crowd, the congratulations, or anything else.
"Walter, I'm terrible in it," I said as we hastened out. Bram
reassured me, "No one likes himself the first time." Walter
said, "It's all much better than you think. You'll see."

Bram turned to go for our car, and I felt a hand on my
shoulder. It was the head usher, red-faced and out of breath.
"Miss Barrymoore, the hospital called. They want you there
right away."

I began running. Someone helped me into my car. Bramwell drove. Out of nowhere two motorcycle policemen materialized and cleared the way through traffic for us, sirens
screaming. I sat numbly in the front seat staring at them
through the windshield. "He's dead," I said. I said it over
and over. "I'll never get there in time."

Bramwell was murmuring words as he drove, but I could
not make them out. Then we were skidding to a stop in front
of the hospital. I ran up the steps and into the huge, square
elevator and waited the eternity it took to rise to the fourth

floor. Someone must have telephoned upstairs because one of Daddy's doctors was waiting as the door slid open.

I heard a voice that sounded like a stranger's ask, "Where is my Uncle Lionel?"

The doctor said, "He left a few minutes ago, Miss Barrymore."

Then I knew the answer to the question I hadn't been able to ask.

"My father is dead?"

"Yes," he said. "Would you like to see him?"

I asked for a moment's time. I felt spent, but calm. "Where are Gene Fowler and the rest?"

"Downstairs," he said. "Having a wake."

A nurse was at my side and led me to Daddy's room. I went in by myself and closed the door and looked down at my dead father.

Mother had said once, "When he was young, your father was the most beautiful man that ever lived. He looked like a young archangel, divinely beautiful."

I began to cry. I was looking at the man she had described. Perhaps I wouldn't have cried then had he looked old and withered. But he looked young! Lying there, his hands crossed on his breast as they had been placed by the priest who gave him the last rites, he looked like the young Hamlet, the young, dead Hamlet . . . All my life I had seen my father's photographs, and now it seemed I saw him as he must have looked in the roles he made immortal. For death had done something subtle and wonderful to him: his chins were gone, his jowls were gone, everything of age and dissipation was gone . . . He lay in death like a beautiful young man!

For three days I walked about like a person under a spell. For three days I couldn't see or talk to anyone. Bram tried to comfort me, but I was beyond consolation. I couldn't forget that face, I couldn't forget it. Thank God, I thought, Death took him that way, not as the old, broken shell of a man he used to say he was. He used to tell me, "I'm an old gadzooks—I'm nothing any more." And I used to say to him, "Oh, no, Daddy, don't think that way!" But he had no confidence, no anything, about his own soul, his own heart, his own destiny. But when he was dead, he was beautiful!

They had to drag me out of his room. I fought and struggled and screamed. They forced me into a chair in the corridor. I didn't know if I would ever get up again, or if I wanted to. I didn't realize his death would affect me so. I hadn't known him well. And it was so terrible, so shameful and terrible, that I hadn't been speaking to him in those weeks before he died.

I thought, all my life I had a father. I knew I had him, though I really hadn't. Yet he was alive then, he existed, and nothing could take that away from me. Now he was dead. And I had not spoken to him before he died! The last words I had said to him had been bitter, nasty, cutting words. I had been too grand . . .

I raged at myself, and the tears overwhelmed me. I was a bloody snob! I shouldn't have been that way about my father! I shouldn't have been such a Goddamned boarding-school bitch! When I let that girl into the house that night I should have said to her, "All right, honey, be kind to him. I'll be here when you come down . . ." I should have realized that my father was sick and broken and lonely and old and unhappy. I thought, oh, if he were alive, I'd know how to be a daughter to him now, no matter what he did, no matter what he asked, no matter how shocking a life he led. But I'd been brought up too bloody much "society" and too strictly and too everything else! And I could not take it, I could not take it, that my own father should ask me to get him a whore!

Oh, Daddy, I prayed, *forgive me.*

I went to the funeral with Uncle Lionel. Aunt Ethel was in Boston, appearing in *The Corn Is Green* and could not reach the coast in time.

If I thought Daddy's death would bring my uncle closer to me, I was mistaken. At the hospital we had scarcely exchanged a word. He had been so stricken that I made no further overtures to him.

The morning of the funeral someone telephoned me. The voice was as impersonal as a hotel clerk's. "Your uncle will pick you up at ten. Please be ready."

At that hour a limousine stopped in front of my house. Uncle Lionel sat in the back, hunched up and silent. Like strangers we rode together to Calvary Cemetery and were escorted through the enormous crowd of spectators to our places in the small chapel. Uncle Lionel spoke only once, when we got out of the car. He looked about, at the green of the trees and the cloudless May sky, and said, half to himself, "Well, it's a nice day for Jack." We stood together, watching, as the coffin was placed in its crypt. Again we rode back together, each with his own thoughts. In the car he spoke once again. He looked at me and said, as though completing a train of thought in his own mind, "Yes, Miss Barrie knew him better." I didn't know what to say. I said nothing.

When the car stopped before my house, I said, "Uncle Lionel, won't you come in? Won't you come in for some coffee or something?"

He shook his head. "No," he said. "I think I'd better go on, thank you."

I felt heartsick. Couldn't he have come in, for a few minutes? Couldn't he have said, perhaps, "We've both lost someone—come out to my place if you're lonely. We'll talk about Jack. Maybe it will make us both feel better." No, nothing like that. And how often I'd telephoned him, saying, I'd like to come out and visit you, Uncle Lionel, and he'd always replied, no, it's too far, I'll come to see you—and he never did. And now, nothing, only the cryptic, somehow rebuking sentence, "Yes, Miss Barrie knew him better."

Was I at fault?

I could understand only this: that he was alone with his grief, and I had no part in it.

I'd been an intruder from the start.

Damn them all, I wept in bed that night, while Moka trembled in his little basket on the floor nearby, and in her room Mademoiselle slept the sleep of the innocent. Damn them for giving me nothing and taking it away before I had it! Damn Mother for her grandness and her indifference and her disdain of me, and damn Daddy for the crazy, mixed-up life he led and the daughter he never gave a damn for, and damn Uncle Lionel for treating me like the boarding-school bitch I am, and damn Aunt Ethel who doesn't even know I'm alive, and damn me for being a silly, arrogant, affected schoolgirl! God damn us all! We deserve everything we get!

CHAPTER NINETEEN

Nobody could stop me now.

I married Bramwell Fletcher. The studio asked me to wait until *Between Us Girls* was released. I refused. I told Walter: "I have nothing to do with the studio once I leave these gates. When I'm inside them I belong to you. But outside, I run my own life."

Mother had done everything to prevent the marriage, and failed. At Daddy's death I had been on the telephone with her. She broke down then. "Oh, Catkin," she wept, "you knew him only at the end! Only at the end!" I listened to her almost without emotion. I was drained of it. She had kept us apart, she had brought me up thinking he was not a man to be loved and respected; she had kept me from my father. That was how she wanted it: that was how it had been. Now, I was sick of sham and pretense and righteousness. Mother was not going to keep me from Bram. I wrote her a brutally honest letter:

I know you don't like Bram. He knows it too. You'd like me to make a better match, to marry someone very social and very successful and very rich. But I'm not. Bram is going to be my husband. Aside from our fights—and we've been through the ups and downs that usually occur the first two years of marriage—we are happy together and I'm going to marry him. And since this is the time for truth, you should know that when Bram was away, I had an affair in New York with Richie Merino, to try to get over Bram. Believe me, in many ways it's a good thing for me that I met Bram when I did . . .

I told her how unhappy Bram's first marriage had been:

I'm going to make him happy. I can do it, because I'm young and strong and have a damn good head on my shoulders, whether you know it or not. If there's anything you want to know about Bram, call Dr. ———. You can have Harry look up his record as a doctor, if you want to be assured on that score too. Put your mind at ease. Find out anything and everything you can about Bram—you'll find a clean slate. But no matter what you say, I'm marrying him. There's nothing you can do or say that will stop me.

Mother capitulated. She and Robin flew to Hollywood for the ceremony. Leonard, on overseas duty with the Navy, cabled me his best wishes.

I hadn't seen Robin for years and I was overjoyed. He had come into a fortune when his father, Leonard Thomas, Sr., died a few years before, and now he was able to indulge his opulent tastes. He had given up his dreams of the theater. Brilliant and talented though he was, he had become a gentleman of leisure, a patron of the arts, seeking his pleasure and amusement with friends in half a dozen countries. His house in Paris was an international rendezvous, with guests ranging from promising young artists to celebrated entertainers such as Maurice Chevalier and Mistinguett, a perpetual house party with Robin bestowing gifts of Cartier jewelry—gold cuff links, jeweled cigarette cases—with the largess of an Indian rajah. Sometimes, listening to Mother's descriptions, it seemed to me that Robin was living more like mad King Ludwig than anyone else—but it was Robin's life, and why shouldn't he live it his way?

From the moment Mother and Robin walked into my house (Bram quietly moved back to his apartment the night before), they took command. "Michael and I will handle everything," Robin announced. "You aren't to have a thing to do with your own wedding. We're even paying for it." He looked at me sternly. "What are you going to wear?"

After I caught my breath, I said, "Why a wedding dress, Robin. What do you think? This is my *first* marriage."

He laughed. "Who's making it?"

"The studio."

Robin looked at me pityingly. "Out of some old wardrobe trunk?"

I explained that Vera West, Universal's famed dress designer, was whipping up a special creation for me. Robin went over the sketches with Vera, suggesting a tuck here, a pleat there. Vera said admiringly, you're so right, Mr. Thomas, and together they designed my wedding dress.

"Now, the guest list," Robin said peremptorily. "Hand it over."

I asked timidly, "Could I have Mr. and Mrs. ——"

"Who are they?" Robin demanded.

"Oh, they're very chic," I said.

"Then it's all right," said Robin. And so we went down the list. "No, no, no," he'd say. "Not these people. We must have a terribly smart wedding. Cross them off."

Mother sat there, listening adoringly. She could listen to Robin by the hour. He'd say, "Don't you agree, Cat?" and she'd say, "Oh, yes, yes, yes. Whatever you say, Robin-cat. You decide. Anyway, you probably know all sorts of people out here Diana hasn't met yet; but you understand, she has to have her directors and cameramen and the rest."

Robin said firmly, "Not at the wedding. At the reception."

I was brought up a Catholic—if not a particularly observing one—and I wanted to be married in the Church. But Bram was divorced, his former wife was still living; it was wartime, and when I inquired, I found months must elapse before we could obtain a special dispensation from Rome. I refused to wait any longer; I couldn't wait any longer. The ceremony was performed in my house by the Reverend H. Paul Romeis, a Lutheran pastor. Three weeks earlier he'd married Barbara Hutton and Cary Grant. Maybe we'd be as happy as they.

The night before the wedding Mother and I had one final fight. She took me aside to tell me that Harry Tweed had asked her for a divorce. I was shocked. "I'm giving it to him," she said. "We haven't been getting along for years, as you know, Diana——"

"Yes, Mother, I certainly do." I added, "The day I left New York, Harry and I had a talk which I never told you about." Before Mother could think what to say, I went on. "He told me, 'Diana, if you want to marry this fellow, go ahead. But please be nice to his friends. And don't try to run the marriage. Let him do it.'"

Mother burst into tears and when she cried, she got angry. "Well," I said, "he was perfectly right, and you know it. You used to give parties and you had all your friends, but you never asked his. And you were always trying to run everything."

"Are you telling me what I have done wrong about my marriage?" she demanded through her tears, and then I grew angry and we shouted hysterically at each other—she, because her marriage was over, and her daughter was marrying against her wishes, and I because I was on edge about my own marriage and outraged that my mother should choose this moment to upset me.

Mother screamed for Mademoiselle, and Mademoiselle came running, and I left the two of them, marched into my room, locked the door, and put on some Shostakovich. I listened to the music. I won't let anything bother me, I told myself. It was the first woman-to-woman fight I'd had with Mother. Until now I was only her Catkin; now I was someone who dared put my foot down. Mother would have to learn to live with it.

The next afternoon, two hours before the ceremony, Uncle

Lionel called. He was making a picture, *Tennessee Johnson,* and could get away for only an hour—hundreds of extras were involved, and even the hour's halt would cost MGM thousands of dollars—but he was hurrying over anyway to see me in my wedding dress, even though he couldn't stay for the ceremony. He came with a wedding gift of two beautiful silver compotes, paid his respects to Mother, and said to me, "My dear, I only wish Jack were here to see you now. It would have been a very happy moment in his life."

That made Mother sniffle, and I sniffled, and we all sniffled. We all had a glass of champagne, Uncle Lionel kissed me, and went back to work. For the first time he'd really acted as my uncle, and I was grateful.

Mother and I went upstairs. Like two children we stuck our heads out the window in my bedroom and watched the guests arrive, exchanging comments about them. There was the Countess de Frasco, Lady Mendl, Louella Parsons, Lloyd Pantages, Maxie Baer—Mother said, "I knew Robin would ask him. Darling, do you really think a prizefighter belongs here today?"

"Of course, Mother," I replied. "Don't you remember what Elsa Maxwell told us: to have a successful party, mix all kinds of people together. And isn't a wedding almost like a party?"

Then we saw my bridegroom coming up the walk. Bram looked perfectly handsome, save that his hair was dyed auburn for his part in *Random Harvest,* which he was making with his friend Ronald Colman. To see your bridegroom before the ceremony is bad luck. I didn't give it a second thought.

Robin gave me away. Mother wept. Bramwell stood by my side, trembling. I put my hand out and took his in mine and squeezed it. It calmed him, and we both went through our lines perfectly. We turned and kissed each other, and we were Mr. and Mrs. Bramwell Fletcher. The date was July 30, 1942.

Photographers descended on us as the reception began on the huge lawn. Mother bristled. "No, we shall have none of this, Diana!" she began, in her best drillmaster voice. "Mother," I said, amused, "you can't stop it. This isn't Newport, it's Hollywood." Outside the gates hundreds of people watched, and in the midst of the gaiety there was a loud splash, and screams from the girls, and there was Maxie Baer floundering in my swimming pool. He'd fallen in, Charvet tie and all.

For our honeymoon Bram and I drove to San Francisco. We stopped the first night in a small roadside hotel. Mother had bought me a white chiffon nightgown, virginal and demure, and as I put it on, while Bram was getting ready, I felt both silly and embarrassed. Then Bram appeared in a bright new robe and pajamas. We looked at each other and fell into each other's arms, laughing. Then we celebrated with a bottle of champagne we'd brought along and, old friends, went to our marriage bed.

CHAPTER TWENTY

FOUR DAYS LATER we were back in Hollywood—I to start a new picture, *Nightmare*, with Brian Donlevy, Bram to begin *The Immortal Sergeant*, with Henry Fonda and Maureen O'Hara. The day we returned, Mother and Robin left, taking Mademoiselle with them. Now that I was married, Mother accepted the fact that I no longer needed a chaperone.

Though I didn't know it, I needed one more than ever.

If you should see *Nightmare* on the Late, Late Show, you'll find the best shot is the first one. I open the door, walk into a room—and there lies Henry Daniell, my husband, a knife sticking from his back. I rush screaming down the stairs and meet Brian Donlevy rushing up.

Mr. Donlevy was handsome and dapper in a blue blazer with gold buttons and a captain's cap—his usual off-the-set costume. He was fresh from his triumph in *The Great McGinty*. We got along famously. *Nightmare* was an old-fashioned melodrama full of secret codes, Nazi spies, and mysterious telephone calls. Brian and I had many love scenes. On the sixth day of shooting he said, "Look, it seems silly, our both going all the way to the commissary for lunch. Why don't we lunch in my bungalow? I have food in the icebox, liquid refreshment——"

This seemed sensible. We began lunching at his bungalow. We took longer and longer lunch hours. He was gay, ready for fun, full of vitality. He began to send me little presents— books, scarves. Bramwell became concerned. "Why should he send you presents?"

"Because he likes me," I said.

Bram used the same inflection he had used when he asked me about Van Heflin. "Is that all?"

"Of course. Really, Bram. He's old enough to be my father."

It was an unfortunate remark. Bram glared at me and returned to his newspaper.

One night I invited Brian to dinner. The two men were charming to each other and to me. I could not help noticing: One was happy, easygoing, devil-may-care—life was a ball to him; to the other, life was real and life was earnest. I thought, Bram is sweet, he has character, he's a fine man—but I wish he'd unbend. I wish he'd have some fun.

Next day on the set Brian said, "Your husband's really a very fine fellow. Rather quiet, though."

I said, "Yes, he is."

"How long have you been married?" I knew Brian knew.

"About nine weeks," I said. I was shocked to hear myself say it. Was it only nine weeks?

My marriage to Bram was a strange thing. We were lovebirds before the ceremony. Though we were happily married in the face of incessant quarrels, a slow disintegration began to set in.

Part of our trouble, I know now, was the difference in age. I was twenty-one, Bram was thirty-nine. He was content to spend the evening at home painting, reading, or playing gin rummy. I'd say to him, "I know you've lived in hotels most of your life—you've always been traveling—now that you have a home, you want to stay in it. But I get bored." The old impatience would sweep over me. I wanted to do the town. I enjoyed going out, seeing and being seen. I'd enjoyed it from the moment I was transformed from wallflower into debutante. I was attracted to men. Like it or not, from girlhood on I had adored handsome men. I reacted instantly to their glance, what they suggested and what they promised. I was married but I loved to flirt. I couldn't help it. It belonged to the excitement of being alive.

Part of our trouble, too, stemmed from the direction my career was taking. No one tells you in Hollywood when you're starting down. But there are signs. I recognized them when I began my fourth picture, *Fired Wife*, with Louise Allbritton and Walter Abel.

Until now I'd had my own bungalow on the Universal lot, like Brian's—complete to bedroom, kitchen, and dressing room. Mine was elegant. It had been Marlene Dietrich's not long before.

The first morning I walked through the Universal gate, the watchman stopped me. "You're going the wrong way, Miss Barrymore. You're in Number Twelve."

"Number Twelve?" I said. I trudged off to find Number Twelve. It turned out to be a single room. I was on the skids, even if my salary was now two thousand a week. I was sure of it later that day when I learned that I no longer had Gwen, my personal hairdresser, who'd been Mae West's hairdresser and used to regale me with stories about her. Gwen wasn't assigned to me on this picture: no one was. I was to use the girl who took care of everyone else.

I tried to make sense of what was happening to me. My *Eagle Squadron* notices hardly surprised me. *Variety* said I had undeniable talent. *Life* thought I played with considerable competence. The New York *Times* (I imagined all my friends at the Stork Club reading it) dismissed me with one sentence: "And Diana Barrymore as the girl friend is entirely inadequate and extremely affected, to boot." Oh, well, I thought unhappily, I knew that the moment I saw the preview. Since I projected neither sex nor beauty on the screen,

I needed a part in which I could act. That's why I counted so much on *Between Us Girls.*

I had worked hard in that picture. Each morning I had dashed down to the studios, to emerge as a twelve-year-old girl in pigtails, middy blouse, and short skirt. Tourists gaped when they saw me nervously puffing a cigarette on the set. I learned to roller-skate for harum-scarum scenes with Bob Cummings. In one scene he couldn't get himself to slap me hard, as the script required. Just as he was about to try for the seventh time, I kicked him sharply in the shins. He swatted me. It stung madly, but director Koster beamed. I sat for three hours while Perc Westmore magically made me into Queen Victoria. I stewed in Joan of Arc's armor. Everyone played up to me—Bob, Kay Francis, John Boles. Koster was magnificent. He even had the grips applaud me after each scene to give me the feeling of theater. I had no excuses, and I thought I did well. Mother phoned me from New York: "Catkin, you were so good, the audience at the Capitol was in stitches." Mother had never been too bad a critic. At the Hollywood preview the audience almost fell out of its seats too. Universal went overboard and spent enormous sums of money advertising me as "1942's Most Sensational New Screen Personality."

But the notices were mixed. They confused me. A San Francisco critic said it wouldn't surprise her if "young Diana Barrymore was to prove the greatest of the Barrymores." I tossed that aside. *Cue* said, "Miss Barrymore evinces the first real evidence of . . . tremendous talent"; but the *Times,* sour again, crushed me: "If she has talent, she should not conceal it in such a frenzied and labored exhibition."

Was I good in films? I didn't know. Tim Whelen, my director in *Nightmare,* touted me as a coming Bette Davis. Melodrama was my forte, he said. Yet *Nightmare* made no box-office records. Walter was silent and embarrassed. His judgment hadn't paid off. My pictures weren't making money. I sat in Number Twelve that morning and decided

I'd been mismanaged. The tipoff was *Between Us Girls*. They shouldn't have given me the part, no matter how much I wanted it, no matter how promising my tests. I wasn't ready for so demanding—and revealing—a role. Even a greatly experienced actress would have thought twice.

I had believed my clippings, and the studio believed in the Barrymore name. We were both wrong, obviously. They should have waited for the right vehicle to come along, they should have nursed me carefully and allowed me to develop. They should have called the tune—not I.

I walked out of Number Twelve and went miserably to work.

When *Fired Wife* was completed, Universal told me I was scheduled for a Sherlock Holmes picture.

I exploded. "I won't do it." A Sherlock Holmes was always the second bill in a first-run house. I wasn't selling the Barrymore name that cheaply!

Would I consider working in an Abbott and Costello?

"I most certainly would not!"

I stalked out, got into my Packard, and drove home. Next morning I was informed I had been put on suspension—without salary.

"Okay," I snapped. "Suspend me." I didn't care. I had enough money. Let them come up with the right picture. I might not be a good judge of what pictures to go into, but I was a good judge of what pictures I shouldn't go into.

During my suspension Bram and I were invited to dinner at Jack Warner's. Ann Warner and I liked each other; we became dinner guests there almost three times a week. Ann's parties, always featured by a showing of the latest Warner release, were gay. I drank, but not more than most. I drove about town on shopping sprees. One day I saw Uncle Lionel driving in the next lane: I waved to him to pull over, and we both parked. I walked to his car, leaned against the door, and we had a little inconsequential chat: how was he, and how were I and Bram, and what was I doing? I said nothing about my troubles at Universal. Then I kissed him good-by and he drove on. I sat in my car watching his car disappear. I wish he'd let me come out and see him, I thought. I wish he would.

The remainder of my suspension, which lasted six months, Bram and I sat out in a cottage we'd taken in Coldwater Canyon, where we painted for hours in a pink and cream studio and discussed the wisdom of returning to New York and the Broadway stage. I was discouraged about my movie career more than I would let anyone—even Bram—know. After so brilliant an entrance, was I to exit as a stooge in an Abbott and Costello farce?

My suspension was over. Walter had a fabulous part for me. I was to play a British society girl in *Ladies Courageous,* with Loretta Young. My role had even more scope than hers!

My spirits soared. I packed away my paints, hurried down to Universal, got Vera busy designing my clothes, and dashed off gay letters to Mother. Walter gave me the bad news ten days later. "It's hard for me to tell you this, Diana," he began. "You're not playing the part. We've hired Geraldine Fitzgerald. We all agree she's bigger box office right now."

I was so hurt I could hardly speak. I was still in *Ladies Courageous,* Walter assured me. I was to play a bitch who made trouble for everyone. No matter how he described it, I knew. It was a completely secondary role. Walter was desperately sorry but helpless. He could no longer gamble on me.

I walked out of his office proudly, my head held high—otherwise, I would have wept. To Vera, who'd followed my meteoric career—over almost before it began—I said, "I guess I've had it."

Vera didn't contradict me. "What are you going to do?"

"Just leave as gracefully as I can." I'd made up my mind. "I can come back. I won't be the first one to make a round trip."

In December, 1943, in the guise of visiting New York for
the Christmas holidays, Bram and I literally sneaked out of
Hollywood. I had been there for nearly two years, I had
made five pictures, I was a has-been—and I had yet to celebrate my twenty-third birthday.

Amazingly enough, I was welcomed back to New York as a
success! Publicity, I thought, is a wonderful thing. It was
exciting to find myself in the society columns again: "What
Mrs. Bramwell Fletcher Thinks of Hollywood Would Burn
Up Wires," to receive scripts from agents, to throw parties
in the luxurious penthouse we took overlooking Central
Park, to catch up on gossip with Robin and Mother. One
night I walked out on my terrace and looked out over the
twinkling expanse of Central Park, the myriad of lights glittering from a thousand windows up Fifth Avenue. "Oh, all
right," I said to myself. "They can have their California and
Malibu Beach and all the rest. I take New York. It's where I
belong. I'm never going back to that factory again!"

Robin said, "Cat, you're absolutely right. Your place is
here, in the theater." Robin had left Paris and bought a
house near New Milford, Connecticut, where he was living
in a fashion that can only be compared to that of Henry
VIII. He was the master of the manor: guests were entertained day and night, weekdays and week ends: Peggy Fears,
Gypsy Rose Lee, John Colton, who wrote the stage version
of *Rain,* Billy Rambo, who was Robin's closest friend, Jackie
Colt, Aunt Ethel's son, his wife Marjorie, and many others.
Robin was in his element. He was forever concocting fantastic feasts for his guests, marinating venison in whisky, then
cooking it in sour cream, churning his own butter, serving
caviar and pink champagne for breakfast, keeping a huge refrigerator stocked with exotic foods flown in from all parts of
the globe.

Mother was unhappy about him—and about me. She knew
the truth about my Hollywood experience and had begun to

suspect the success of my marriage. Robin, however, distressed her. His shining career in the arts had never materialized. His friend Tyrone Power had gone on to great things, but Robin had become an eccentric country squire, trying to live a fifteenth-century life in the twentieth century.

Mother had made a new life for herself after her divorce. She had bought a house in Easton, Connecticut, where she lived with a companion, Margaret Wise Brown, a well-known writer of children's books. Mother still lectured, but now she toured the country giving readings from the Bible, to a harp accompaniment. Though she had a career, Robin was the core of her existence. She literally lived for him, yet he had managed to break away from her—first Vienna, then Paris, and now, though she had a house with ample room, he insisted upon taking his own. Robin worshiped Mother, but he told me, "I can't live with her. I don't know how you did it all those years at Gracie Square."

For Bram and me things unexpectedly fell into focus early in 1944. We were cast as leads—Mr. and Mrs. Maxim de Winter—in Victor Payne-Jennings' Theatre Guild subscription production of *Rebecca,* in which, to my delight, Florence Reed also had a part.

I came down with grippe during rehearsal in New York. Robin sent over a continuous series of little gifts, all kinds of special foods done up in lovely little boxes, and usually at the bottom a gold bauble from Cartier's. Then one afternoon he dropped in to see me with his friend, Billy Rambo, and they brought me a basket of champagne and caviar. I sat up in bed and the two men watched as I delightedly opened my gift. They were going to the theater that evening. Billy didn't seem to be his usual vivacious self. Ordinarily he took on Robin's character, and Robin was always gay and ebullient.

Robin had to leave. "Billy, stay with Diana, I'll meet you at the theater," he said. He leaned down to kiss me. I drew back. "Don't, Robin, you'll catch my grippe." He said, "Oh,

I don't give a damn. You can't give me anything anyway, and I love you." He kissed me and left.

"What's the matter, sweetie?" I asked Billy. "You seem sort of depressed. Is anything the matter?"

"No," he said somberly. "You'll know soon enough."

"Well, don't be so mysterious," I chided him. "What is it?" He changed the subject and, after a little while, rose to leave. He kissed me good-by. I thought it a strange kiss. He left his lips against my cheek longer than usual, he put his hand on my shoulder, and then he left.

At a quarter of nine Robin called. "Is Billy there?"

"No, Robin. Isn't he at the theater?"

Billy hadn't shown up yet. "Oh, well," said Robin, "I'm going in." If Billy called, he'd left his ticket at the box office.

I was awakened from a deep sleep by the shrilling of the telephone. It was 1:00 A.M. Mother was on the wire. "Diana, Billy has jumped off the Empire State Building. I have to go down to the morgue and identify the body because Robin is completely shattered."

I hung up numbly.

In the morning mail there was a letter to me from Billy—obviously mailed just after he left me. "I'm sorry to do this to Robin," he wrote. "But I just can't take life." He had tried suicide before, I learned, when he had been in the Navy.

That afternoon my doorbell rang. It was Robin. He was pale and distraught. He looked like a marble angel, damp and white. "I can't go anywhere," he said huskily.

"Oh, Robin, darling, come in, come in! You're here, aren't you? You're with me." I took him into what Bram and I called our French room, a beautifully paneled study with a little red sofa that was also a bed. "Now, darling, sit down."

He sat down. "Are you here because you want to stay for a while?" I asked. He said, "I can't go to Mother." He knew Mother was jealous of Billy. Before this it had always been

Mother to whom he returned, Mother to whom he told everything.

I put him to bed, and he fell asleep.

Mother telephoned. Was Robin there? She wanted him at her place. I said, "Mother, at this moment he should go where he wants to go, and he seems to want to be here." Hurt and angry, she hung up. When Bram came home, I said, "Thank God, Bram, he came to me because I understand him."

We went to bed. I awoke in the middle of the night. I heard Robin crying; he sobbed like a child who has been hurt so terribly nothing can help. I couldn't stand it. I got out of bed and went to him. He was like someone in a daze: the light was on, he didn't know it was I, he knew only that someone was there, and he put his arms around me. I got on my knees, because the sofa bed was small and Robin was a big boy. "Baby, quiet, shhh," I said. I rocked him in my arms until he stopped. He said, "Don't leave me, Diana. Please don't. Is it all right for me to be here? I just can't face Mother."

I said, "You're here, darling, for as long as you want, ever. You know we're catkins and always have been, darling. You are here and I love you."

"Don't leave me," he murmured again.

"I won't, darling, I won't," I said.

He said, "Now. I mean now. Don't leave me now."

I didn't leave him. I slept on the floor by his bed that night. In the morning when I awoke, he was still asleep. He lay all curled up like a little bear, his eyes closed, all swollen and pink, and his blond hair was all over his face.

I sat on the edge of his bed and put my arms around him. "Catkin," I said softly. "Catkin, wake up."

He opened his eyes and sat up. "I'm hungry," he announced.

"Wonderful!" I cried. "Good, good!" I fixed him some eggs, but I knew they couldn't simply be boiled or scrambled for Robin, so I made him shirred eggs with sausages and potatoes, and topped with *orégano* and sour cream.

Robin stayed with us three days, until he was in control of himself, and then left for New Milford. I never asked him why Billy did what he did. Bramwell was distant about the entire matter. He had never approved of Robin. "It's depraved for any man to behave like that about another man," he declared.

I said, "It's my brother and it's not depraved. Aren't there some things you can find it in your heart to understand?"

It led to a bitter quarrel, and we were still quarreling when we left on our tour of *Rebecca*.

We played Cleveland, Detroit, Pittsburgh, St. Louis. We fought. We had heart-to-heart talks. I confided in Florence Reed. Maybe what I needed was a baby. Maybe that would bring us together. Florence said, "It would be wonderful for you." When we reached Chicago, she told me, "If you're going to have a child, you want a background for it. You were born a Catholic—you should be married in the Church. I'll talk to Archbishop Stritch."

Florence visited the registry and made an appointment for me. I spoke with a high Church authority while Florence waited for me in a cab in a blinding rain outside. When I emerged, I exclaimed, "My God, Flo, what I must dig up! My early life, everyone who knew me, my family—they'll all have to be investigated and the information sent to Rome." What Bram and I hadn't had time for in Hollywood when we were married, we would have to have time for now. A committee of priests must investigate my background, Bram's, the story of his first marriage, everything. Maybe a baby would be the answer. I would retire from the stage for a year or so. I needed my own child to lavish love on, to mother, to make up for the mothering I hadn't had.

But though we saw doctors and I took tests, nothing happened.

I began dreaming about the child I wanted. Like my dream at Garrison Forest, it came again and again. I lay in a hospital bed, seven months pregnant, my husband beside me, and in some inexplicable way, he was also my doctor. There was one other bed in the room, and in that lay another woman, also pregnant. She expected her baby before me. One day she gave birth; as she did so, my stomach grew smaller. I looked down at myself, in dismay. Many people were in the room watching me. I heard a voice say, "Well, try again."

I saw the woman who had been in the bed rise and walk out with her new baby. The room emptied; the people left, all holding their little sons and daughters by the hand. Suddenly I was no longer pregnant, and there was no one lying beside me. Then I saw myself walking out of the room—alone—no husband, no child—alone.

In Cincinnati I was backstage, dressing for the performance, when Florence hurried up to me. "Your mother is on the phone and she says it's urgent."

Mother's voice came over the line, choked and anguished. "Diana, Robin's dead." She gave me no warning.

Standing there, holding the telephone, my knees buckled and I nearly collapsed. But I went on that night. At one point in *Rebecca,* playing a scene with Margaret Bannerman, the English star, I had to cry. I began and couldn't stop. Margaret held me in a vise to help me control myself. I started to cry as an actress, playing make-believe, but when the tears came, I was myself, I wept as a human being. How much had gone with Robin! We were alike in so many ways, and, like two lost children in the woods, we could hold on to each other and comfort each other.

Mother called again the next day. She was bringing Robin's body through Cincinnati. He had said, after Billy's death, that when he died he wished to be buried next to him, in the Rambo plot, in Indianapolis.

When I met Mother at the station, she was utterly broken. I slept with her that night, my arms around her as she wept. "Oh, Robin, my baby, my baby!" That was all she could say, all she could talk about. "They've taken the one thing I love!" She repeated it again and again. I tried vainly to comfort her. "Darling, you have me, you have me." I could not resent her words. They were true. I knew I could never replace Robin in her heart.

How did Robin die? He literally destroyed himself. In his Connecticut home he drank and he ate, and there was no stopping him. He took sleeping pills to sleep, and Benzedrine to wake, and he lay in bed for days, his guests coming and going, and he drank straight whisky, the cases piling up outside his bedroom, and one morning he was found dead. He had died in his sleep. He was twenty-nine years old.

I sat in my room, in my hotel in Cincinnati, and read over and over again from Mother's book of poetry. When Robin was small she had written a poem entitled "For Robin."

A while ago when my little son was ill
Three evenings he pulled down my head to rest on
   his narrow white breast—
As his light child's hands so transparent with
   illness wavered in and out through my hair—
O he held me   my little son did   in
   the curve of his unborn tenderness—
And I knew in that moment his sweet child's mind
   was securely forever imprinted—
With the yearning face of my love.

I don't know if Mother was a good poet or a great poet who is yet to be discovered. But she loved Robin so!

CHAPTER TWENTY-ONE

My AGENT'S LETTER came just after V-E day. Would I be interested, to the tune of one thousand dollars a week, in going on the Jack Carson comedy show on the NBC radio network, originating in Hollywood?

I leaped at the offer. We'd been on the road for months. We had taken *Rebecca* to New York and then back on tour again. I had had my fill of tears and tragedy, make-believe and real. I desperately needed a change. Robin, Mother's utter misery, my own marriage—I had to get away. Here was a chance to return to Hollywood through the front door. Bram agreed to remain with the show until the tour ended, then join me. I flew at once to Hollywood, rented playwright Clifford Odets' house on Fairfax Boulevard near NBC, and started a new career. I couldn't know that it was also to mark the end of my marriage to Bramwell Fletcher.

Big, affable, and full of laughs, Jack Carson bolstered my spirits the moment we met. We'd have fun on the program. I was Jack's foil—I played myself or what people thought was me: a haughty, temperamental lady star who looked down upon Mr. Carson as something of a buffoon. Jack's butler was Arthur Treacher, as grand as I, and my weekly entrance was built up with a roll of drums and a clash of cymbals, and Arthur's announcement, as lordly as only he could make it, "Miss Barrymore is on her way . . . Miss Barrymore approaches . . . Miss Barrymore has arrived!"

My hours were incredibly short: 9:00 to 10:00 P.M. on Mondays, when we read our script, and a few hours on Fridays, when we went twice before the microphones—at 5:00 P.M. for the West Coast, 9:00 P.M. for the East.

It didn't take me long to realize that for the first time in my life I was really on my own. There had been Miss Gerdes, then Mother, then Mademoiselle, then Bram. Now, no one. I had nothing to do but play—and all week to do it in.

I filled my time with men and parties. I was invited everywhere. I was no longer bored. I was meeting all the gay, exciting people I'd wanted to meet. I had the feel of success without the challenge of the camera. I made every important party—Ann Warner's, Lady Mendl's, Ouida Rathbone's, Cobina Wright's, Atwater Kent's. I dated every eligible man in Hollywood. Some were names, some were not.

For a while I spent a lot of the time with Rory Calhoun. Here, I thought, was one of the most beautiful boys I'd ever laid eyes on. Look at it, I used to marvel at myself, look at the face, Diana! Did you ever see such lashes? Isn't it enough to make your heart burst? Rory was an outdoor boy. I adapted my wardrobe to match his. When he came over he found me bouncing about in flat shoes and bobby socks, blue jeans turned up at the ankles, a three-inch-wide Buster Brown leather belt with a huge brass buckle tight about my waist, a black form-fitting sweater, my hair sleeked back in a pony-tail and tied with a bright red ribbon. I matched the mood of my romances—evening dresses to Western boots, checkered shirts, and a sombrero.

I met George Brent when Ann Warner selected him as my dinner partner. George, just divorced from Ann Sheridan, appealed to me. I'd seen him on the screen with his black patent-leather hair: now it was gray, and he was handsome with his dark eyes and courtly manner. He talked about his experiences in Hollywood, he had charm, intelligence, and a kind of world-weariness that enchanted me. He was the type of older man who attracted me. With George, my bobby socks and jeans vanished: I was the sophisticate in décolleté.

The tempo of my social life heightened. I dated Henry Fonda, Jimmy Stewart, director Freddie de Cordova, Jack La Rue, Baron Eric Rothschild. An old beau from my debutante days, John Galliher of Washington, D.C., breezed into town, just mustered out of the Navy. "Johnny!" I cried happily. "I have this wonderful big house—Bram's on the road —move in!" He did. There was no romance between us. Johnny reminded me of Robin—witty, ebullient, an enchanting guest. Every hostess wanted him, and we became a twosome invited everywhere, though both of us led separate private lives. Gaily we met for breakfast each morning on my patio and compared notes about the night before.

As the days passed, almost as though taking a page out of Robin's fabulous entertainments, I turned my home into a continuous house party. I wasn't thinking of Robin; I was thinking of Lady Mendl and Atwater Kent. I wanted Diana Barrymore's parties to be as well known. I wanted my name to represent star billing—if not on screen, then in Hollywood's social life.

Lady Mendl had open house only on Sunday. I had mine every day. I had overnight guests and week-end guests. My food and liquor bills began to run into staggering sums: fifteen hundred dollars a month. I kept enormous turkeys and hams on hand for buffet luncheons, dinners, suppers. People were always dropping in on their way home from the studios as they might drop into a bar. I had five telephones spotted about the house. I wanted to be near one when it rang. I couldn't be alone a moment; it was as though I had suddenly sprouted wings to fly off in any direction my heart desired, with no one to say, "Now, Diana, now Catkin, I won't have it!" Nevertheless, Cobina Wright, Sr., as she had in Palm Beach, tried to warn me. "The people you invite here, really, Diana, they're such a hard-drinking crowd and they make you drink with them——"

I shushed her. "Don't lecture me, darling. I'm a big girl now."

Many of the men I dated drank heavily. I kept up with them. It was gayer that way. Once Tony Duke and I had had our table at the Stork Club; now, at the Mocambo, everyone knew the Barrymore table—third banquette to the right as you entered. I dropped in there almost nightly with my current escort of the day or the week.

On a San Francisco week end I entered an elevator at the Mark Hopkins Hotel just as a startlingly handsome young coast guard stepped out. We recognized each other. It was Victor Mature, the "beautiful hunk of man" in *Lady in the Dark*. Who could forget him? Victor was between marriages; he'd just been divorced from his second wife, the former Martha Stevenson Kemp. "I'll be in Hollywood in a few weeks," he said. "May I call you?"

I never thought he would. But he did—and that began a three months' romance. Victor and I held court nightly at my Mocambo table. We watched the starlets dancing with male stars, hoping to be seen by the right producer. I remember watching them with a strange combination of superiority and frustration. How hard they struggled to open doors that swung open for me without raising my little finger! And what had I done so far? Oh, skip it, Diana, I'd say to myself. I'd down a shot of Pinch Bottle and go gaily off on the floor with Victor or with Johnny who was never far away.

Victor wanted a dramatic career. We rehearsed Shakespeare and read scripts together. I helped him improve his English. Like Brian Donlevy, though, life was a ball to Victor. One Friday night I came home from my broadcast to find thirty people in my living room. Everyone was high. Not a single face was familiar. I looked around and there was Victor, the happy host. He was throwing a party with my liquor! "Darling, I'll pay for it," he assured me. I laughed. "Oh, don't be silly." And I joined the drinking. After all, I was earning a thousand dollars a week for less than five hours' work—and I spent as little time at NBC as possible.

This, I discovered, was to plague me. Usually the full cast adjourned to the sound room after our first Friday broadcast to listen to a rebroadcast and check their performance. After the first weeks I rebelled. "It's boring enough to do the same show twice in a few hours, but to have to listen to it, as well . . ." I begged off. I preferred to return to my guests. Politely the director suggested that I do as everyone else.

"Am I reading my lines badly?" I asked. "Is there anything I should change? If not, why listen to the rebroadcast?" No, he admitted. He had no suggestions. "I guess you don't have to," he said.

Word got around that the front office felt I was not taking my work seriously enough. Now and then I showed up at Monday rehearsal a little shaky from a hang-over. (Sunday nights were big nights in Hollywood.) But I was convinced I could drink without showing it—a lady always held her liquor. I never slurred my lines. Nonetheless the front office built up a dossier on me. Little by little my part on the Carson show dwindled. I realized it, but I felt that there was nothing I could do without losing face. I was too grand to ask favors of anyone. I was fulfilling my contract; I would continue to fulfill it.

The writing on the wall became clear when my agent called me. Jack was taking the entire show to the Strand Theatre in New York. "You'll have a very small part," he said. "Do you want to go like that into New York, where everybody knows you?"

I knew what he meant. The Carson show would appear on stage, playing second billing to a motion picture. Like vaudeville. I'd never done vaudeville. It would be humiliating for me to do that in New York. I told my agent I'd sit my contract out in Hollywood. Sooner or later something else would come up after the Carson show. I was sure of it.

One step I did take. I had been seeing too much of Victor. I spoke to him. "Look, Vic, it's no good. We're not going anywhere, we're not getting anywhere. You once asked me, in an offhand moment, to marry you. It was sweet of you, Vic, and I adore you but—no. Let's call it quits."

And Victor, who took these things in his stride, kissed me and went his way.

In January, 1946, several weeks before my contract expired, Mother came out for a visit. Her first remark was to Johnny, whom she liked. "John, really, the way you and Diana live in this horrid house." She looked about the room. "What have they done this in—early Pullman?" She turned to me. "And who are these terrible people you allow yourself to see?" Had she heard reports of the mad life we'd been leading? Johnny proceeded to charm her back into good humor.

Mother had been busy. She had brought Robin's furniture to her home in Easton. She had reconstructed his bedroom and study there and made a shrine of them, keeping everything exactly as it had been when Robin was alive—his paintings, his antiques, his books and music. Even his desk remained as it had been the morning he was found dead. Mother had made only one change. She took Robin's bed into her bedroom and placed hers in his—and for the rest of her life she slept in Robin's bed. She still wept when she talked of him.

I tried to cheer her up by inviting her to go with us to a party the next evening given by John Decker, Daddy's old friend. He was to unveil a new statue. The list of invited guests read like a Hollywood roll call: Paulette Goddard and Burgess Meredith, David Selznick and Merle Oberon and Jennifer Jones, Harpo Marx and Errol and Nora Flynn and Ida Lupino and Jack La Rue, Lawrence Tierney, Lon Chaney, Jr., Aunt Ethel's son Sammy Colt.

Mother was Mother. "No," she said, "I'm tired. Besides, it will probably be a dreadful bore. That man Decker's a monster anyway, and something's sure to happen."

"Mother," I said, "I've been going to these Hollywood parties for months and nothing's happened yet."

But this time she was right. Johnny and I walked into a rough affair. A great deal of drinking went on; guests came and left. Several abortive fist fights broke out. The statue was knocked over before it could be unveiled. It crashed to the floor, the head broke off and rolled away. Decker uttered an anguished cry, swooped down and picked up the headless figure, and hugged it to him. Lawrence Tierney, who had made a success playing bad man Dillinger on the screen, accused Sammy Colt of stumbling and knocking it over. He took a punch at Sammy. Jack La Rue jumped in to defend my cousin, and Tierney's fist crashed into Jack's face. Blood spurted. When I saw blood on Sammy and Jack, I exploded. I rushed up to Tierney—he'd ripped off his shirt and stood like a belligerent Tarzan—"You dreary, dreadful actor!" I cried. "If you want to fight, hit me! You're punching everyone else, so why don't you hit a woman?" I slapped him with all my might, half a dozen times. I was wearing two rings and they must have hurt.

A woman egged me on, screaming, "Hit him, Diana! That's the girl! Tell him where to get off!"

Someone telephoned the police. Johnny's voice was in my ear. "Diana, you can't have publicity with Michael here. Let's get out of here."

As the police came in the front door we ran out the back door and through the garden to Johnny's car.

Next morning at breakfast there were the newspapers—the story and my picture on the front page! I had to show the papers to Mother before she saw them herself. I took them up. "Here, Cat," I said. "You were right about last night's party."

She was sitting up in bed. She fluffed her pillows and said, "Well, I have to get comfortable, I suppose, to see this."

She read through the accounts silently. She turned to me. "It's exactly what I thought would happen to you in Hollywood. It's disgraceful! You're following the same disgusting pattern as Jack!" I was very ashamed. She went into a tirade. "Obviously you're on your way, Diana—God knows where you'll end!"

I didn't quite know what to say to her.

Bramwell's letters had been piling up on my desk. Now and then he telephoned. I found it difficult to talk with him. He was so—sedate. I was bored even to talk to him on the phone.

Mother had been gone, back to New York, about a week when Bram's voice—eager and enthusiastic—came over the long-distance wire from Chicago.

"Darling! The show's closing and I'm coming out!"

Oh, no, I thought. I can't face him. No woman in love could have behaved as I had these last months. We were finished. I said to him, "Bramwell, don't you think you'd better go back to New York and see about a job there? There's nothing out here."

"Oh, no, my dear!" he exclaimed. "I'm coming out on a wing and a prayer. I'll be there tomorrow!"

Next morning I hustled Johnny out of the house and drove to the airport. I stopped in the bar to fortify myself, then strolled out and stood waiting for Bramwell's plane. I watched as it circled and came down, then I saw him emerge. He was wearing a brown tweed suit, and it was too early for him to be caught in the pitiless California sun. I thought, all the young, vital men I've known these last months—poor Bram! But I kissed him dutifully and drove him back to the Odets' house, which he'd never seen.

As we came up the driveway, he saw one of my cars. "Who's here?" he asked. "Nobody, Bram," I said. "What's that other car doing here?" he went on. "That's mine too," I said. "They're both mine."

"Well, was anybody here?" he demanded. For a moment I wondered if his friends had written him.

"Here? Here when?" I countered. "Nobody's been here, Bramwell."

"Well, who have you been seeing?"

I opened the door. "Hardly anybody, dear." We walked in. The Odets' sunken living room was three steps down, with a guest bedroom at the right. Bramwell looked about. "Well, I say—" he exclaimed. "Rather an attractive place you have here." He walked into the guest room, then came back. "What's upstairs?"

I said, "Come on, dear, I'll show you our bedroom." I led the way. The moment we were inside, he took me in his arms. "Darling," he said. As he drew me to him, I thought, this is a lie, Diana. How long can you keep it up?

I tried my best, though I had to drink to do it. One night Bram was in the bedroom, and I sat downstairs, sipping a drink and trying to think how I could break the news to him. Suddenly I looked up: there was Robin standing in front of me, dressed in one of his beautifully tailored English suits.

I didn't want to lose the vision. I said aloud, "Don't go away, Robin-cat. What did you come back for? Is anything wrong?"

There was no expression on his face. It was blank, like a mask.

Then he vanished.

Bram came to the head of the stairs. "Who were you talking to?" he asked.

"Robin," I said.

He came down and put his arm around me. "Come to bed," he said gently. "You're tight."

I knew I'd seen Robin—for perhaps the count of eight seconds—and Bramwell wouldn't understand. So I went to bed and I lay there in the darkness and wondered if I'd ever see Robin again. Time after time I tried to conjure him up sitting in the same room, in the same chair, at the same hour of night. I'd say, "Come back, come back, Robin." He never did.

The storm broke during Bram's second week home. We went to a dinner party given by my old friend, producer Luther Green, then engaged to marry Judith Anderson. Katina Paxinou, the Greek star, cooked dinner to perfection. I wasn't thinking of food. As we walked into Luther's house, I knew something terrible would happen. How odd, I thought. At Luther's apartment in New York I'd met Richie Merino, almost on the eve of my marriage to Bram. I'd loved Bram then. That brief encounter made no difference. Now, here in Luther's home in Hollywood, my marriage was coming to an end. I knew it.

Bram and I scarcely exchanged a word all evening. I drank everything put before me, from highballs to oriental wines and liqueurs. Miss Paxinou and Miss Anderson were so vital they filled the room. But Bram and I were like strangers and like strangers we drove home.

I drank again at home. When I reached a point of absolute bravery—and absolute indifference—I stumbled over to my husband, who was reading his paper.

He looked up and began to rise, perhaps to support me.

"Sit right where you are, Bram," I said thickly. "I have something to tell you. What do you think I've been doing in Hollywood all the time you've been away? Playing dominoes?"

Bram gazed at me with distaste. "You're drunk," he said.

"Of course I'm drunk! If I wasn't, I wouldn't have the guts to tell you this, Bramwell. I've been sleeping around. I have slept with——" The names poured from me. Bram's face grew white. He leaped to his feet. "Shut up!" he roared. "For God's sake, shut up!" I stopped, taken aback by his vehemence.

"This is the most disgraceful thing I have ever heard." His voice trembled. "I can't believe it. Are you serious?"

"Of course I'm serious! Would I bother to tell you all this if it wasn't true? I don't love you any more, Bramwell. There's nothing left between us. That's why I did what I did.

I knew nothing of life when I married you. But I've learned plenty since." I turned around, found a chair, and sat down heavily. "I suggest divorce," I said.

Bramwell looked at me. "*Suggest* divorce? After what you've told me I wouldn't remain here if you were the last woman on earth."

I waved my hand. "All right. Pack up, dear. There's no problem then."

"I will," he said grimly and went upstairs. I lit a cigarette and sat smoking. Nothing particular passed through my mind.

He came down carrying a suitcase. He did not look at me. "I will send for the rest tomorrow." The door slammed.

I drew hard on my cigarette. I know where he's going. He's going to his good friend, Frank Tours. Frank, a musician who once conducted for Irving Berlin, had been Bram's best man at his wedding to Helen Chandler. He lived a few blocks away.

I got to my feet. I felt jumpy at the pit of my stomach. I poured another drink, put on my Capehart, and played the Rachmaninoff No. 2 in C minor, which always seemed good for me in stress. The music filled the room. I listened dreamily. Suddenly the enormity of what I'd done struck home. My God, I thought, I think I've made a mistake.

I reeled to the telephone and shakily dialed Tours' number. Yes, Bram was there. No, he wouldn't come to the phone. The receiver clicked. I went back to the Capehart and leaned against it and cried. There was no way out, now. Bram was decent, and I was a slut. Mother was right: God knows where I'd end. I thought, tearily, well, *noblesse oblige*. I'll do away with myself. It serves me right. At least I know how to act handsomely when I must.

I managed to get a pencil and paper and wrote laboriously, "To Whom It May Concern—" I left all my worldly goods to Mother. My tears splattered the paper. What a mess you've made of your life, I thought. I felt like a sweater that has become unraveled. What a fool you've been, you ass! You were insane! Only a crazy woman would tell such things to her husband . . .

I left the letter on my desk and telephoned George Lloyd, a night-club entertainer whom I'd known since my El Morocco days. "Darling," I said slowly and distinctly, "come over, because I am going to kill myself." I hung up.

Glass in hand, I climbed the stairs slowly, the lovely spiral staircase, step by step. In the bathroom I opened a bottle of sleeping pills and poured thirty of them into my hand. I counted each one carefully. They were yellow jackets. Thirty should do it. Then I waited.

I heard the door downstairs flung open and George's excited cry, "Diana! Diana!"

The spell was broken. I knew I wouldn't do it. I dropped the pills on the floor behind me and walked to the head of the stairs. George rushed across the room below, caught sight of me, and started up the stairs.

"No, stay there. I'm coming down."

He stood there, frozen. He asked hoarsely, "Have you taken anything?"

I put my hand on the rail and majestically descended the stairs. I was Lana Turner in *The Ziegfeld Girl*. I was Bernhardt in her magnificent death scene—I wasn't sure which one, but no matter. I came down the stairs slowly and, at the bottom, crumpled gracefully in a faint.

I was pretending, but when I felt George try to pick me up, I really blacked out.

I was lying on the sofa before the fireplace and an old friend, Dr. Hugo Weinberg, was working on me with a stomach pump. I wanted to cry out, "No, no, I didn't take them." I tried to scream, but I was paralyzed and no sound came. Yet I was undergoing the most agonizing experience, as though a live eel had been forced down my throat and into my very bowels until I could stand it no more. It was writhing inside me and I wanted to retch and could not . . . I thrashed about, moaning and choking. I caught a glimpse of my left hand. The skin was blue, the veins stood out. I thought madly, it's like a canvas by Picasso.

Then suddenly I wasn't struggling any more. I lay gasping.

"What were you trying to do?" Dr. Weinberg was leaning over me.

"I don't know," I whispered. "I was an ass." I began to cry. "Oh, Hugo, please call my husband and tell him I'm dying. I'm so ashamed. I've been so incredibly awful to him."

Dr. Weinberg shook his head. "You didn't take any pills, did you?"

"No," I said. "I guess I really didn't mean to. Oh, God, maybe I should have——"

"Let's have no more nonsense, Diana," he said. "I'll call Bramwell. I won't tell him you're dying because you're not."

"Call him!" I begged. "Tell him it was all on account of him because I made a dreadful mistake and wanted to kill myself, because I realized the error of my ways too late." I thought, I'm even thinking in Bramwell's language.

Dr. Weinberg called. I heard Bram's voice, thin and sharp. "She's all right? I don't want to see her. Good night."

All right, I thought. I began it—instigated it—did it. Bram has every right to think as he does. Dr. Weinberg interrupted my thoughts. "You're not going to do anything silly after we leave, are you?" He gave me a sedative. He and George helped me to my room. I fell asleep.

At noon the next day I called Mother in New York. "Mummy, number one, I tried to kill myself. As you can attest from this voice, I did not succeed."

She screamed, "What do you mean, tried to kill yourself? Are you all right?"

"I took an overdose of sleeping pills." I wanted Mother to feel sorry for me too. "It never got into the papers."

"Diana! Will you talk sense? For God's sake, what happened?"

I calmed her, told her what happened, and added that I

was going to get a divorce. And Mother, who had been so against my marriage, counseled patience. "Diana, we must think this through carefully. Divorce is a very serious thing. You had better come to New York." I would have time for a flying trip: I wasn't due at rehearsal for four days. "Okay, Mother," I said. "I'll come. I know what I want to do though. It's my life."

After I hung up I called Bramwell. He refused to talk to me. I gave Frank a message. "Please tell him I'm going to New York to see my mother about a divorce." I added, "I don't think he'll contest it."

Mother drove me to her home. When we were alone: "All right, Diana, let's get down to facts. Why are you doing this?"

"Mother, I'm bored. And, anyway, there's nothing left between us."

That was a good enough reason, she admitted. "But you went through so much to marry this man—I can't understand what happened, and how it happened so quickly."

"Five years isn't so quickly, Mother."

She looked at me and something strangely akin to pity seemed to lurk in her eyes. "Catkin, dear, what's happened to you in Hollywood?"

I tried to answer her. I couldn't reveal the entire story. She had glimpsed something of it in her brief visit. I indicated there were other men I liked. Mother, too, had had men in her life, but she would look differently upon me than upon herself. I concluded, "Mummy, Bram is just too old for me."

She smiled sadly. "I told you that before you married him."

"Yes, but I was only twenty-one then—now I'm older and I realize it won't work."

"Well, all right," she said, and we understood each other completely. She pondered for a moment. "Now, where ought you go? Harry went to Reno. Do you think you'd like Reno?"

I couldn't help smiling at her quick change of mood. "Oh, Mother!" I said. "I want to go to Las Vegas." Only three weeks remained of my radio contract. I'd go there then and get it over with as quietly and decently as possible.

I returned to Hollywood. In those three weeks I met Mr. John Howard. I wish I hadn't.

CHAPTER TWENTY-TWO

I WISH I COULD dismiss Mr. John R. Howard by saying that he was a handsome, six-foot-two tennis professional whom I met, married, and divorced, after living with him as man and wife for six months. I have made many mistakes: Mr. Howard was a dreadful one. At least the record shows that I left him long before he was jailed for white slavery.

Looking back now, I can only explain him by saying that I married him on the rebound from Bramwell Fletcher— that it was a combination of youth, sex, and wishful thinking.

Two weeks before I left for Las Vegas and my divorce, my telephone rang. "This is John Howard," said a voice. "I was at your house last night."

I remembered no John Howard. "The only John Howard I know is the motion picture actor," I said. "He wasn't here last night."

"My," said the voice, "I sure made a jazzy impression." He laughed. "And you even gave me a couple of drinks."

I'd had a cocktail party the night before, but I still couldn't place him. "You saw me playing tennis last week," he went on. "I know because I saw you in the grandstand."

Then I remembered. He was the handsome blond tennis star. Every woman's eye had been on him. Over the phone he sounded easygoing, slangy, and very young. He was to play an important match in Palm Springs next week end, he was saying. Wouldn't I like to come out as his guest and watch him?

I was restless, I had nothing better to do until Las Vegas. Why not? "Sure," I said.

The address he gave me turned out to be a motel. No one met me. "Miss Barrymore?" the clerk asked. "Cabin Number Nine." I began to unpack. Suddenly, with a great screeching of brakes, a red roadster slithered to a stop, and out of a cloud of dust stepped Mr. Howard and another striking young man, tennis star Frank Kovacs.

"Hi," said Howard breezily. "Get here all right?"

"You might at least have been here," I said stiffly.

"Y'unpacked?" he asked. I nodded. "Well, then, c'mon, kid, let's go out and eat."

"I'm afraid I don't dine at this hour," I said with dignity.

"Okay," said Howard. "Then let's make love."

I tried to wither him with a glance, which was difficult, because Mr. Kovacs burst out laughing and Mr. Howard seemed to find it very amusing too. "Is that what I came here for?" I demanded.

He slung a white sweater over a brown, muscled shoulder and grinned. "What else do you think I asked you for?"

I could either stalk out or play it as a gag. I chose the latter. "Let's eat instead," I said. Mr. Howard intrigued me. I'd never been talked to by anyone like that before.

I watched him play Kovacs that afternoon. He had told me, "I know just where I want you to sit—center court." He took me there before the game. I thought, just like the theater—third row, center . . .

He did not win that afternoon, but I wasn't following the play. I was watching this handsome boy out there on the court, bursting with health and beauty. I was looking at his legs, so hard-muscled, so suntanned . . .

After the match he said, "C'mon, kid, feel like eating?"

I said, "Yes, I'm hungry." And we ate together. He was

simple, direct, uncomplicated, absolutely refreshing. I thought, he's the antithesis of Bramwell: young and athletic, brusque instead of polite, simple instead of complex, a man whose conversation is crude and ungrammatical. He'd say, "I come in and I see——" I was fascinated. He told me about himself. His father owned a gasoline station. He'd learned tennis and made a name for himself as the fifth-ranking tennis professional in the country. He was two years younger than I; he'd been married before. He had little to say about it. He was charming when he wished to be, extremely attractive—wavy blond hair, blue eyes, a beautiful sensuous mouth, a body that was Grecian sculpture come alive.

Next day we drove back to Hollywood. He was to play a tournament in El Paso the following week. I thought, yes, tennis players *are* like actors—always on the road. But they don't work in grease paint and make-believe; they don't live in the jaded, inbred world of the theater . . . "Want to come down to El Paso with me, kid?" he asked.

I went. I fell in love with him. Everything helped: the speed with which he courted me, the sharp contrast between him and the man I was divorcing, the fact that he represented another world—health, simplicity, unabashed animal vigor. He'll be good for me, I decided. He'll bring me back to normal living again, normal hours, normal people. I'll be outdoors all day, playing tennis, swimming, riding. Perhaps my life will take a saner direction. Bramwell wasn't right for me. Maybe what I need is someone as simple and uncomplicated as this boy.

In El Paso, Johnny said, "Want to try something for kicks?"

He pulled out half a dozen small cigarettes.

"What are those?" I asked. He grinned. "I figured you didn't know. Marijuana."

Strangely enough, with all my Hollywood experience, I'd never smoked one. When Johnny lit a cigarette for me, I drew back. "Wait a minute. What are these things going to do to me? I hear that people go berserk and God knows what —I don't think I want one."

He laughed. "Take it, kid, just for kicks."

The first puffs meant nothing. "Try and pick up that pen from the table," Johnny said. "It'll be heavy."

"Really?" I said. "I mean, three or four puffs on an old tired cigarette? How's that going to make anything heavy?" I picked up the pen, and it *was* heavy.

Johnny was enjoying himself. "Try and write something," he suggested. I tried. Everything went slowly—like an LP record gone wrong. After a few seconds, or it may have been minutes, I said, "I can't do it. But Johnny, I don't think it's right for anything to affect a person like this. This isn't what I want. I want *food*."

He grinned again. "Yep, that's one of the reactions. What do you want?"

"I want a couple of milk shakes and scrambled eggs made with lots of cream." I was surprised to hear myself. That combination ordinarily would make me sick. Johnny laughed lazily and began to move toward me. He seemed to grow before my eyes. God, I thought, what a beautiful man! What a sexy, beautiful man . . .

For an insane thirty-six hours we played records, laughed, giggled at ourselves—everything was funny, everything was relaxed, everything was amazing. I thought of nothing in the past. All was like a dream. Only the fantastic present remained.

Then we gave up marijuana. I never touched it again. Johnny had to play tennis and the two didn't mix.

He played his tourney. When I went to Las Vegas, Johnny came to spend the first three weeks of my six-week stay there. He had savings of twenty-five hundred dollars; he lost it all at the roulette tables. I knew he did it to impress me. I began to loan him money. Before he left for his next tourney, in Boston, he had helped me lose five thousand dollars of my own.

When my decree came through, I was so eager to be with him that though my plane stopped en route in New York, I didn't pause to see or even telephone Mother. I flew direct to Boston. There I discovered he had told the newspapers we were engaged. We hadn't even talked about it. I didn't care. I was mad about Johnny. At a press conference he called that night at the Ritz-Carlton, we announced it officially. Before Mother could read the news, I telephoned her. "You must come up to Boston and meet him."

She wouldn't believe it at first. "My God, Diana. Not again! And so soon? It's indecent!" And after a little while: "A tennis player? Is this a gentleman tennis player? Someone like Bill Tilden or Fred Perry? Is he English?"

"No, Mummy. He's a full-blooded American boy. I think you'll like him because he's giving me health."

She sighed. "Well, all right. I'll come up tomorrow. If you're serious about this young man, obviously I must meet him."

In her suite at the Ritz, where once I'd rehearsed *Romantic Mr. Dickens,* John and I had our audience with Mother. She began, "Of course, you realize that Diana has no money?"

This wasn't altogether true. While I had spent my NBC money as soon as I received it, Robin's estate had been settled not long before. Robin left Mother and me one hundred thousand dollars each. After taxes my share was forty-seven thousand. I'd already gone through about a third of it but I had nearly thirty thousand left. No fortune, but I wasn't penniless.

"I don't care if she hasn't," said Johnny. "All I want from your daughter, Miss Strange, is her love."

Mother tried another tack. "But Mr. Howard, what will your lives be like? Will she follow you on your tennis matches or will you follow her on her theatrical tours?"

I interrupted to say that this would work itself out. We would follow each other whenever either of us was working.

Finally Mother asked Johnny to go downstairs so that she could speak to me alone. "Well, he's terribly good-looking," she said grudgingly. "But Diana, you can't be happy with a man like that. He's so *common*. Are you in such a hurry that you can't wait to find a gentleman?"

"Don't you worry, Mother," I said. "This boy is all right."

I took Johnny for a week end at Mother's place in Easton. He was decorative but indolent. Once she asked him to mow the lawn. "Sorry, Cat, no can do," he said. "I'd use the wrong muscles."

Mother stomped out. She resented his familiarity. She came back to find him sprawled across the sofa, in white shirt, white flannels, white socks, and sneakers. He'd brought his own jazz records: jazz was blaring from Mother's Capehart, Johnny was happily immersed in a comic book, and the floor was strewn with half a dozen others. Mother sized up the scene and took me aside.

"Diana," she said crisply, "I want you to get rid of all three—those picture books, that young man, and the noise he makes." She looked at me. "Oh, Catkin, you could do so much better!"

I became Mrs. John Howard on January 17, 1947, at the Park Avenue Central Presbyterian Church. The Reverend Dr. Spears had questioned us closely before consenting to perform the ceremony. How serious was I? Did I intend to make a home and produce a family? I told him Bram and I had wanted children and were unsuccessful. This marriage, I said, would be permanent.

Mother implored me not to marry Johnny. "He's not for you," she warned me over and over again. "He's not part of your world. Keep him as a lover if you must, but for God's sake, don't marry him!" I refused to listen.

The ceremony was impressive. My brother Leonard, who

had left Paris to live in New York, gave me away. Now that Robin was gone, Leonard and I, almost strangers through the years, were really beginning to know each other. Leonard also took a dim view of Johnny, but nonetheless he had prevailed upon Dr. Spears, who rarely married divorced persons, to officiate. The guests included Mrs. Cole Porter; Mrs. Cass Canfield, my godmother; Leonard's wife, Yvonne; and many of Mother's friends. None of Johnny's guests were on hand—neither his parents nor his friends. He had no money for a wardrobe, so I bought him a dark striped suit and a striped Guards tie at Saks Fifth Avenue. I bought myself a fabulous hat at John Frederics, and Mother bought me a simple, charming print at Henri Bendel's. "This is a nice dress to get married in," she said.

I felt very proper as we walked down the nave to the little chapel. Saints and martyrs looked down on us. We knelt and I said the words I'd once said before. I thought of the other time with Bram. If I meant them then—and I did—did I mean them now? I had answered Dr. Spears truthfully. Yet a curious sense of unreality stole over me as the ceremony went on. My marriage vows rang false in my ears, and I didn't know why. "But I've said these lines before," I thought wonderingly, "Why am I doing the same play?"

Mother stood as if she were Joan at the stake. At my first wedding she had wept. She had been the mother. This time it was: *Oh, well, Diana wants it, what else can I do but allow her—and suffer.*

I moved through the reception in Leonard's Park Avenue apartment in a rosy haze of champagne. We spent our wedding night, Johnny and I, in the hotel suite in which we had been living together for months. As I removed my hat and earrings, through the mirror I could see John undressing. He was staring straight ahead of him. Does he feel as I do, I wondered? How *did* I feel? How can my emotions change so swiftly? How can I ever trust my judgment if what I want so desperately becomes something I'm not sure I want the moment I get it? We'd been lovers only last night. Why should the solemn marriage vows suddenly put butterflies in my stomach that even champagne could not stop? Mother was right. He didn't belong at that reception. I didn't belong in his world. I remembered an episode in El Paso. Johnny had introduced me to a friend, Mr. Richard Short. I knew nothing of Mr. Short's criminal record. The two men eyed a diamond bracelet I wore. Harry Tweed had given it to Mother, and she had given it to me. "You know, we could turn that into dough," Johnny had remarked. "Why don't you let us have it? We'll conveniently lose it, split the insurance money three ways, and then give it back to you." I'd been indignant, and they dropped the subject. Yes, Mother was right. I didn't belong with him—not as his wife.

I turned suddenly and spoke to Johnny. "My God," I said, thinking aloud. "You're *common!*"

He looked at me expressionlessly. "You knew that before you married me. Now that you're Mrs. Howard, you're going to know it even better."

"Obviously," I said. "But you may be called Mr. Barrymore. Did that ever occur to you?"

"I'll never be called Mr. Barrymore," he said coolly. "I'm too well known in the tennis world."

"Well, I'm too well known in the theatrical world to be called Mrs. Howard," I retorted.

He came up to me. "Oh, c'mon, kid," he said roughly. He kissed me hard. I wanted to slap him. He grabbed my arm and kissed me again. I did not fight him.

It was not love. It was lust.

We spent part of our marriage in Saint Augustine, Florida. I discovered my husband had arranged for a month's free stay at a hotel by telling the management they could advertise the fact that Diana Barrymore was honeymooning there. When we went to restaurants, when we entertained Johnny's friends and admirers in night clubs, I picked up the check. Johnny never had money.

After St. Augustine he got a job as a tennis pro at the Louisville Boat Club. In a Chrysler I bought because Johnny wanted one, we drove to Kentucky. Our home was the tennis pro's quarters—a two-room shack about thirty feet from the courts. I tried to make the place cozy and attractive. I bought lamps, drapes, a record player: I made the beds and cooked. Johnny did nothing. When he wasn't playing tennis he played the pinball machine or lounged around reading comic books. I cleaned up after him—he couldn't use the wrong muscles. I'll try to be a good wife, I told myself, I can't renege now. My duty is with my husband.

I wanted to meet his family. Johnny refused. "They live on the wrong street for you," he said.

"You're an arrogant s.o.b.," I flung at him, "not to introduce me to your family!"

He sneered. "You? Out of the *Social Register?* If you ever saw them, you'd drop dead."

We fought. There was no denying the fact that I was out in the sun all day—playing tennis, swimming, riding, feeling healthy, but only pretending I was happy. I turned to a drink to comfort me. Then I taunted him: "That garrragge-keeper, your father." Once he slapped me across the mouth with his open hand, my lip bled, and I screamed. Johnny left for a week. I was told he'd been seen at a motel with a girl. I never knew if it was true. When he returned, we made up.

One night we were driving home; we had both been drinking. Suddenly we heard the whine of a siren behind us. After a while we pulled to the curb, and two policemen leaped out of the patrol car that had been pursuing us. Johnny swung at one of them, only to have the other bring his gun butt down on his head. Johnny crumpled, bleeding. I rushed at my husband's assailant and found myself thrown unceremoniously back into the car. I fought and screamed and kicked all the way to the station house. We spent the rest of the night in jail. The story hit the front pages next morning. We were released on bail. The charge: assault and battery, and drunken and disorderly conduct.

On the telephone Mother only said, "Oh, my God, Diana! Hollywood and now this!"

My way out came a few days later with an offer to star in the summer-stock production of Maxwell Anderson's *Joan of Lorraine,* a role that attracted me tremendously. Rehearsals were to begin immediately in Salem, Massachusetts.

"Aw, stay here for the summer, Diana," Johnny said. "Stick with me."

I said, "Johnny, you have your business, I have mine. I can't give up the theater just because I married a tennis player. This means a new start for me. Thank God they still want me in spite of the scandal!" I packed, kissed him good-by, and flew to Salem. I arrived there June 17, 1947. It was six months to the day, almost, since I'd married John Howard.

When the case came up in the Louisville courts, I wasn't there to fight it. The fines and damages claimed by the policemen ran to nearly fifteen hundred dollars. I paid. Weeks later, when I asked Johnny for a divorce, he said he'd give it to me—for a price. I never paid it, but I got my divorce anyway. It took me three years, but I got it.

CHAPTER TWENTY-THREE

Tᴇɴɴɪs ᴀɴᴅ John Howard were far away from me in Salem. Very near was a man named Robert Wilcox, who was to mean more to me than any man but my father.

Mr. Wilcox was anything but prepossessing when the producer introduced him to me. He needed a shave, he was unkempt, his clothes were unpressed. He apologized with a slow smile. "I had no idea I'd be up here today," he said. He came as a last-minute replacement for my leading man.

When, shaved and washed, Mr. Wilcox dined with me that evening, I thought him terribly attractive. He was about thirty-six, tall, slender, dark-eyed, with aquiline features, and a dark hairline mustache. He seemed a strange combination of George Brent and Fredric March—and perhaps even Daddy. His voice was deep, and he was slow-moving and courtly of manner. He apologized again for his appearance that morning. "I just came out of the Payne Whitney Clinic yesterday," he said.

"Oh, I'm sorry," I said politely. I had never heard of the Payne Whitney Clinic. I had no idea it was a place where alcoholics often went to take the cure.

He grinned a little self-consciously. "I celebrated by buying a pint of whisky and killing it on the train coming up from New York," he said. "My first drink in six months. I really wasn't in shape to get shaved or anything else this morning."

I said, well, I could understand a man going on a little bender after not having had a drink for six months. With that we both ordered another martini and began talking about the play.

Bob was a good actor. When I told him so after rehearsal he smiled. He had been in more B pictures—twenty-six, he said—than anyone he knew. He left Hollywood to enlist, entering the Army as a private, emerging as a captain. He was wounded and assigned to Special Services in Brussels, where he organized shows for the troops. He began to drink heavily. "I lived like a king," he told me later. "My driver used to bring me two bottles of cognac a day. I was entertaining VIPs from the States, I drank with everyone and everyone drank with me." Then it got worse.

His father, a Rochester, New York, physician, died when Bob was sixteen. "My mother tried to be father and mother to me and my brother, and never quite made the grade," he went on. "I became a problem to everyone, including myself." He did odd things. He quit the University of Southern California after one year to become a mucker at Boulder Dam. He tried summer stock; a talent scout saw him as Duke Mantee in Robert Sherwood's *The Petrified Forest*. Overnight he was in Hollywood. "How do you get into B pictures and never get out?" he asked. "I don't know. Maybe I was typed, maybe I never got the breaks." In 1937 he married Florence Rice, daughter of sports writer Grantland Rice. They were divorced two years later. "I've been a bachelor for a long time now," he said with a smile, "and I like it that way."

During those first weeks Bob and I talked endlessly. I needed someone to talk to. Now and then I telephoned Johnny, but the calls became shorter and fewer. We had nothing to say to one another, and I knew he must be doing the town with his girl friends. Bob, on the other hand, was part of the theater, as I was. He was quiet, modest, even a little defeated. When he said, "I became a problem to everyone, including myself," my heart went out to him.

He began wining and dining me. At the end of the week he asked me, a little sheepishly, for a loan of fifty dollars to pay his hotel bill. I knew he'd spent his money on me. At dress rehearsal he showed up on stage, weaving. I rushed down to Leonard Altobell, the producer, sitting in the back of the house. "He's not loaded," I cried. "It's the pills and medication he's taking. He's just come out of the hospital." I drank, too, but only after the show. I still felt as I had with Laurette—it was disgraceful to drink before a performance. Bob apologized to me. "Diana, you know I went away to stop this. Getting out and getting this job so quickly made me nervous. I took too much. I won't do it again." I could understand that. My heart went out to him the more. Opening night he was fine.

We became inseparable. I thought, I can't go on like this with Bob here and my husband down in Kentucky. I telephoned Johnny. "Look, you and I made a mistake from the word go, Johnny. You know it as well as I do. It's not that I've met someone else, although I have. I won't lie to you. But that's not it. I just think we're all washed up."

Johnny's voice was cool: "If you knew it was a mistake at the beginning, why'd you stay as long as you did?"

"Pride," I told him. It was only partly true; I didn't want to give him the satisfaction of knowing that it was sex too. I went on: "Because Mother said it wouldn't work and my brother said it wouldn't work, everybody said it wouldn't, and I was doing my level best to make it work. But it can't, it hasn't, so let's forget it." I talked about getting a divorce as soon as my tour ended.

"Sure," said Johnny agreeably. "Only it's going to cost you, kid."

"Oh, no, it won't," I snapped. I hung up. A few days later

I received a demand from Johnny for a settlement. I turned the matter over to an attorney.

Mother had fought bitterly against Bramwell. She'd been unable to bear Howard. She was wretched when she learned about Bob. Mother was unwell. She still went on tour with her readings, entitled "Great Words to Great Music," but her incredible vitality seemed quenched, she tired quickly, she was even more irritable than before. "Oh, Diana" she lamented. "What have you found now? An actor nobody ever heard of, from God knows where——"

I refused to let her upset me. "You might as well get used to him, Mother," I said. "Something tells me this is it."

I asked Bob, "When did you fall in love with me?"

On the fifth day, he said. "I want you to know I have a certain integrity, Diana," he added seriously. "I mean I don't try to sleep around with every woman I meet." So he had talked to me and listened to me but remained aloof. On the fifth day we took a walk together. I strolled on ahead. I was wearing a pair of red pedal pushers—I was walking an adorable little fox terrier I'd bought—and Bob looked at me and said to himself, "That's for me."

I laughed. "With my bowed legs?"

He nodded. "You're ashamed of them, but I think they're wonderful. Funny, isn't it?"

Funny? I thought it was adorable.

"How about you?" he asked. I smiled at him. "The moment I saw you," I confessed. "I thought you were the sexiest thing I'd ever laid eyes on—whiskers, hang-over, and all."

We were in love. As the weeks passed, I was sure of it. When I was offered a winter tour in *Joan of Lorraine,* I refused unless Bob was signed as my leading man—a condition I was to insist upon many, many times. Bob was signed. I received seven hundred and fifty dollars a week, Bob two hundred and fifty dollars. I wrote Mother happily, "After two errors I've finally made a home run. This is what I hoped for and never thought would happen."

We returned from the tour to an apartment I rented on Park Avenue. I decorated it with salmon-pink walls, gold-and-black curtains, gold-and-white sofas, a pink-and-white rug. Mother gave me a life-sized turbaned blackamoor that had belonged to Robin. At the entrance I set up a slot machine for guests to make contributions. With Bob as host, I began giving parties for all my friends in the theater.

Mother by this time seemed almost resigned, although now and then she flared up at me. "My God, Diana, the way you live openly with this man! You have no morals; you don't seem to care what anybody says!"

"They're all hypocrites, Mother," I'd retort. "Everybody does it, only they do it behind locked doors." I wasn't ashamed. Bob and I would have been married now had I been able to untangle myself from Mr. John Howard.

Some things I couldn't understand in Mother. She asked Bob and me for a Christmas week end—and insisted that we take her bedroom! On another week end she invited us again —and there was Bramwell Fletcher! We greeted each other politely. Mother said only, "Diana, I've rather come to like that man." She had had him up several times before, giving him her guest house in which to live and paint. It was all incredible. Bob told me later that Bramwell asked him if he understood me. "She's a problem," he quoted my ex-husband. "Difficult to manage, self-centered, selfish, eccentric." Bob told me, with a kiss, "I haven't found it that way yet. I don't think you're eccentric. I just think every one thinks you are, and you do your best to live up to it." Perhaps he was right.

I never knew why Mother chose to invite Bramwell and us. I never understood her conduct some weeks later in Atlanta, when I gave what I think was my finest performance in the theater, in *Joan of Lorraine*.

Mother had originally named me for Joan. The Maid of Orléans was part of her life. She admired her above all

women. She had written plays about her. She never forgot
that George Bernard Shaw thought she would make a magnificent Joan—she had the passion, the spirit, the superb assurance. Therefore when I came to Atlanta and found Mother
visiting friends in Charleston, I telephoned her. "Mummy,
please come down and see me. It would mean so much to
me." She had never seen me as Joan. She agreed. The cast
was excited: Michael Strange would be in the audience and
we'd have a party in her honor in my hotel suite after the
show.

I played my heart out that night. Any actor will tell you
it is unusual when members of the cast, finished with their
roles, crowd into the wings to watch you do a scene. It was
the last, the most moving scene, when Joan, alone in her cell
before she goes to the fire, dedicates her armor to God. Her
last words are: "If I had it to do over again, I would do what
I have done. I would follow my faith even to the fire." I
was Joan: I felt the flames about to sear my flesh, I knew
Joan's exaltation, tears streamed down my face. When I
walked off the stage, I was still under the spell. I stared with
astonishment at my fellow actors: tears were running down
their cheeks too.

In my dressing room I waited, exhausted. There had been
innumerable curtain calls. Now people streamed in to congratulate me. Everyone but Mother. An usher brought a
message: she would see me at the hotel. I thought, she's so
moved, she can't come back. But when we all adjourned to
my suite, Mother wasn't there either. She was in her own
room a few floors above. We waited and waited and finally
Bob went to investigate. He found her pacing the floor, distraught. "What is it, Michael?" he asked. "Everyone's waiting
for you." Mother tossed her head. "I'm not going," she said.
"She's more interested in those people about her than she
is in me." Bob stared at her. "You're absolutely wrong,
Michael," he said, trying to control himself. "She gave that

performance tonight for you—she was so great because you were watching her and she wanted to make you proud."

Mother finally came. When she entered the room I was in the midst of a group. She stood at the door, her face like a stone. Then she strode up to me. Her lips brushed my cheek. "I won't hold you, Diana, you're so busy." Before I knew what to say, she had turned and left. She hadn't looked at anyone there, she hadn't said a word to anyone.

In the terrible silence I ran into the bedroom. Behind the closed door I began to cry. The nervous tension of the play, and now Mother. "What have I done to her to deserve this?" I wailed. Bob held me. "Let her go. I won't go after her and I won't let you." Nor did we.

Could she not bear my moment of triumph? Or was it that she had never played Joan and was jealous of me? Was it that she alone had to be the center of attention—always?

It was while on tour that I walked into Bob's dressing room to find a bottle of whisky on his table. "Bob, you know that's *verboten*—really, one doesn't do this in the theater."

"Oh, I probably won't touch it," he said casually. "I just like to know it's there."

Some days later I was putting away his laundry when I found another bottle hidden under his shirts. "Bob, what are you doing?" I cried. "Bramwell went through this with a wife who hid it under the clothes too. If you want it, for God's sake, take it. Don't hide it."

That started a new era. Bob carried a bottle of liquor in his make-up case and the case was always in his dressing room. Between acts he would take a nip or two. We talked about it. My friends drank, I drank, we enjoyed becoming amusingly and charmingly tight. The problem was when not to drink. Obviously not when you're due on stage in ten minutes. Bob explained, "It gives me energy. Don't worry, I won't go up in my lines." Nor did he. Why had he drunk that first night coming up to Salem after having taken a six-month cure?

"I was frightened," he said. "My first job in over a year, and I'd heard you were so damned temperamental——"

So it went. We toured from city to city, and there was little to do on the long rides but play poker and drink. No one in the cast spoke to me about it. I was the star; they were frightened to bring it up, and anyway it was none of their business.

During the performances I began popping into Bob's dressing room for a nip too. Presently the time came when we both showed up on stage, weaving. We defended each other hotly. Bob was dizzy from medication, I told the producer. Bob explained that I couldn't sleep worrying over his health and the pills I'd taken to catch up that afternoon made me stumble on stage.

I came to count on a friendly shot of Four Roses between acts. In Akron, when I hurried into Bob's dressing room, he'd just finished the bottle. I was in my heavy Joan of Arc armor, I was uncomfortable, I needed a drink. "Oh, never mind," I said. "There's a bar around the corner." And as I was I clanked out the stage entrance and into the bar. People gaped at the Maid of Orléans, standing there in her chain mail and silver armor, demanding impatiently, "A double whisky, please, and make it quick." Bob was so choked with laughter when I returned that he couldn't even bawl me out.

The critics didn't overlook the obvious. In Colorado Springs I read, "Miss Barrymore seemed a little unsteady on her pins, but if she hadn't been—how superb she would be." And in a small Illinois town our review consisted of one line: "Tch-tch-tch-tch-tch-tch!"

"Bob," I said, "this is no good. We'd better watch ourselves."

We tried to stay on the wagon.

When we were back in New York, Mother took a hand. She invited us to tea. We arrived to find a surprise guest— Bob's brother, Dr. Ross Wilcox, resident surgeon at New York Hospital. Instinctively I knew why Ross was there.

Mother could have invited him only to play Macbeth to her Lady. She was wearing a white hostess gown trailing to the floor, and I had never seen her look more saintly, with her dark eyes and pale skin, which in recent weeks had taken on a pallor suggesting that she really was ill. But over the cakes and tea she began to browbeat Robert in front of his brother. He was living off me, she charged. We were living together openly, shamelessly. We were drinking too much. It was scandalous!

Ross, who expected nothing like this, sat silent and embarrassed while Mother raged on. Then Bob spoke. I had never heard him so grim. "Michael," he said in his low, measured voice, "you were once married to a man named Leonard Thomas. By all accounts he was a fine and decent man. He went away to war. He was no sooner out of New York City than you started taking up with John Barrymore. And you dare talk about us?"

He turned to me. "Shall we go, Diana?" I said, "Yes, darling." We rose and walked out.

For days after that debacle Mother telephoned me, but I would not speak to her. After a week, though, I went over and we made up. No one had ever talked back to her like that. I was proud of Bob.

Drinking is insidious. It creeps up on you. I can't trace back to the month, the week, the day, when my social drinking went over the line. In Hollywood, when Bram was away, I drank heavily. During my John Howard period I tapered off. I was on a health kick, out on the tennis courts at eight-thirty every morning and feeling very noble. Now and then I drank. I knew Mr. Howard wasn't for me and I had too much pride to admit it. The one night we went on a bender, we landed in jail—and on the front pages. I wasn't happy about that. Liquor had made Daddy alternately sentimental and belligerent. Apparently it had a similar effect on me. And I was learning something about myself. Boredom drove me to the bottle. Boredom and a wish not to think about tomorrow.

Now, with Bob Wilcox, whom I loved, a subtle change took place in my drinking habits. For long periods neither of us worked. When we did, it was I who was hired, and I who insisted that he must go along as my leading man. If they wanted Barrymore, they had to take Wilcox.

This was galling to him. It lay behind much of his drinking.

I had never taken a drink in the morning. My breakfast, no matter how late, consisted of coffee. Bob's was a jigger of whisky in black coffee.

Three hours later or so we had coffee again. I followed mine with a chaser of whisky. Bob took only whisky.

Then, one morning, I poured a jigger of whisky into my coffee as well as into Bob's.

And finally one morning I found myself tossing off a whisky neat—while waiting for the coffee to perk.

Morning drinking was the key, I know now. Sometimes, when I was to join my chic friends for lunch at Twenty-One or the Colony Club, I began drinking hours before. I knew I'd have martinis at lunch, but I took an extra one beforehand. Looking back, I can find no reason and no excuse. I didn't need it to be clever, I didn't need it for courage, and in those early days I didn't need to shake off a hang-over. I didn't need it. Yet I took it.

Once I tried to explain it by saying it was the chameleon in me. I took on the coloration about me: I always changed with my surroundings. In Hollywood, not only had I changed wardrobes to match the mood of the men I dated; I transformed my personality as well. It was as though in my desire to be one with them I became a reflection of them: I smoked their brand of cigarettes, read their kind of books, ate their favorite food, even mimicked their speech. When Bob Wilcox, in pajamas and bathrobe, made his way to the pantry in the morning and remarked, as his fingers closed around a bottle of vodka, "Guess I'll have a shot of this to wake me up," I heard myself saying agreeably, "Pour one for me too." I really didn't want vodka then. Had Bob taken milk or orange juice or Ovaltine, I think I would have said with equal agreeableness, "Pour me some too."

Always I complemented, I paralleled, I became the female counterpart of the man I loved. Perhaps this was part of the way I gave myself—part of the way I loved.

Bob and I toured the summer of 1948 in *The Philadelphia Story*—I in Katharine Hepburn's role, Bob in Van Heflin's. When we returned to New York, there were no jobs.

My money was beginning to run out. We took a less expensive apartment, a duplex above a restaurant, in East 52nd Street. It sounded grand, but actually the only grand thing about it was the flight of thirteen steps from the kitchen to the studio living room. Nothing remained of the money Robin had left me, and our few weeks' summer salary soon vanished. I started to borrow on a trust fund Daddy had set up for me. From it I had received my five-hundred-a-month allowance for many years. Now, I was told, I would come into a sum of twenty-five thousand dollars on my thirtieth birthday—still more than two years away. I borrowed steadily. Each time Mother had to give her permission and cosign my request. Each time became an ordeal for me.

With nothing to do but rattle around in our apartment, the bottle took over. Vainly Bob tried to get parts on Broadway. His drinking was too well known. He tried to drown his humiliation in whisky. "I can't support you the way a self-respecting man should," he'd say abjectly. "Oh, darling," I'd cry. "Don't say that. Don't think that way. All you need is a chance, and it will come along." He had to have money for small purchases and was ashamed to ask me. I set up a checking account in his name. He was very moved. "I'll not forget this, Muzzy," he said, using his favorite term of endearment for me. "I'll make it up to you." Of course you will, darling, I said. Of course you will. Just think of it as a loan.

We were both cheered when an agent proposed "The Barrymore Theatre of the Air," a weekly radio program in which I would play dramatic scenes, with Bob as my leading man, from the lives of famous women: Cleopatra, Marie Antoinette, Empress Carlotta of Mexico. Since the material was almost inexhaustible, the show could continue indefinitely, I thought. We would both make new careers. But the producer of the show tested Bob and decided he preferred to use Arnold Moss, an actor who was more skilled in portraying foreign-speaking figures. Bob took this very hard. It was one more blow to his ego. At considerable cost I taped a complete show and took it to Bill Paley, president of CBS. Bill was kind but had to reject it. No one person could successfully play so many roles, CBS thought.

Nor could I sell it elsewhere.

We drank. We waited for the jobs that didn't come.

CHAPTER TWENTY-FOUR

THE NEWS Mother announced stunned me. The doctors at Memorial Hospital had finally identified the cause of her weariness. Leukemia. "Of course, they're perfectly insane," she said with a toss of her head. But when she left, I was close to hysterics. Leukemia! That was cancer of the blood cells! That was incurable!

I telephoned the distinguished cancer specialist whose name she gave me. Yes, he said. The diagnosis appeared certain. And she refused to take treatment.

When Bob returned from walking our little poodle, he found me slumped on our gold-and-white sofa in a stupor. In half an hour I'd finished nearly half a fifth of vodka we had in our pantry. I had no apologies! My mother was going to die!

Nothing my brother Leonard nor I could say would persuade Mother. She refused to submit to treatment. Instead, she turned more and more to the Bible. Her lecture readings now included "The Lord's Prayer" and "The Lesson of the Prodigal Son." On tour in Indiana, she came to a decision. She had Robin's body disinterred and removed to the Oelrichs family plot in Woodlawn Cemetery, in New York, where he was laid to rest next to the place reserved for her. She recalled that, years before, Robin had said he wanted to be buried next to her. She felt this took precedence over his request, made in a moment of grief over Billy Rambo, to be buried next to him. In Woodlawn Cemetery she placed twin headstones over Robin's grave and over hers. On her stone she had engraved the first half of a stanza from Solomon's "Song of Songs":

> For, lo, the winter is past, the rain is over and gone;
> The flowers appear on the earth; the time of the singing of birds is come, and the voice of the turtle is heard in our land.

On Robin's she had engraved the remainder:

> Arise, my love, my fair one, and come away.

I had met the news of Mother's illness by getting drunk. Now a second reaction set in. I was literally shocked into sobriety. Bob and I took ourselves in hand. We joined a health club in Rockefeller Center and swam, played handball, knocked ourselves out with calisthenics. We had a doctor inject Vitamin B-1. I began reading new scripts. Summer stock was all very well, but it meant only two or three months' work, and always in a role someone else had made a name in. If I was to return to Broadway, I had to find a new play.

Meanwhile I enjoyed my apartment. I delighted in preparing exotic dishes for Bob. Once he said, "I don't know whether you really want the stage. All you need is a man and a cookstove and you're happy." I ran over and kissed him. "If it's a man I love and a stove that works," I said. Perhaps he was more right than either of us knew.

I was busily whipping up an elaborate snack one afternoon when I heard a sound like rending wood above me. I had no chance to look up. Suddenly the top of my head exploded in a blinding crimson flash of pinwheels.

When I came to, I was lying in my bed and a doctor was examining me. Bob hovered nearby, white-faced. I writhed in pain that not even morphine could deaden. A six-foot, four-inch-thick section of ceiling plaster had crashed down on me. For ten weeks I suffered excruciating headaches; my vision played tricks on me. Now and then I blacked out for seconds at a time. I knew this only because when Bob spoke to me I found myself losing entire sentences. Work, a new play, both were out of the question.

The day I felt myself again, we celebrated my recovery with a small champagne party in our duplex. After everyone had left, I cleaned up tipsily. I hummed to myself as I filled a tray with empty glasses and began descending the stairs to the kitchen. My heel caught, I lost my balance and tumbled headfirst down the flight of steps, crashing into unconsciousness at the bottom.

When I awoke, I was in the hospital, and it was three days later. My eyes were blackened, my face cut by splintered glass, my back wrenched, my front teeth—the teeth I'd had so beautifully capped in Hollywood—knocked out. The doctors said I had suffered a fractured skull and lacerations of the brain. That I was alive and my eyes intact was something of a miracle. To Bob I mumbled, "I guess it takes a lot to kill a Barrymore," and lapsed into a nightmare world of hallucinations.

When I woke again, there was Mother bending worriedly over me and I heard the nurse's protest: "You mustn't disturb the patient." Mother didn't even glance at her. "Oh, go away," she said impatiently. "This is my daughter!" And to me: "My poor little Catkin, why didn't you tell me! Why didn't Bob let me know?"

"I didn't want to worry you, Mummy," I managed to reply.

"Really!" she said. "I *am* your mother. Now, look, Diana. You're going to be all right. And don't worry about money. Leonard and I will take care of it." Meanwhile, she went on, in a few days she was going abroad to be cured. "There's a marvelous man in Switzerland," she explained. "He'll tell me, of course, that it's not leukemia. They keep on saying it is, here, but they're wrong. I know they are." She kissed me and left. She was in excellent spirits.

When I returned to my apartment a month later, there was a letter from Mother in Zurich. She had taken our old friend, Ted Peckham, with her as secretary and companion. The Swiss specialist, she wrote triumphantly, assured her that it wasn't leukemia. She had lost considerable weight. He was building up her strength.

She and Ted, who was tall, blond, and handsome, took long walks through the peaceful Swiss countryside, dressed —as once she and Daddy had been—in similar hats, coats, and scarves tied about their necks, Windsor fashion. (I learned this from Ted later.) They drew stares wherever they went. It was Mother who suggested they dress alike. Was she trying to recapture the long-lost days with Daddy, during what she knew (though she would not admit it) were the last months of her life? I don't know. It was one more facet of the woman called Michael Strange, who was my mother.

My hospital regime—regular hours, food three times a day, and no alcohol—worked wonders. I celebrated my return with another champagne party, notified agents I was ready for a job, and waited. But the word was out that Barrymore and Wilcox sometimes appeared rubbery-legged on stage. It wasn't easy to book us.

I borrowed—and borrowed again—from my trust fund.

Early in 1950 Hardie Freiberg, a TV producer, dropped out of the sky like an angel. He had an idea: "The Diana Barrymore Show." I would be hostess on an 11:00 P.M. program, playing a few records and chatting with guest celebrities. "Diana, you know everyone," he said enthusiastically. "You can have any name you want. You'll need to learn a few lines, and the rest will be kicking it back and forth with your guests. You'd be so right for it." He was sure he could sell it to a sponsor.

TV disc jockeys were just coming into their own then. Compared to "The Diana Barrymore Theatre of the Air," which I had failed to sell to Bill Paley, this would be a lark.

"Go ahead, Hardie," I told him. "I think it would be wonderful!"

He called twenty-four hours later. "Honey, we've got it! Ansonia Shoes!"

They were prepared to sponsor my show on a thirteen-week deal, with options all the way. I was overjoyed. Here was a new career! For my first show I invited two friends with whom I'd be comfortable: Earl Wilson, the columnist, and Nina Foch, the actress. I chose a closetful of shoes at Ansonia, posed for scores of publicity pictures, and was launched.

Three days before the program I began studying my script, It was only six pages, yet I felt strangely queasy as I read. I had memorized scripts five times as long, but this was different. I had to ad-lib in the midst of it. This wasn't acting—it was wit and repartee . . .

I studied the script, put it away, studied it, put it away. *Well, really, Diana,* I thought, annoyed. *You've had hard parts before. This is a snap. You did them in Hollywood before the cameras. Yes,* I answered myself, *but a television camera doesn't stop. Make an ass of yourself, my girl, and everyone will see it. There's no taking scenes over here.*

The day of the show Bob stayed with me until four o'clock. I sat in a huge green chair next to the window, going over my lines. I might as well have been reading another language. Freiberg had said, "Don't really learn it, Diana. Ad-lib it." This made me more nervous. I could learn lines as an actress or I could ad-lib—but this was half and half. I was confused, unable to decide what to memorize and what to ad-lib.

Bob knew how nervous I was. "Darling," he said, "I'm going out and leave you alone. You learn those lines. And for God's sake, don't drink." I promised. "Just stay steady. I'll be back in a couple of hours. You're going to be great."

Alone, I sat in the chair. I was becoming panicky. Outside, it grew dark. The minutes were rushing by. Soon it would be time to leave for the studio. I looked at the clock and realized, with a sinking heart, it was seven o'clock already!

But I wasn't to go on until eleven. Four hours. "Oh, Diana, tonight is your night to give it. Now, study. Four hours is plenty."

I thought of the day before when I visited CBS. The elevator starter tipped his hat. "Well, Miss Barrymore, I'm glad you're going to be with us. It will be nice to have you part of the family."

I said, "Thank you very much, darling. Forgive me, but what is your name?" Tom, he said. "Well, thank you, Tom. I'll be seeing you every week."

I felt comforted as I went up. They know me, they like me, they want me.

I watched the dusk now—pink, then gray, then blue-black, then black. A strange apprehension tugged at me. I need something to settle my nerves. I don't think one little old brandy will hurt me. Not at seven o'clock, when I'm not on until eleven.

Across the room stood the coffee table, with liquor and glasses. I walked to the table, poured myself a brandy, and swallowed it. It went down, glowing and reassuring. I felt the warmth spread over the knot in my stomach and dissolve it. Of course, Diana. That's all you needed. I began to return to my chair. I thought, I'd better pour another one to take back and study with. When I returned to my chair, I carried my brandy with me in a water tumbler—six ounces instead of one.

I settled down to study, brandy in my left hand, script in my right. I read the script, closed my eyes to fix the lines, sipped the brandy. I read, I memorized, I sipped from the lovely tumbler. I don't know how many times I went to the table.

Suddenly it was nine-forty-five. I had to leave for the studio. I put on my coat. Bob came in just as I was pouring one for the road. He strode up to me and tried to snatch the glass away. I clung to it. "I've got to have it for my nerves!" I cried. I gulped it down.

"Diana," he said quietly, "you're drunk. You can't go on."

I became indignant. "What do you mean, drunk?"

"You're slurring your words," he said.

"Slurring?" I drew myself up. "Of course I'm not slurring."

"Look, Muzzy," he said cajolingly. "Call them and tell them you're sick, but please don't go to the studio tonight."

I flared at him. "If you won't take me, I'll go myself."

The telephone rang. With one eye on me, Bob answered it. "She's not there yet?" he asked as if in surprise. "She left at least twenty minutes ago." He hung up. "All right, come on, you better hurry—that was Freiberg's secretary. They're waiting for you."

At the CBS building I said, "Don't come up, Bob. You'll make me nervous."

He kissed me good luck. "I'll find a bar with a TV and watch you there," he said. "All the luck in the world, Muzzy."

I swept by Tom, who smiled at me, and into the elevator and up to the studio. I pushed open the door. Someone said, "Hello, Miss Barrymore." I called out, "Hi!" A moment later Freiberg materialized from nowhere. "Diana, sit down, will you, honey? Please sit down." Someone steered me to a chair. I sat there, looking about me. It seemed people were in corners, whispering.

Unexpectedly I found the director of our show, a blond, handsome young man, sitting next to me, talking. "Won't we be late?" I asked, worried. He placated me. "Don't worry about it, Miss Barrymore. Everything's under control."

I peered about. "Where is Earl? And Nina? They aren't late, are they? Not our first night!"

Nobody replied. Then Freiberg came through a door and over his arm he carried a blue satin dress—the dress I was to wear on the program. "Here's your dress, darling," he said.

I thought, he doesn't expect me to put it on here? Then the thought struck me. He's giving it back to me. It probably means I won't go on. Does he think I'm loaded? Well, by God, I guess I am! I spoke aloud. "Aren't I going on?"

He took me by the arm. "I'm sorry, dear. I don't think you should. You'd better go home."

The dress was on a hanger. I looked at it.

"How about next week?" I asked. I spoke carefully and distinctly. "I promise you this will never happen again."

"We'll see, honey," he said. "You go home and sleep and we'll talk about it tomorrow."

Then I was in the elevator and suddenly in the lobby; the smiling face of Tom, the starter, was before me, but it was a strained smile. They must have all heard about it, I thought. He said, "Good night, Miss Barrymore. Shall I get you a cab?"

I said with dignity, "Isn't there a doorman?"

"Not this late, Miss Barrymore." He called a cab and helped me in. It took me to my apartment, which was just around the corner. I could have walked it.

Later I learned that while I waited, Freiberg had consulted with Earl and Nina. He told them I was in no condition to go on. The show was canceled. He asked Earl to print nothing. Earl proved a friend and didn't.

I was sitting in the chair by the window in the darkness when Bob came in. At the bar they had turned on the much-publicized Diana Barrymore show. The announcer appeared: "Ladies and gentlemen, due to circumstances beyond our control, the program scheduled for this hour will not be seen. Now, the eleven o'clock news."

Bob walked over to CBS and paced back and forth waiting outside for me to appear, but I had already left. He returned to the apartment.

He made his way through the gloom to the kitchen and switched on the light and saw me. He stood there, looking at me silently. "Well," he said. "I begged you."

I said dully. "Yes. You begged me."

"Look, darling," he said. He sat down next to me and took

my hand. "This isn't the end. There'll be a lot more where that came from."

I shook my head. "No, Bob. I'll never find work again. I'm finished."

"No, you're not finished, Diana."

"I'm through," I said, and I began to cry and shake. I couldn't stop; my body was rigid and I shook uncontrollably. Bob carried me to bed and gave me a sedative, then he held me close. I lay in his arms. "Oh, Bob, I'm finished. They know how we've been in the theater. Now everyone will know here, too, how Barrymore was too loaded to go on her own show when she had a terrific chance . . ."

"No, you're not finished," he repeated. "You've just started. This is just an experience. You'll learn from it."

He lied—and he knew he lied—and I knew he lied.

Next morning Freiberg called. "Honey—" he began.

I interrupted him. "Hardie, I know what I've done, for the love of God, give me another chance! I don't deserve it, but will you?"

"Diana, if it were me, I'd do it," he said gently. "But Ansonia is so mad . . . We're going to try another girl—a girl called Faye Emerson."

The name didn't mean much to me.

I tried to be gay about it. "Hardie, of course you're right and Ansonia is right. I don't blame you one bit," I said lightly. "It's just too bad, all those free shoes I could have had!"

For months everywhere I looked, stories and interviews and photographs of Faye Emerson leaped out at me. Her name was like a dagger. *You fool, you idiot! It could have been you on the cover of* Look, *of* Cosmopolitan . . . *It could have been you.*

CHAPTER TWENTY-FIVE

I MARRIED Bob Wilcox. Mr. John Howard did not contest my divorce action: in fact, he seemed to have vanished from sight. The FBI, it developed, was looking for him. They even tapped my telephone, hoping he might call me. He never did. Then I read of his arrest in a Chicago vice raid. Why the FBI wanted him I learned much later—when he pleaded guilty to transporting a Hollywood starlet to New York for purposes of prostitution. He needed her earnings to enable him to go into business. The business wasn't specified. I learned then, too, that his good friend, Richard Short, who had eyed my diamond bracelet so hungrily in El Paso, was also put behind bars for procuring.

"You're well rid of that crowd," said Bob. "Now forget it, Mrs. Wilcox." Bob warned me before I married him: "I'm not sure I'm the right man for you, Diana. You need someone strong. I can't do anything for you. I have no money, all I own is what I have on my back. And it looks as though I'll never get another job in pictures. But I do know you'll never find anyone who will love you more selflessly or more completely."

"Darling," I said, "no woman could ask for more. Not a single thing more."

The ceremony was performed by a justice of the peace in Newark, New Jersey, on October 17, 1950. Mother was not there nor was she told about it. She lay in Massachusetts

Memorial Hospital, slowly dying yet refusing to believe it, fighting for her life against impossible odds. She had spent nearly forty thousand dollars fleeing from one doctor to another here and abroad. Now, a shadow of herself, yet still magnificently in command, she held court daily in her hospital suite. It was decked with flowers, packed high with books, records, and gifts. A stream of friends poured in and out, with my brother Leonard and Ted Peckham, taking turns playing at major-domo, and Ethel Malcolm, her maid, bustling about on errands. Mother's meals were delivered from the outside—she abhorred hospital food. Fresh flowers were brought in every other day; her florist bills alone exceeded twenty dollars a day. Sometimes, if she felt up to it, Ted chartered a limousine and took her for a drive or to a movie.

Each week end I left Bob and journeyed to Boston—I had not worked now for months—to stay with her. I read to her from her favorite poets, Shelley, Keats, Browning. As usual, we fought. No illness could temper Mother. If I ventured to bring up Bob's name, she snapped, "I won't listen; I don't want to hear about him!" Or, "Diana, don't mention that man in my presence!"

She had never forgiven him. Nor could she forgive me for remaining with him in New York while she was ill in Boston. She was jealous of Bob for taking me away from her, as she had been jealous of Billy Rambo for taking Robin from her. It would have been too cruel to tell her I was now Mrs. Robert Wilcox. No matter how much Mother and I whipped each other, I managed to keep that secret from her.

In these weeks she talked about herself as a mother. "I failed Robin," she said once. "I should have been more of a mother to him in later years and less of a mother before."

"That's right," I said relentlessly. "You never cut the umbilical cord."

She looked at me, deeply hurt. Then: "I failed you too. I gave him too much affection and you not enough."

I said, "Yes, Mother."

Her eyes filled with tears. "I failed you both. And now you're going the way your father did—drinking, drinking, drinking!" She berated herself and I could no longer be hard. "Don't say that, Mummy!" I cried. "It's all past and gone. And I'm not drinking!" Of course I was. Several times Ted Peckham halted me at her door. "You're not in condition to see her," he said. I lashed out at him. "How dare you say I can't see my own mother!" But he stood firm, and I found my way to a restaurant and filled myself with black coffee so I could return to the hospital. Who wouldn't drink? My mother dying, and my own career . . .

Once when I called on her, I found her surprisingly subdued. Her visitors that day included a family friend, a priest who had attended parochial school with Daddy when both were boys. He revealed something she had never known. Daddy, at fifteen, was apparently a probing student, original, a hater of sham. Sensitive, moody, questioning, he was trying to find his own way. His teachers thought he might have a brilliant career in the Church. They thought he had the makings of an eloquent divine.

One afternoon he met a woman; she flirted with him, encouraged him—and seduced him. It was his first sexual experience. Then, to his horror, he learned that she was his father's mistress.

Fellow students discovered him later, sprawled on his bed in a stupor. He was fifteen, and he had drunk himself unconscious.

He never knew why she had done it. He would not speak to his father about it then. He was unable to speak to him about it when he was older, for three years later Maurice Barrymore lost his mind and was committed to a mental institution. There he died soon after.

"My dear," the priest said to Mother, "I knew Jack. I have wondered so often—who can know how tormented he was, what conflicts were set up in his heart and soul by that awful experience, at that crucial age? What must it have meant to see his father reeling down Broadway, drunk, a chorus girl on either arm . . . We know his own drinking began about that time."

Mother turned her face away. "Yes," she said. "Poor Jack! Poor Jack!"

In my apartment I sat with a drink and wondered too. Was this behind his savage irony, his love and hatred for women, his self-mockery, the burlesque he made of what he felt most deeply? And his drinking?

I could ask the questions but I had no answers. Neither for him nor for myself.

Everyone I have loved has died while I was at work. Daddy, when I was attending Universal's *Eagle Squadron* preview; Robin, when I was playing *Rebecca* in Cincinnati. And now Mother, as I was on stage in Moss Hart's comedy, *Light Up the Sky*, in Miami, the first week of November, 1950.

As with Daddy, the doctors assured me that I could go. It was a one-week engagement, and one of the few jobs offered Bob and me. It meant a thousand dollars to us—and we needed the money. Mother said, "Of course, Catkin, by all means go." She had been so disdainful of her illness, there was no reason to believe that seven days later I would not find her, as much Michael as ever, presiding in her flower-decked room.

But when I came off stage that Saturday night and Bob walked toward me, I knew instinctively. Out front the audience still rocked with applause. I was to return for a curtain call. Instead, I faced Bob. "My mother is dead, isn't she?"

He nodded and took me in his arms.

Leonard had telephoned him from Boston an hour before.

Boston, I said. I must get to Boston. I had only my summer dresses. I borrowed a black suit from a girl in the company and I took the midnight plane from Miami. As I boarded it, I carried in my purse a medicine bottle of whisky.

The flight itself is a confused memory. I sat in a window seat and my mind was like a phonograph turntable. It revolved endlessly, but all I could remember was the moment I first knew, knew surely, that my mother was going to die. It had been at her final recital, in Times Hall, in New York, just before she went to the hospital.

I was sitting with Bob as the curtain parted. There, on a severely simple stage, stood a rostrum and on it the Old and New Testaments. Beside them, a bound notebook. I knew it contained the Communist Manifesto. Mother loved to read them together—the word of God and the word of the Godless. She had always liked to shock.

Then she appeared from the wings. I sat bolt upright. I drew in my breath so sharply that people turned. Bob's hand gripped mine hard.

I was looking at a dying woman. She had become so thin, so fragile! She, who had been so healthy, so vigorous, whose incredible vitality extinguished everyone about her—now, a wraithlike reflection of herself. Pale white lights played upon her as she moved forward, making her appear even more ethereal, so that she seemed to float before us. She wore a long, flowing white robe, appliquéd with leaves of gold, the robe of a Grecian priestess. It had split sleeves that trailed to the floor, and a gold cord braided about her waist, with long golden tassels at the side. I could have encompassed her waist with my two hands! Only her magnificent shock of black hair was the same, and her eyes, dark and flashing. But her face was gaunt and her skin seemed to have taken on a translucent quality, almost as I remembered Robin in boyhood. She stood on that stage and death stood beside her. I kept my eyes averted and listened to her voice as she read, so hauntingly musical, so unbelievably melodious, a voice that sang like a low violin. Mother could recite the alphabet and send shivers up and down your spine.

Later I went backstage. "Mother—" I began, holding her hand, searching for words. She took one look at me and pushed me on almost roughly. "Diana, you're drunk. I'll see you later." And she was already greeting somebody else. I wasn't drunk. I hadn't been drinking. The one time in my life I was overcome and wanted to pour my heart out to her, she thought I was drunk!

Leonard waited for me in his hotel room. He stood there as his father, Leonard Thomas, Sr., would have stood when faced with tragedy—calm and strong. He was my rock to cling to. We looked at each other. I said, "All right, Leonard. What do we do?" He said, "We go to the funeral parlor to see Mother." I said, "Okay." I opened my bag and took out the bottle. I didn't hide it from Leonard. He said gently, "I've had a few myself. Let's have one together, shall we? This is not going to be a very amusing day."

I watched him as he brought two tumblers from the bathroom and poured drinks for us. He turned to me. "Let's sit down," he said. "Don't do this on the run. There's no hurry any more."

"You're quite right," I said. We drank together, slowly, then together we went to the funeral parlor.

I looked on Mother, dead. She had asked to be buried in her Grecian robe, and so she was dressed in it. But her face was pale and yellow, made up as she would have hated. I turned to the undertaker. "My mother wouldn't wish to be seen this way. Please send in the man who does the make-up."

He came in with a little box. "Leave that here and go away, darling," I said. "I will stay and make my mother up."

Though it was against the rules, I made her up as she lay in her coffin: Michael's face, Michael's eyebrows—the swallow-wing eyebrows that were her mark. I spoke to her as I worked. "Oh, Mummy, I wish I'd known you better, I wish I had been closer to you all these years. Oh, I wish so many things." I thought of her, always restless, always seeking else-where the harmony she could never find in herself. Now at last she was at peace. I made her up as she made herself up in life, as she would have wanted to be seen in death.

When we read her will, dated October 27—only nine days before her death: only then had she accepted the verdict—we discovered that the last thing Mother wrote was her own funeral scene. She planned the services in every detail, down to stage directions. Her body was to lie in state in her Easton home. Wagner's *Parsifal* was to be played continuously on her Capehart, screened off from the rest of the room. The funeral was to be conducted from the house.

For three days Mother's body lay in state in her enormous, high-ceilinged living room banked with thousands of flow-ers, the flowers she loved. I arranged them as a designer might fix a stage set. Mother would have wanted it that way. Peo-ple came and went and the Capehart played softly. Bob sat behind the screen and saw to it that the records were played as Mother wished. The huge room, the music, Mother in her priestess' robe—there was something strange and medieval about it all. Each night I placed a little French praying stool next to her coffin, and I knelt on it and prayed, and then kissed my mother good night. Her lips were cold, cold, cold . . .

Then the service was held, and the coffin closed, and we rode through the dark November day to Woodlawn Ceme-tery, and I saw Mother lowered into the grave she had pre-pared for herself, next to Robin, under the headstones bearing the words of Solomon's "Song of Songs."

I was not sober when I stood above her open grave and threw earth upon her coffin. I heard it fall, and something of my own life, my own faith in myself, died with the sound.

BOOK THREE

CHAPTER TWENTY-SIX

THERE WAS NO REASON for a crab to be on the ceiling.

I lay in bed, suddenly awake, staring at it. An enormous white crab slowly crawling across the ceiling.

How can that be, I wondered. Can it get there all the way from the Atlantic?

I reached and turned on the light. I stole a quick glance at the ceiling. Obviously, nothing there. Of course not. I switched off the light. Don't be an ass, you fool! There's nothing there. I shut my eyes for a few seconds and opened them —and that obscene thing was still going across the ceiling. A white crab.

Why should it be white? There aren't any white crabs unless you throw them into boiling water. Then they turn pink. Or is it the other way around? I watched it as it crawled. It reached the opposite wall. I said conversationally, "Turn around now. Come back." I wasn't frightened. And it did. The crab reached the wall, extended its feelers, waved them gracefully from side to side, then turned and slowly crawled back across the ceiling. I felt annoyed. I said, "You know, you don't belong here. Go away, please. Get lost." After a moment I stole another glance at the ceiling. The crab had vanished.

Well, I said. That's a relief. Now really, Diana, this is too much. You know very well there was nothing there. It's nerves and imagination and worry and too much liquor. Diana, honey, this is the time to pull yourself together. You've been drinking steadily for weeks now. *It's no good, Diana!* I was shouting at myself when I suddenly fell asleep again.

Next day I was more frightened than I admitted, even to myself. I said nothing to Bob. I thought, this can't be the DTs. Can you get DTs when you're only thirty? Isn't that rather young? I've not been drinking so much, not for so long anyway. I don't see things. I don't hear voices.

But what I had seen—or thought I saw—shocked me into sobriety for days afterward.

Not only Mother's death had started me on a drinking spree: I drank to forget but also to push away my growing panic over money. It knotted my stomach every time I dared think about it. Money had always come easy to me; I had never worried because there were so many sources. Now, suddenly, all the springs had dried up. I had earned nearly two hundred and fifty thousand dollars in Hollywood: it was gone, as was Robin's legacy of forty-seven thousand. I had borrowed to the hilt on my trust fund—we'd lived that up, Bob and I. I could count on some money when Mother's estate was settled, but that was two or three years off, and because of the staggering expenses of her illness, the sum could not be too large.

And Bob had no income, no savings, no job.

All at once money became terrifyingly important, not for the childish delight of having it in my own hands, but as a necessity—for food, clothing, and a roof. And over money Bob and I began to quarrel. It wasn't easy to fight with Bob. He was amiable, gentle, and though like Daddy—always a little rolling on his feet—never belligerent, unless he thought I had been insulted. Then he leaped to my defense, ready to swing blindly at any producer, stagehand, anyone who dared

say Diana Barrymore was drunk. Most of the time, as the
day wore on, Bob moved from a state of mellowness—"I feel
no pain," he put it—to drowsiness and sleep. He rarely tried
to make producers' rounds now. Rather than risk the humiliation of rejection, he stayed in the apartment. As for me, a
Barrymore couldn't traipse from office to office asking for a
job. No name did. Agents handled names—and agents were
reluctant. No producer wanted a repetition of Ansonia.

When I first met Bob he had said, "I'm all washed up,
Diana. You should know that now." I brushed it aside. "Oh,
goody, so am I!" I said gaily. I still had money then. My
hopes for Bob and myself were fantastically ambitious. We'd
become the new Lunts, a sophisticated husband-and-wife
team who would make a single shining name for themselves.
What I failed to realize was that Bob was in dead earnest.
He had given up.

Now, worrying about money, I saw nothing funny in our
situation. Almost in panic I cast about. I began to sell things.
Robin had left me a dozen valuable modern paintings. I dis-
posed of them through Ted Peckham. Ted now bought and
sold, for socially prominent clients, anything ranging from
objets d'art to once-worn Mainbocher evening gowns and
used mink bedspreads. One of Robin's paintings, worth two
thousand dollars, went for seven hundred. "Must you?" Ted
asked unhappily each time, and each time I said, "Yes, I
must." The sight of the empty spaces on the wall depressed
me. I hurried out and bought an armful of prints to cover
them.

When that money was gone, I began to pawn my jewelry.
My diamond bracelet found its way to the Provident Loan
Association. Then a stunning ruby and diamond pin Jimmy
Clark, one of my chic beaux, gave me for Christmas after my
coming-out party. (Mother had said, "It's in such good taste,
Catkin, you can keep it.") Then a magnificent and unique
diamond-studded cross, fashioned of gold and crystal, which
Daddy himself had designed as his gift to Mother on their

first wedding anniversary. I pawned them all, consoling myself with the promise that I would redeem them the moment Mother's estate was settled.

Bob watched all this, utterly wretched. "Goddamn it," he exploded one afternoon. "All these things you've loved, and now you're selling them because I can't support you!"

"Bob, I don't want to talk about it," I said.

But he brooded. He whipped himself. "If I were any kind of a man, if I had any self-respect——"

That did it. That set me off. His frustration made me sorry for him, and then furious because I was sorry. I didn't want to be sorry for my husband. I didn't want to pity my own husband!

"You're Goddamned right!" I yelled at him. "If you were any kind of a man I wouldn't have to do this! You'd get a job, if not on Broadway, then anywhere. Why don't you go out and get a job like other men!"

"All right," he said doggedly. "I'll go out tomorrow. The hell with acting!"

An inspiration came. Francis Kellogg had married Fernanda Wanamaker Munn, of the department-store family, in 1943, a year after I had married Bram Fletcher. Now Francis was an important executive at Wanamaker's. Swallowing my pride, I telephoned him. "Fran, darling, things are terrible . . . is there anything you can do for Bob?" And Francis, a friend as always, said, send Bob up.

I tried not to think how my husband felt, begging a handout from his wife's former beau. Bob returned a few hours after he left. He had obviously stopped at several bars on the way home. Francis, he said, could not have been more gracious. He had taken him down to the shoe department and introduced him to the manager. There might be a position open as a shoe clerk—at forty-five dollars a week. Bob looked at me. He lit a cigarette and his hands trembled. "I don't know, Muzzy . . . Start selling shoes, at my age?"

It cut me to the heart. "Oh, darling, no, no, of course not!

What are we thinking of! You're an actor, and by God, you'll stay an actor!" I held him close. "How dared they!" I cried. "They should have offered to make you a vice-president!"

Who else was there? I called Bill Paley at CBS. To Bill I couldn't admit we were broke. "Bill," I said, "my husband's bored with doing nothing. He's an actor, he can direct, he has a beautiful voice. Maybe you can use him."

Bob returned even more crushed. The only position he could be considered for was that of an usher. He had been taken down and shown the bright young men, twenty-one and twenty-two years old, in their musical-comedy uniforms, guiding guests from studio to studio. "Me, at forty, doing that?" He took a stiff drink. "Christ, I wish I'd never become an actor! What in hell am I fitted for?"

Then *I* got a job. In vaudeville.

How indignant I'd been in Hollywod at the idea of going in vaudeville! Now I jumped at the chance when Jerry Rosen, an agent, said he could book me on a tour outside New York. People would always flock to see a Barrymore, and I was a good mimic. The routine I prepared was suited for both night clubs and stage shows. I opened as Ethel Merman singing "There's No Business Like Show Business." Then I impersonated Aunt Ethel, caught in a moment of regal dismay as she learned that her wayward niece, Diana, had signed to do a five-a-day vaudeville act. Then I did impressions of Daddy, Tallulah Bankhead, Judy Holliday, and Katharine Hepburn, and closed, in a startling change of pace, with a reading of the potion scene from *Romeo and Juliet.*

It was a fantastic potpourri, yet my tour was successful. My check was one thousand dollars a week, which sounds far more than it really was. My agent and my manager took 25 per cent, 20 per cent went to the government, and from the remainder I paid hotel and traveling expenses, cost of my costumes and songs. When from that I subtracted my lengthy long-distance calls every night to Bob in New York, who had nothing to do but wait for my call, I wasn't left with much.

I forgot my pride. In Watertown, New York, I followed a juggling act. A Barrymore following a juggling act! What had Daddy told me: "They say I'm a buffoon. I probably am. But it's paying the rent and I'm paying back what I owe." I thought, it's the same with me. The important thing is that money is coming in.

Then Jerry announced that he had booked me into New York's Palace Theatre, top vaudeville house in the country. "The Palace!" I cried. "Are you out of your mind? I'm not ready for the Palace! I'm not good enough for New York. I'll be doing something foreign to me in a place where everybody will come to see me!"

There was no way out. Opening morning, despite the sedative the house physician gave me, I stood in the wings, shaking. Until now I had had people to play with on stage. Here there was only that monster of a microphone, and I knew it could never throw me a cue. Yet my first show went beautifully. The second was disastrous. But by the third and fourth I had gotten hold of myself. And people came, people applauded.

Now Jerry brought still more exciting news. The Celebrity Club in Sydney, Australia—the best-known night club down under—wanted me for a three-week engagement. They'd pay seven hundred and fifty dollars a week—an enormous salary by Australian standards—plus my round-trip fare!

After I calmed down I asked, what about Bob? No, they wanted only me. For days I struggled with myself. I didn't want to leave Bob. He said, "I love you, I worship you, and it will be hell when you're gone, but this is a wonderful chance—you go ahead, Muzzy, and be sensational." But that night when I turned and looked at him as he slept, at his black head against the blue pillowcase, I knew I loved him and that I could not go eight thousand miles away from that man and do anything good. I needed him for strength. He had so little himself, but strangely, he gave strength to me.

I took my last painting from the wall, a Diega Rivera, and called on Mrs. Bror Dahlberg, in whose Chicago stock company Robin and Tyrone Power had acted years before. Gilda was one of the richest women in America. Perhaps she would loan me fifteen hundred dollars—the cost of a round-trip ticket for Bob—on the painting. Gilda, however, thought it wiser for me to go alone. If I proved successful, she would pay Bob's fare to Australia to join me. "And three weeks really isn't so long, my dear."

"It is for me, Gilda darling," I said and went back to the apartment, my mind made up. When my round-trip passage arrived, I promptly exchanged it for two one-way tickets and together Bob and I left for Australia in the fall of 1951. If we couldn't be Lunts in New York, we might manage it on the other side of the globe!

Australia was a fantastic series of triumphs and fiascoes. We went for three weeks: we remained six months. Our entry into Sydney, Australia's largest city, was a production— crowds jamming the airport, photographers' bulbs flashing, a huge bouquet of roses thrust into my arms. The newspapers splashed our photographs over page one and recalled that Daddy had toured Australia forty-five years before with William Collier in *The Dictator*. They remembered him well, especially since he and Collier had been arrested one night for "laughing too loudly in the street." Yes, I thought, that was Daddy. I was described as "the most dynamic stage and screen personality ever to visit Australia"—Bob, my director and leading man, as "the star of twenty-six films." "Darling," I whispered to him, "maybe they think we *are* the Lunts!" We'd do all right, I told myself.

My first two weeks at the Celebrity Club were fine. The owner, Joe Taylor, a big man with thick black horn-rimmed spectacles, couldn't have been more considerate. My songs and mimicry went over beautifully. These gay and carefree Aussies liked me, and who minded if I was a little gayer, a little more carefree than anyone else? After the wretched months in New York, after my lonely tour in vaudeville, I felt like a suddenly freed prisoner: I was eight thousand miles away from money problems, from suspicious Broadway producers and doubtful Broadway agents. I felt even better when a tentative bid came from the famous Princess Theatre in Melbourne for Bob and me to costar in our favorite play, *Light Up the Sky,* after my club engagement. Bob promptly flew to Melbourne to negotiate.

For the first time I was alone. Not having Bob at my side upset me. I wasn't due on stage for my first show at the club until 9:30 P.M. I had nothing to do. I went there early and sat at a table. Like everyone else, I ordered drinks. Gin and more gin. I managed to get through my performance. Then I sat again and ordered again. When I rose to go backstage for the midnight show, I found Joe Taylor suddenly standing in front of me. His black shell-rimmed spectacles seemed enormous. "Diana, you are not going on the late show."

Oh, oh, I thought, I think I've done it again.

"Why not?" I asked aloud.

"Because you can't. You're drunk."

I drew myself up. "Who says I'm drunk?" I demanded. "Show them to me!"

Joe looked at me sadly. "It's no use, my dear. I can't permit you to go on."

I went to my dressing room, got my clothes together, and left. I knew I wouldn't return.

Bob hurried to the club the moment he came off the plane from Melbourne the following night. I wasn't there. He found me in our hotel room, sitting as I had after the Ansonia episode—by the window, looking out into the darkness, thinking nothing.

"You're through at the club, aren't you?"

I nodded.

"Why?"

"You know why."

"Couldn't you have played fair with Joe Taylor?" he demanded angrily. "Jesus Christ! He's been a prince to you! You let him down. Why? Why?"

My nerves gave way. "Goddamn it, don't be so —— righteous!" I screamed at him. "Who in hell do you think *you* are!" I looked around wildly, grabbed a glass, and threw it at him with all my might. It crashed against the wall. The liquor made a huge blob of bright yellow on the yellow wallpaper. "I don't know why!" I screamed. "I don't know! I didn't mean to, I didn't mean to hurt him, to hurt you, to hurt myself, but I've done it." I sat down. "I don't want to talk about it. You let me alone!"

Later, over a bottle, we made up. "Muzzy, don't worry," he said again and again. "The play's coming through in a day or two. Anyway, you never belonged in night clubs."

I thought, as well as I could think, he's right. If I had been a good entertainer, okay. But I wasn't. And I didn't belong.

That night I woke suddenly before dawn. Bob was sound asleep. Something had awakened me. Something to the right of my bed. I turned my head slowly—and I felt the hair raise on the back of my neck. Mother stood there, clear as life. She was in the white priestess' robe in which we had buried her. I smelled the delicate perfume, the lemon verbena scent she always wore in her hair. She was looking down at me. She spoke. "Oh, Catkin, Catkin, what's to become of you! Look at the way you're going!"

"I'm not doing anything wrong, Mummy," I said.

"Wrong?" Her voice sang in its familiar low violin tone. "It's disgraceful! The cheap spectacle you're making of yourself!"

I felt ashamed. "I know, Mummy. I'm so sorry I let you down. I hadn't meant to let you down." As I heard myself say the words, I became angry. "It's not my fault, really! Not the way I've been brought up! I've had no family life, no home life, I've had nothing but stepfathers all my life! You kept me away from you, you kept me away from my own father, you gave me the wrong set of values! Damn you!" I cried. "You were a bad mother to me! You made me wear old-fashioned dresses that made me miserable when other girls were wearing lovely clothes at dances! You always beat me down! You kept me under your thumb! You never let me grow up——"

"No, Diana, no," she said. Her face was suddenly the suffering face of Joan of Arc. "It isn't true. It isn't true."

"And what about Atlanta, Mummy!" I cried. "Bob begged you to come to the party. He went to your room. You didn't want to. You were jealous of your own daughter! . . ."

Bob's voice cut through the haze. "Diana! What's the matter with you?" He was sitting up in bed. "Who are you talking to?"

I looked at Mother. She was gone.

I began to cry.

Bob took me in his arms. "What is it, Muzzy?"

"My mother, my mother, I saw my mother," I wept. "She was standing there as clear as you are."

Bob was very gentle. "I think you should sleep," he said. He held me close and after a little while the tears stopped. I fell asleep. And in the morning, I still asked myself: was it a dream? The scent of lemon verbena still seemed to linger in the room . . .

That afternoon both Joe Taylor and I gave prepared statements to the press about my abrupt closing. We had ended our contract by mutual agreement, we announced. I had suffered severe laryngitis, the result of late hours and smoky atmosphere. I said, "Laryngitis always attacks me when I perform in night clubs. I've always preferred the legitimate theater but unfortunately one has to eat." Mr. Taylor's statement read, "I could not ask Diana to risk ruining her voice permanently by singing when she has such a persistent laryngitis."

In Melbourne the announcement of my appearance, with Bob as my leading man, sold out the Princess Theatre three weeks in advance. My spirits soared. They were paying us seven hundred dollars a week—more, they assured us, than Laurence Olivier and Vivien Leigh had received when they appeared in Australia. We played to crowded houses. Garnett H. Carroll, owner of the theater, suggested we try a second play. While still playing *Light Up the Sky,* we began rehearsing Noel Coward's *The Marquise,* only to learn, seven days before opening, that he wouldn't release it because he expected to rewrite it into a musical. We had seven days to learn a new play. We threw ourselves into rehearsals of another Coward comedy, *Fallen Angels.*

On opening night everyone forgot lines, as was to be expected. Daphne Winslow, an Australian favorite, and I played two women getting drunk while they awaited the arrival of an old lover they'd once shared. I ad-libbed. I swore. After all, I was playing a tipsy woman. I said, "Goddamn," instead of "damn." I interpolated words. One line read, "This thing is killing me!" I read it, "Oh, heavens to Betsy, this thing is killing me!" The audiences roared, but the director, Eric Reiman, was furious.

Next morning at rehearsal he upbraided me. This, though the reviews spoke of my "superb drunken clowning." "Tonight, Miss Barrymore," he said stiffly, "You'll do it my way."

"I won't," I said.

He lashed out at me. I lashed back. "Why, you arrogant s.o.b.," I cried. "You're only mad because I didn't take your direction. I did it my way and got those wonderful notices."

He threw the script on the floor. "I'm calling Garnett."

"Don't bother," I snapped and walked off. I told Bob. "Good for you," he said. "You've got to be judged on the stage by what you do. If you do it badly, because he wants it that way, nobody but you will be blamed. You did right."

Garnett was firm. I must obey the director. But I had made such a scene before everyone that I couldn't back away now. "I'm sorry," I said.

That was it. I left the play after one performance. And after such glowing notices!

We lounged about, enjoying ourselves for several weeks. We flew to Brisbane, where I was booked into a vaudeville house with a girlie show called "The Nudie-Cuties." I'd seen better chorus lines at the penny arcades in Atlantic City. But we needed the money. I worked out a skit with Bob, who hated vaudeville as much as I. His American jokes fell flat; the audience wanted broad burlesque; this, I felt—acting in a cheap skit amid the bumps and grinds of the Nudie-Cuties— was as low as I'd ever reached in front of an audience. I was depressed, Bob was depressed. Our Australian adventure that began so brightly . . . We drank. When we arrived for the noon show on our third day, I found that our photographs had been taken down. The theater owner said, "I can't attend you, Miss Barrymore."

"What does that mean?" I asked.

"Brisbane isn't like Melbourne, where you did a legitimate show. People have complained that you were intoxicated."

He was right, and they were right. "I'm sorry," I said, turned on my heel, packed, and left.

Still they wanted me. We went to Tasmania, where everything became confused. I opened on March 2, 1952, the eve of my thirty-first birthday. The house was half empty. After the show Bob and I dined at the hotel. We were served superbly made meat loaf. "I'm going down and congratulate the chef," I said. "Even Robin would say this was divine. I want more."

I found my way to the kitchen. The chef was delighted. He fixed up a tray with a second helping, and as I was taking it out, the hotel owner hurried into the kitchen. "You can't take that upstairs," he said. "We don't permit that here. No food in your room."

"Get out of my way, little man," I said.

He swore at me. "I know all about you, you Jezebel! You

American Diana Barrymore! I've read in the papers what you've done! Now put that tray down and get out! Leave my hotel!"

"How dare you!" I exclaimed. "You monster!" And I gave him as good as he gave me.

We flew back to Melbourne and spent the next week basking in the sun. One afternoon I said to Bob, "I don't see us getting any more offers. I think we've had it. Let's go home."

Of the money we'd made, we had our return tickets and seven hundred dollars. We spent five hundred dollars of it in three days in Honolulu, at the Royal Hawaiian Hotel. We'd never had a honeymoon: this was ours. We spent wildly, almost frantically. We knew the ship was sinking, and we wanted it to go down in a blaze of glory.

When we landed in the San Francisco airport at 6:00 A.M. of a cold, rainy March 13, 1952, we had twenty-five dollars in cash and a hundred-dollar traveler's check between us.

CHAPTER TWENTY-SEVEN

"Okay," I said. "We start all over again."

Bob gave me a sad grin. "With thirty-five dollars?"

I tried not to be frightened. Yes, I said. Maybe we could make another career in pictures. For our first two weeks in California we'd been guests of Bob's brother, Ross, who now practiced medicine in Los Angeles. But we'd been unable to take the noise of his two young children rising at seven o'clock; we were impatient, we desperately wanted to be in Hollywood. We had thanked Ross for his hospitality and had taken the cheapest lodgings we could find on the Sunset Strip —a small room with two studio beds in a tiny hotel. The single room looked out on the chic Sunset Towers across the street, where I had often stayed. The moment I walked into the room I pulled the blind down and kept it down. I didn't want to be reminded.

On the telephone with agents I tried to sound gay and indifferent, as in my opulent days when I had my enormous house, my swimming pool and tennis courts, my cars. The agents were not enthusiastic. I hadn't realized how much bad publicity preceded us home. With astonishing naïveté I thought we had been so far from the United States that nothing would get back. But everyone knew. I had made headlines in Hollywood. I'd been fired from Sydney's Celebrity Club. I'd walked out at Melbourne's Princess Theatre. My contract canceled at the Theatre Royal in Brisbane. Thrown out of my hotel in Tasmania. Yes, all true. But somehow it sounded much worse, I thought, than it really had been.

We tried to get jobs. Bob tried—even as an extra. I went with him because he refused to go alone. Bob had given me a scare. Shortly before dawn one day I had been awakened by his groaning. "I've got the most horrible stomach-ache," he gasped. I gave him two aspirins. They didn't help. He took two nembutals, and so did I. I fell asleep but through my deep sleep I felt something was wrong. I woke to find Bob doubled up in agony, like a woman in labor. His face was the color of putty; sweat literally poured from him. "Oh God," he moaned, "I can't stand the pain!" I stumbled into the hall, shouting for a doctor, who diagnosed it a few minutes later as colic and gave Bob a shot of morphine. Hours passed; the pain refused to go away. Finally Ross was there, examining his brother. When Bob fell asleep, Ross asked me, his face grave, "Has he ever had anything like this before?"

I remembered. In Sydney, Bob had awakened with the same savage pain. I thought it was a hang-over. The doctor there had diagnosed it, too, as colic.

Ross shook his head. Bob had suffered an attack of pancreatitis, a liver ailment, caused by too much alcohol. "This is your second attack," he told Bob later. "Pancreatitis is very serious. A third or fourth attack can be fatal. I mean it." Bob paled. "You have to stop drinking," his brother said quietly. "Keep it up and you're signing your own death warrant."

Shocked, we both went on the wagon. But in a few days we were drinking beer. At least it wasn't hard liquor—right away.

Now, still shaky, Bob needed encouragement. When his job applications were turned down, he grew miserable. We traveled by bus and trolley instead of taxi to save money. It galled him. At night when we returned to our little room, he brooded over it.

"God," he would say, "how awful this must be for you, Muzzy. Remembering what you had here——"

Perhaps he wanted to make me feel sorry for myself, so that he could feel sorrier for himself. Bob, I'd learned, could solace himself with misery. I wouldn't play the game. "Darling, it doesn't matter," I'd say. "We'll probably own the Sunset Towers in a few months. Don't think about it." But when he belabored himself, it was all I could do not to burst out, "Yes, you're damned right I feel awful! I miss everything I had, and I wouldn't be in this filthy hole now if you could support me——"

We were two people fighting against reality. We refused to believe our own situation. Night after night we called a restaurant six doors away and ordered a dinner of spareribs sent us—which cost a dollar additional for the service. We could have gone to the restaurant and eaten there. But we were still trying to save a vestige of grandeur, even if it cost a dollar each time—a dollar we couldn't afford.

Once we ate well. With only change in our pocket and our rent two weeks overdue, we were invited by Harry Crocker, a well-known Hearst writer, to dinner at Mike Romanoff's restaurant. We swept in, playing the very successful bit. Mike greeted us royally. He couldn't know we'd been munching peanuts all day long to save money, and that we'd come by trolley and not Cadillac limousine. We were ceremoniously shown to a banquette, reserved for VIPs, and I gushed and darlinged everyone in sight. I ordered a dish Sir Charles Mendl had often had when he took me there—*potage Cyrano*. It made me feel chic again.

Several people wandered over. What was I doing in Hollywood?

"Oh, just passing through." I wasn't going to say, I'm looking for a job. I wouldn't say, Damn it, I'm broke, do you know anybody who'll give me a job?

When we returned to the hotel our key wouldn't work. Bob laboriously got down on his knees and peered through the keyhole to see if it was obstructed. "Now really, Bob," I said. "You look ridiculous. Let me try." The key wouldn't fit. Bob went downstairs to the desk. When he came up his face was gray-white. I knew the truth at once. "We're locked out?" I said. "That's pretty." I became very grand. "And in a place like this?"

I marched downstairs. The clerk looked unhappy.

"Give me the key to our lock, please."

"I'm sorry, I can't let you in your room, Miss Barrymore," he said miserably. "I'm under orders. Not until you pay the bill."

"Well, can I use your phone, or do I have to give you ten cents?" I acted bitchy, though it wasn't the poor man's fault. I called Harry Crocker. I didn't know who else to call. "Harry, I'm locked out, we don't even have the money to go around and try to borrow from anyone. Would you be an angel and send me the rent for tonight so I can get in and get some sleep?"

In fifteen minutes a messenger was there with two hundred and fifty dollars in cash.

When I walked into the room I pulled up the blind for the first time and gazed at the Sunset Towers. I thought, funny, how one little lane can take you from one side of the tracks to the other.

The next day I racked my brain. Who might loan me money? I could think of no one.

Then Tyrone Power's name leaped into my mind. I'd gone to his parties here; he and Annabella had come to mine. I telephoned him.

"Look, Ty," I said after a little while, "I'm flat broke. Can you—will you—help me? Anything you can spare?" The only way to ask for money, I was convinced, was to be honest.

"Oh, I'm sorry, Diana," he said. Then: "I guess we all go through these things. I'll send you a check." I hadn't specified an amount, nor did Ty ask. He added vaguely, "I'd love to see you—let's get together some time."

A few hours later a man in chauffeur's uniform was at our door. "Miss Barrymore? Mr. Power sent me." He handed me an envelope and was gone. I opened it wondering, how much has he sent? Perhaps as much as one thousand dollars?

Out fluttered a check for one hundred dollars.

I was so hurt. If only he'd told me, "I'm sorry, Diana, darling, I have a wife and child and I can't do anything now, but the moment I can there's nothing I wouldn't do for you. Michael and Robin were so wonderful to me when I needed it . . ."

Who else dared I try? I thought of Huntington Hartford, Jr., the A&P heir. Huntington had taken me out in Palm Beach in my debutante days. We'd danced together at El Morocco and the Stork. We'd been at each other's parties. Really, he shouldn't miss even five thousand dollars. I telephoned him, and after we both had exhausted our conversational powers and I sensed he was about to get off the phone, I said, "Huntington, I'll tell you why I called. It will strike you as an odd request, and you may not even think it's true, but I'm absolutely flat broke."

Before he could say a word I hurried on: "I'll be getting money from Mother's estate soon and I'll pay you back. Huntington, I literally need money for eating." I tried to be gay. "Of course, you could probably send over the A&P, but I think I'd rather have something green."

There was a long silence at the other end. I felt my face flush; perspiration broke out on my scalp. It was so humiliating to do what I had to do! Then Huntington's voice came. "Well, sure, Diana," he said uncertainly. "But, you know, things are tough right now. I have so many projects going . . . Will one hundred dollars help?"

I said, "That will help a great deal. Thank you very much, Huntington."

I hung up ready to cry. Yet, I thought, I can't really blame them. They know what a mess I made of things in Australia. All that consoled me was the knowledge that Mother's estate

would be settled in November, 1952, her attorney had written me. That was a few months away, and surely I'd be able
to repay my loans. I wasn't begging, I was borrowing . . .

We reached the end of our money again. I remembered a
brilliant young set designer, Tom Oliphant. He proved an
angel. An apartment was empty in a building his mother
owned. Bob and I could move in, temporarily, and forget
about rent. "I warn you it's not like anything you're used
to," he said. We were enormously grateful just to have a roof
over our heads, I told him. And Tom, who was not working,
had one hundred and fifty dollars waiting for us when we arrived.

He was right about the apartment. It was painted stark
white, like a hospital operating room, and the building
trembled with the trucks that roared by endlessly, day and
night. Oh, God, I thought. There was nothing I could do
about the trucks; but as the days passed, I grew to loathe
more and more the white walls and ceiling about us. Finally,
broke as we were, we bought paint and Bob and I set to
work to repaint the walls dark green, the ceiling Chinese red.
Maybe it would help me think I was back somewhere, somehow, in elegance. We started enthusiastically on the ceiling
while the pile of empty beer cans mounted in the center of
the room. We never got to paint the walls. Tom's mother
dropped in, looked about in dismay, and ordered her son to
put us out. "We only wanted to make it chic!" I cried. Tom,
painfully embarrassed, could do nothing.

We moved to a motel. I tried to promote dinner invitations, at least, to cut down our food costs. I called the gay
people I'd known who once made my table and my bar their
own. No invitations came, though I continued to read about
their parties in the columns. On impulse I telephoned Dolores Costello. I had not seen her for years. She sounded
genuinely delighted to hear from me. Her daughter, my
half-sister Deedee, was expecting a second baby. And John,

Jr., my half-brother, was in town too. We'd have a family reunion.

When I saw Dolores at her home, she looked as I remembered her in the silent films—smartly groomed, her hair with scarcely a touch of gray in it, beautifully golden blonde—a magnificent, lovely woman with an angelic serenity about her. I could understand why Daddy fell in love with her.

The last time I'd seen my half-sister Deedee she had been a gawky girl. Now, at twenty-two, she was beautiful and radiant and a mother too. Then Johnny entered—a tall, handsome, vital young thing. I thought, this is what Daddy must have been like at twenty. Johnny hadn't Daddy's profile, but there was something electrifying about him—an air, a dash. He burst into the room like a comet; he took stairs three at a time; he bounced about; he'd sit, then be up, then pace the room like a caged animal. He sent off sparks of restlessness.

We talked family talk while Bob listened quietly; Johnny wanted to know everything about Daddy. I recalled what Cobina Wright, Sr., once told me. Johnny had come to her, years before, and besieged her with questions about Daddy. "He never really knew his father," Cobina had said. "He asked me, 'How can I find out about him—what he was like?' I said, 'Talk to your father's friends who are still around—John Decker, Gene Fowler, and the rest.' " And it was true; for in addition to Daddy's remoteness from his children, when he died Deedee was only twelve, Johnny only ten. How much could they remember? In those last months of my father's life I had gotten to know him better than any of us —and how little I had known him!

Dolores broke into my thoughts. Had I seen Aunt Ethel?

I shook my head. I had no idea whether she was here or in the East. She was living in Hollywood, Dolores said, although she saw her rarely. I gathered that Dolores, like Mother, had never been too friendly with Aunt Ethel. Was it because my aunt resented the women who had been close to Daddy, because he was always her little brother and she worshiped him and thought none of them had been worthy of him?

I said nothing of this to Dolores but asked her for Aunt Ethel's telephone number. I will call her, I told myself. I will talk to her. If I can borrow from strangers, I can borrow from my own aunt.

I telephoned her the next day. That magnificent voice came over the wire: "Oooooh, Diana, so nice to hear from you."

"It's nice to hear your voice, Aunt Ethel," I said. "I'd love to see you."

"Come out any time—come out for tea this afternoon."

"I'd love to, but I don't have a car." I didn't want to confess I couldn't even afford a taxi. I added, "I didn't expect to be in California—I was just passing through and haven't had time to do anything about a car."

"I'll send mine for you," she said.

"May I bring my husband?"

She asked, "Which one?"

Now *really*, Aunt Ethel, I thought. "Well—" I made an attempt to laugh. "The latest one, Aunt Ethel." I added, with some dignity, "It's been five years now."

Bob, as it happened, had one of his few appointments that day and so I went alone. Aunt Ethel sent her long black limousine driven by her chauffeur, Fred, whose wife was Aunt Ethel's secretary. They had been with her for fifteen years, he told me on the way out.

Aunt Ethel's house turned out to be of lovely pink stucco with black shutters, and green ivy growing everywhere. The interior seemed all pink, with tones of gray; a pink living room leading into a dozen other pink rooms. She was waiting for me upstairs.

I was ushered into her bedroom—and there she was, almost as on stage, propped up in bed, wearing a pink bed jacket, masses of pale pink lace pillows behind her, pink and gray everywhere, and a black phone, strangely modern and incongruous, on a table next to her. She looked older but still indescribably regal.

She put out her arms. "Diana, hel-lo, my dear child!"

I ran to her and threw my arms around her. I thought, Diana, be careful not to rumple the bed—Aunt Ethel is doing so beautiful a piece for you.

Then, pointing to a chair at the foot of her bed, she said, "Sit there." It was like a command performance. I sat in the chair.

We talked about her sons, Jackie and Sammy Colt, about Dolores and her children, about Bob—was I happy with him? Near the telephone I saw a manuscript, some pages covered with handwriting, some typewritten. I had heard that my aunt was working on her memoirs.

"Aunt Ethel, I'd love to hear some of it. Could you read me a little?"

She was pleased. "Would you really like to hear?" And as I sat there in that pink and gray room, feeling like a character in a Victorian play, feeling that I should be in bonnet and hoop skirt as I had been in *Romantic Mr. Dickens,* Aunt Ethel, propped up on her pillows, her head high, her eyes shining, began to read to me. I scarcely listened to the words: I listened only to her voice and its cadences. If Mother's voice had been a low violin, Aunt Ethel's was a viola, with tones within tones, with an indescribable echoing quality as though you heard it inside an enormous seashell.

Then tea was brought, and over tea and cakes Aunt Ethel got around to asking what I was doing in Hollywood. "I know you've been in Australia," she said. "I saw it in the newspapers."

I felt ashamed. She was kind to say no more than that. I had been interviewed at the airport when I arrived. A reporter had asked, "Did you know your Aunt Ethel is to star in a television program?" "Star?" I retorted brightly. "She'll take the whole show over!"

There was no reason for me to say that about my Aunt

Ethel. But the reporter's words were like a cue thrown me on stage: automatically I caught the line and threw it back.

"It all began so divinely," I said, "but we didn't do so well later." Then I came out with what I had to say. "Aunt Ethel, I know you and Mother never got along, and you and I certainly haven't seen much of each other, but I need to ask you something important." I paused. "It's terribly embarrassing——"

She lowered her head and looked at me from under her brows. It could have been Daddy. "Yes? What is it?"

I spoke bluntly then because my aunt was a woman who detested beating about the bush. "Aunt Ethel, I'm broke. I'm so bloody broke, it's not funny. The reason I haven't done anything about a car is because I haven't the money. Everything I made in Australia I spent in Australia. We came back with about seven hundred dollars, and we went through five hundred dollars in Honolulu in three days. It was so beautiful—it was a honeymoon for us because we never had one and I couldn't resist it."

She smiled. "That sounds so like Jack," she said. "He couldn't ever hang onto a penny . . . How much do you need?"

"It's not what I need, Aunt Ethel, it's what you can spare."

"Would three hundred dollars help for a little while?"

I felt enormously grateful. "It certainly would. It would keep me in groceries for months if I'm careful."

She wrote the check and was very sweet about it. She kissed me good-by. "I hope something works out for you," she said. "If it doesn't, I wouldn't stay here too long. I'd go back to New York and look for a job there. It never does you good to stay in a place where nothing happens for too long." If I returned to New York, I might get something and then Hollywood would want me. "It always happens that way," she said. "Keep in touch with me and let me know how you make out."

I promised. And I promised I would repay her as soon as

Mother's estate would be settled. As Fred drove me home, I wondered, why hadn't we gotten to know each other? Why couldn't my family be like other families?

In November, 1952, I sat with Winfield Huppuch, Mother's lawyer, in his office in New York. I had left Bob in Hollywood, where he had been signed for a one-shot TV show, "Public Defender." When I came back we'd really start anew; maybe this was a beginning for Bob.

Mother, Winfield told me, had left an estate of roughly thirty thousand dollars. "Your mother was a strange woman," he said. "She was always overdrawn at the bank." He looked at me through his rimless spectacles. "Each month she insisted that we go to the bank and go through her canceled checks, and invariably she'd toss aside two or three and say, 'I never signed those!' " He smiled. "But, of course, she had."

For a full afternoon, it seemed, I signed checks: tax liens against the estate, judgments that hadn't been paid, repayment of my borrowings in Hollywood, repayment to my brother Leonard—Leonard had come on the scene in California a few months before, when I'd exhausted every name I could think of, and bailed me out. When Winfield gave me the final grand total, it amounted to roughly eight thousand dollars. I could draw on it, through him, up to five hundred dollars a month as long as it lasted.

"Well," I said. "At least, I'm debt-free."

Winfield nodded. If I would meet him at noon tomorrow at the Lincoln Warehouse, he would open a trunk full of Mother's papers left to me. I couldn't explain why, but I was frightened. On the way to the warehouse the next day I stopped for a drink and then another. Then we were examining the contents of the trunk.

There were Mother's manuscripts, the accumulation of a lifetime of writing—unsuccessful writing, really. While Winfield watched, I went through them. Three unpublished plays about Joan of Arc, five typewritten copies of each; copies of *Clair de Lune* and *The Byrons;* music scores, annotated by her, for her readings; pages upon pages of notes for books and poems yet to be written. I remembered how she had said, perhaps more to herself than to me, "Those critics! They're all asses! One day they'll appreciate me. I've given them too much. They don't understand." As I rummaged through the trunk, I came upon a heavily bound Manila envelope. It was filled with Daddy's letters to Mother, from their first meeting through their courtship, their marriage, and the final separation. And in another envelope, my childhood letters to her, written from school and camp, all signed with—I'd quite forgotten—a sketch of a little kitten. She had saved them all.

I placed the letters and the annotated music scores to one side.

"The rest," I said, "goes into the incinerator."

Winfield looked at me, startled, but said nothing.

A boy brought a huge basket, and one by one, I let them fall into it—the plays, the manuscripts, the notebooks. I turned to Winfield, "Do you think I'm being callous?" I asked. "Am I doing wrong?"

He shook his head noncommittally. "They are yours," he said.

I could not tell him what strange emotions shook me at that moment. I wanted to begin a clean slate. God help me, I wanted my mother to be gone—gone away from there, gone away from me, gone out of my life. I wanted to be free.

CHAPTER TWENTY-EIGHT

It was FEAST after famine. In the fashionable Hotel Madison, where the doorman used to take me, as a little girl, once around the block for my daily airing, I set up Barrymore headquarters. I telephoned Bob in Hollywood—he had received no other offers—"Pack up and come East, Bob. We're both finished there. Let's face it. TV is in New York anyway, not L.A. We'll try to struggle through here."

For the first few weeks it wasn't a struggle. It was El Morocco, the Stork and Twenty-One, cocktails, parties, and dinners. I invited everyone I knew. I made new friends, among them Nita Naldi, the silent-screen beauty who had acted with Daddy and been Rudolph Valentino's leading lady. Now in her fifties, she was a big, magnificently handsome woman, her eyes like coals, her skin still startlingly white, creamy, and glowing. I called her Mother Moonbeam, after the "Li'l Abner" comic character. She called me Deen-ya—never Diana. Ann Andrews dropped in as did people from both worlds, the *Social Register* and the theater. Sometimes fifty and sixty guests milled about my suite. I'd call the Madison's Café Lounge and order forty-seven dollars' worth of *hors-d'oeuvres* without turning a hair. It was divine not to worry about money.

Winfield Huppuch, watching all this dubiously, began to warn me, and finally delivered an ultimatum. I couldn't continue living at the Madison. I was spending money at a fantastic rate. Bob and I moved to a kitchenette apartment on Sutton Terrace, overlooking the East River, the neighborhood where I'd grown up. It was on the ground floor with a large French casement window opening on a garden. At least I could see grass and trees. Here I began reading play scripts, but most of them were embarrassingly bad, sent by producers who evidently wished only to capitalize on my name. I sent them back.

Suddenly one afternoon the thought struck me like a blow between the eyes: Diana, you're going to be broke again! No money coming in, everything going out! And you can't count on Mother's estate now—you've had it. Almost panic-stricken, I called every agent I knew. Jules Ziegler, Louis Shurr's assistant in the happy days when I first went to Hollywood, threw me a life belt. Armando's Restaurant, one of the most popular Café Society night spots, wanted a lady disc jockey, a name to interview names in a radio program to originate in the restaurant. Armando was delighted when he suggested me. "Everybody knows her in show business," he cried. "Fine. Bring her in tomorrow and we'll do a test show."

"Jules," I said gaily. "You know Barrymore. She never stops talking. And no lines to learn? Wonderful!"

At 8:00 P.M. Jules and I arrived. Everybody said hello, how nice to see you, how are you, I remember you with your father on the Rudy Vallee show. The program was scheduled for 10:00 P.M., over WABC. Newspapermen, radio executives, potential sponsors, crowded the restaurant. While Jules moved about, lining up contracts, I held court at my table, chatting happily with everyone who dropped by. People joined me, ordered drinks for themselves and me, and wandered on. Diners at other tables sent drinks to me, with their compliments. Things began to get a little hazy. All at once I found a microphone in front of my nose and, seated opposite me, a pretty, dark-haired girl. She was my first guest, Beverly Paterno, the talented night-club singer. I saw a signal. I spoke. "Good evening, ladies and gentlemen, this is Diana Barrymore. I hope you'll like me. If you do, fine. If you don't —who gives a damn?"

Someone waved his hands and Jules' agonized face was in front of me. "Diana, what's the matter with you!" I heard a buzzing of voices and laughter in the back of the room.

"Oh, was the mike on?" I asked. I knew it had been. "I was only kidding. I thought it was dead."

"All right," Jules said nervously. Again the engineer across the room brought his arm down and pointed at me. We were on. I said, "I'm so delighted to meet you, Miss Paterno," in my best Newport manner. "Now, tell me, Miss Paterno, just what makes you think *you're* a singer?"

Miss Paterno didn't quite know how to take it. Someone waved his hands again, and then Jules had me by the arm; there was no microphone before me, and I knew . . .

That began it all over again.

Days passed. My money dwindled. I read a few scripts, but nothing decent came along. Bob had gotten nothing since his one-shot job in Hollywood, and was too beaten even to bring up the Armando incident. He seemed to have reached a stage of indifference to everything. "Oh, God!" I'd cry. "I'm so damned bored! Let's do something—let's get out of here, take me somewhere, do anything!" Bob didn't want to. He didn't even want to take me to dinner: I'd have to pay the check, and each time I did, I grew more vitriolic. I couldn't help it. He wouldn't fight back. I tried to goad him, goad him out of his apathy, goad him into being a man with self-respect, a husband. "Goddamn it, can't you go out and get a job?" I'd scream. "No," he'd say. "You need me. You can't be alone." He was right, and it made me the more enraged. "Go out anyway!" I'd yell at him. "We're just no good for each other this way. We're just pulling each other down!"

Often, when I returned in the late afternoon from lunching with friends, I'd find him in the bedroom, passed out on his bed, in his clothes. I would sit around, impatient, wretched, lost. I turned on the TV, turned it off. I picked up a book, riffled its pages, put it down. I played my records, paced the room, telephoned everyone I could think of—anything to keep myself occupied. Bob would be all right by 8:00 P.M. and we would eat; then perhaps go out, see people, break the monotony that tortured me.

Slowly this schedule changed. When I found Bob asleep when I came in, I said, "Oh, the hell with it," and took a drink, then another. I was lonely. After the gaiety of the Madison, it was depressing to sit in an apartment with no one to talk to. I couldn't stand being alone.

By eight o'clock, when Bob awoke, fairly sober, he found me tight. Then I went to bed to sleep it off, and Bob sat, reading, trying to occupy himself until I awoke—only to give up and return to the bottle. When I did awake a few hours later, he was asleep, passed out again.

It was a seesaw in hell.

Sometimes we became synchronized, both awakening about two or three in the morning, sober. Then we could not fall asleep until long after dawn, and sometimes not then. When the wakefulness was too much to bear, we took pills to sleep. And when we woke, we took pills to stay awake.

The results began to show. My face bloated; I looked ten years older. I was going downhill and I knew it. I tried to get hold of myself. One night when I awoke to see Bob sprawled across his bed, in his clothes, passed out, I thought, "Oh, this is disgraceful. We should both be horsewhipped!" I shook Bob violently. He came to, slowly, groaning. "Bob, get up!" I shouted. "Goddamn it, this has got to stop! *It has got to stop!*"

We talked it over. We'd go to AA.

We sat in the fourteenth row (Ooooh, I thought, is this the best we rate?) at the Lenox Hill branch of Alcoholics Anonymous. It was 9:00 P.M. I sat huddled next to Bob. We'd both fortified ourselves, but I was frightened and embarrassed. Somebody is sure to recognize me and say, Why is she here? Sure, we know she drinks, but does she drink that much? Yet, who am I kidding? Here I am at an AA meeting, and I'm drunk!

The seats were straight kitchen chairs and uncomfortable. I had to crane my neck to see the small stage. A man was speaking, a thin woman seated silently next to him on the platform. The man said softly and waved his hand, "As I looked, I saw a white light come through the window. It scared me. I looked, and I thought I could almost see Jesus Christ our Lord. I realized then that I could no longer be a drunk."

Well, now, I'm a Catholic, I thought—not a good one, but I am one. I know something about religion. I know AA has helped many people, but really, I don't believe I can go for this. They say if you look around you'll find the right AA group for you, but really—if they're going to snip around and talk about religion and white lights coming through the window—oh, no. I want the frankness I expected to find here. Someone who would stand up and perhaps be a little like me, perhaps have my problem. The point is, who here could be like that? How could anyone be like me? Who had my parents? Or my problem? They'd have the drinking problem, sure. So many of them have that. No, these people won't understand me. I'm a special case and they'll be on my back more than on anyone's. Oh, no. And all this talk about God . . .

I turned to Bob. "Let's go, let's go. This is too much."

He held me back. "No. Everybody knows who you are. We'll have to wait this thing out."

A heavy-set woman with blonde hair was speaking in a singsong voice. Her story was one of steady drinking, of DTs and empty bottles piled outside her hotel door, of shame and jobs lost because she drank and drank and drank. I listened, miserable. I only wanted out.

We left there finally and made straight for a bar. I sat watching the amber lights play in my glass. Standing up there, before everybody, talking about how much they used to drink. They're exhibitionists—each one trying to say he was a bigger drunk than the other. And they're such *bad* actors!

Perhaps, I often thought later, we didn't give AA a chance. We should have tried to find the right group for us. Instead, we never went again.

CHAPTER TWENTY-NINE

THEN, on a soft May night, in the York Inn, a restaurant and bar on the ground floor of our apartment house, Tom Farrell came into my life.

He was seated at the bar with a drink before him, staring at himself in the mirror when we entered—a young man of about twenty-five, wearing slacks and a white sport shirt. Bob introduced us. "How do you do?" I said. Mr. Farrell tore himself away from his reflection in the mirror and turned slowly to me. "Hi-yuh," he grunted. His eyes flickered over me as if I were something unpleasant. He turned back to the mirror. "The barflies Bob picks up!" I thought angrily and paid no more attention to him.

We sat drinking for about ten minutes. Farrell said nothing. I whispered to Bob. "Let's get out of here. This man gives me the creeps." When we walked out, Farrell was still staring into the mirror.

In the apartment I turned to Bob. We'd been quarreling and bickering for days. "Why must you pick up such *common* creatures! That man hasn't the manners of an ox!"

"I didn't pick him up, he picked me up," Bob protested. "He said he saw me in pictures and bought me a drink." Bob lit a cigarette. "A rather strange guy but a nice fellow, I think. It's only that he fawns on people he thinks have been somebody."

"You mean you?" I said. I couldn't help it.

Bob looked at me. "You've been awfully bitchy to live with lately," he said. "I'm taking a walk." He slammed the door.

I put on the record player, refilled my drink, and was listening to Shostakovich when the house phone buzzed. A man's voice, low and husky, asked, "Is Bob there?"

"No. Who is this?"

"It's Farrell." There was a pause. "I just met you in the bar. Can I come over and have a drink?"

Really, I thought. Then: "Sure. Why not?" Even Farrell was better company than no one. He might even talk.

He walked in with a mad arrogance, as if he wore a train held up by a retinue of little girls behind him. "Where's Bob?" he asked. "Taking a walk," I said, thinking idly, this boy *is* rather attractive. He was tall, six feet two or three, and built like a polo player. His hair was jet black, tousled, over thick black eyebrows. A black Irishman, I thought, a moody black Irishman.

"Can I get you a drink?" I asked. To reach the kitchenette I had to walk by him. He stood motionless, but as I passed him and returned with a glass of Scotch, his eyes followed me into the room and back like a hunter's gun tracking a bird's flight. I placed the drink on a table near him and sat on the sofa.

He ignored the glass. Instead, he sat down beside me. "You know," he said slowly, his eyes still fixed on me, "you're a very sexy broad."

I looked at him. I was becoming unnerved by that unblinking stare. But I spoke up in my best Newport manner. "Really? How nice of you to think so."

There was a dead silence. Suddenly he grabbed me and his mouth was on mine. His voice came hoarsely, "Goddamn you, the first minute I saw you I wanted you!"

I struggled, but I was excited. No one had talked like that to me for a long time. I heard myself protesting, "But suppose Bob walks in?" My mind whirled and in it a little pro-

tecting thought went round and round: *He can't answer that.
But if he does, what else can I say?*

"He walks in and I'll kill the son of a bitch!" he said chokingly. *"You haven't been loved yet.* I'll show you."

I could not fight him.

Later he said, "Baby, if you think this is a one-night stand, it isn't. I've known actresses before. I want to see you tomorrow. There's a place a block away on the East River. Will you meet me there tomorrow at eight?" He told me where.

I was still able to think. "No, Tommy. I don't want to get involved in a love affair. And you're the type I could get involved with."

He kissed me hard. "Diana." He spat the words: "You-are-not-going-to-lose-me. Understand?"

I thought, shouldn't it be the other way around: I'm not going to lose you? Who did this man think he was? I pushed him away. "Look, Buster, go home. Good-by. It's been charming. I'm not seeing you again."

He wouldn't go. I made for the door and shouted for the doorman. "Martin, would you get this man out of here? He's making a nuisance of himself."

Suddenly Farrell towered over me. He pushed me back into the apartment with little, abrupt shoves, using the heel of his hands against my shoulders. "Take it easy, baby," he said softly.

The next moment Farrell was advancing on me, his eyes staring, his hands outstretched, half-clenched. I rushed wildly into the hall, screaming, "Martin, he's going to kill me!" Farrell leaped after me. I turned and kicked him just as Martin came running up. "Out, Buster!" I said furiously. I was shaking. "You've had it! Get!"

Farrell stopped short. He looked at Martin, trembling but ready, and then at me, tensed like a spring. "Relax, Diana," he said. The shadow of a smile played about his mouth. He pushed back a curl of hair that had fallen over his forehead. "Eight o'clock. I'll be waiting."

I ran into the apartment and slammed the door.

In the morning I told Bob that his friend Farrell had dropped over.

"Did you have fun?" Bob drawled and turned his back to me.

I said, "I wish you wouldn't meet such *common* people in bars."

I was raging inwardly—at Bob for his indifference, at Farrell for his incredible insolence. Bob did little but drink that day. By seven o'clock he had passed out on his bed. I won't meet Farrell, I told myself. He's a monster. He's John Howard all over again. But at seven-forty-five, with nothing to do, no one to talk to, intrigued despite myself, I went to meet Farrell.

Our rendezvous was a concrete embankment overlooking the East River, reached by an arched bridge that spanned the busy East River Drive. Farrell was waiting for me on a park bench, smoking. He wore a leather windbreaker.

"Hi-yuh," he grunted as he had in the bar.

"You seem pretty sure of yourself," I snapped. "You could have been stuck here all night without my showing up."

"No," he said. "You'd show up."

I laughed. His arrogance was so impossible it was funny. "I shouldn't even talk to you after your behavior last night. It was disgraceful. It was absolutely inexcusable!"

He lit a cigarette for me but said nothing.

"Look, I was loaded or it wouldn't have happened," I said. "I don't know a damn thing about you. Who are you? What do you do?"

He laughed, the first time I'd heard him. "Baby, I'm nobody. You're Barrymore, but I'm just nobody. Do? I do nothing. I manage somehow."

"How perfectly enchanting! I know one thing you probably do, Tommy. You beat up women."

He inhaled deeply. "Yeh," he said. "I've got a bad temper. Specially when I drink." It was not an apology. We sat, silent. A soft wind came off the river.

"Ever hear this?" he asked casually. He began to quote:

> "Afoot and light-hearted I take to the open road,
>   Healthy, free, the world before me . . ."

I gaped. "Well, now, *really!* How would you know Walt Whitman?"

He didn't reply. Instead, he went on, in a not unmusical voice:

> "Henceforth I ask not good-fortune, I myself am good-fortune;
>   Henceforth I whimper no more, postpone no more, need nothing. . . .
> Strong and content I travel the open road."

I thought, this is John Howard with a Bramwell Fletcher technique. I said aloud, "It's unbelievable that you should quote poetry to me. That's what my first husband did."

"Yeh?" he said. "Tell me about it."

I found myself telling him about Bramwell, then about John Howard, and then about Bob, our surrealistic life, the insane routine we were living because I couldn't help Bob and Bob couldn't help me.

"Tough," he said. He crushed out his cigarette and stood up. "Diana, look at those boats on the river, the moonlight painting the water like old ivory. Old ivory, blue-white ivory, a million years old . . ."

"Why, Tommy! You're a poet! First Whitman and now that lovely figure of speech. Who *are* you?"

He laughed. "All right, baby, I'll tell you. I'm a professional vagabond. I vagabond all day. When night comes I spend my time feeding pigeons in Central Park in the lamplight. That tunes me up with the world."

I was enchanted. "Now I understand. A vagabond poet. My crazy vagabond poet."

He took something from his pocket and held it up. It was a rosary. "You don't have one, do you?"

"No, Tommy, I don't," I said.

"But you were brought up a Catholic, weren't you?"

I nodded.

He kissed the rosary and pressed it into my hand. "From me to you," he said softly.

Oh, Diana, I thought. Bramwell could learn from this boy.

We sat gazing at the water, the boats slowly passing by. *I've been here before,* I thought. Of course. Tony Duke, Tony and I used to sit hand in hand watching these patterns in the dark water, so long, long ago. Was it me then? No, it was another girl, in another life, on another planet. It never really happened . . .

Farrell began talking almost dreamily, as though to himself, and I came slowly back to the present. I fell in with his mood. "Look at the water, Diana," he was saying. "Ever think that it's like the universal soul—God Himself—and how we're all part of it? Suppose you filled a bottle with that water and let it float in the river. I think our souls are like that. We're all individual souls—like the water in the bottle —but we're also all part of the universal soul, the river, God. When we die the bottle breaks and we become part of the universal soul, we join it . . ." He paused. "Maybe it's not Catholic dogma, but it's the way I think when I see the water and the moonlight. It does things to me—I feel I'm part of everything, growing with everything, the trees, the leaves, the grass—I'm alive, more alive than any other living thing . . ."

He turned to me, his voice urgent. "Baby, I want you. Now. We can't go back to your apartment. I know a place on Sixty-eighth Street."

He had broken the spell himself. "Oh, God," I said. "Is it some kind of a house?"

He shook his head. "Don't worry. It's a hotel and nobody asks questions so long as you have the money."

"I don't know, Tom," I said. "I could think better if we had a drink." I looked at him. "You and your soul."

When I slipped into our apartment, the clock by my bed showed nearly 7:00 A.M. Bob lay asleep, sprawled in his clothes on his bed. Later I learned that shortly after I had left the night before, he awakened and questioned the doorman. Martin told him he had seen me meet Farrell over on the embankment. Bob turned on his heel and returned to the apartment.

I undressed and fell into bed. I slept most of the day.

Next night I met Farrell again. This time he waited for me on the overpass. He stood in the center of the arch, high above the passing traffic, silhouetted against the night sky. There was a ramp leading up to the overpass: when he saw me, he stretched out his arms, wide, and I began running, and I ran to him and he enfolded me. It was like a scene in the theater—the dark sky, the dark trees and shining stars as a backdrop, and Farrell waiting for me. Oh, I thought, Mummy and Daddy used to have their rendezvous in the shadow of the Bridge of Sighs, in Venice. Isn't it strange how I'm doing it all over again? . . .

Farrell took me to dinner that night and then I went with him again.

This time when I returned, Bob was waiting. He was not drunk, but he was not sober. "Well," he said. "Martin tells me you were with Farrell again."

"He's right," I said.

"I'm not going to make a scene, Diana," Bob went on conversationally. "After all, this is the twentieth century. But would you tell me why you're doing this to me?"

"I don't know, Bob," I said. I thought aloud. "Maybe because this man has a physical attraction for me."

He said, "What do you want me to do?"

"I don't know what I want you to do. You do anything you want to do."

"What do you suggest?" he asked sarcastically.

I put into words exactly what went through my mind. "If you were any kind of a man, you'd walk out on me."

Bob was silent for a moment. "You're a whore," he said.

It was like a blow in the face. Bob had never, no matter how vitriolically we fought, used that word to me.

"Maybe so," I said lightly. "I won't argue with you about it. But, Bob, you don't understand. I love you very much. It didn't mean a thing to me. I'm like a man about those things. It meant absolutely nothing."

He didn't understand. "I would never do it," he said hotly. "I couldn't sleep with another woman, the way I feel about you. How can you do this to me if you love me?"

"Love you!" I cried. "Darling, if I didn't love you, how could I be with you twenty-four hours a day? Other husbands are away all day. Even actors get out to make rounds. If I didn't love you, could I stay with you day and night for six years?"

He tried another tack. "Diana, how can you possibly think that man is attractive? He's a hoodlum."

"Well, you picked him up, didn't you? You must have liked him."

"He was all right to drink with—he's okay with a guy."

I was growing furious—furious at him, furious at myself. "Well, I have news for you, Bob!" I shouted. "He's okay with a woman too!"

Bob looked at me. "You *are* a whore," he said.

"All right," I said. "You're beginning to repeat yourself. You take me into bars and introduce me to people like that . . ."

I went to bed.

At six o'clock that evening the telephone rang. Bob, in the sitting room, answered it. He came into the bedroom.

"Your lover is on the phone," he said.

"Which one?" I retorted. It was a filthy lie, of course. There was no one else.

Bob didn't deign to answer. "I'll hang up on this extension when you pick up yours," he said.

"Be sure you do," I snapped. "I'll wait for the click."

Then I heard Farrell's low voice. "Honey, how do you feel?"

"Just fine, doll."

"Well, tonight again? There's a new night club you've never been to, and I'm told you used to sing in night clubs. We'll have a swell dinner and really enjoy ourselves. This place has a terrific piano player and if you feel like singing, you can. I've talked to them about you. They'd love to have you."

"All right," I said. I felt as though Farrell was pulling me out of quicksand.

It was the first night club I'd visited in months, a place in the Village, and not too bad. He seemed to be well known there. I drank. Farrell kept remarkably sober. I drank because I felt guilty. Who knows why I drank now? The owner escorted me to the bandstand and I sang. "Can't Help Lovin' That Man of Mine," and "St. Louis Blues." Farrell was fascinated, I fascinated myself, I was in divine voice, I bathed in adulation . . .

About midnight Farrell called for the check. He tipped handsomely. "Baby," he said. "Let's go back to the hotel."

"Oh, no, Johnny," I protested. "You don't know what I had to go through this morning with Bob. I don't dare."

"Then get rid of him." Farrell put his hand on mine. "Look, you're supporting him. I watched you sign the check at the bar. How can you respect a man you have to keep?"

Yes, I know, I said. Didn't he understand that's why I was with him now?

That night I went with Farrell again . . .

Bob was waiting when I came home. He had been on beer.

"I see you're rather embroiled with this young man," he began as soon as I removed my coat.

I said, "Yes, I am, Bob."

He pleaded with me. "What's the matter, Muzzy. Don't you love me any more?"

"I love you, Bob," I told him. "But I'm not *in* love with you." There was an extraordinary difference, I said, though I couldn't quite explain it. "You've done something to me through all my years of supporting you—I can't describe it. Yes, dear, I love you. God, if anything happened to you, I think I'd die. But you know what?" I continued to think aloud. "I think you had better go to Rochester. Stay with your mother for a while. I think you ought to get out of my life for now, at least. We're not doing either of us any good."

His lower lip began to quiver. "No, Muzzy, I won't go," he said. "I know how unstable our lives are. But there's a stability, at least for you, in having someone here you can count on to be here when you come and go. And if I walk out, it will only hurt you. Shall I hurt you and hurt myself— or shall I stay and help you? I'm sticking it out." Hadn't he told me the day we were married that he'd never leave me? He meant it.

All right, I said. Then I grew livid. How could I cope with someone so sweetly reasonable, yet so wrong for me as I was wrong for him? "Any man in his right mind would bat me over the head and walk out!" I shrieked. "You just haven't got the guts!"

Bob turned from me, took a bottle of Imperial off a shelf in the kitchenette, threw himself on his back on his bed, and began to drink.

In the weeks that followed we had utterly mad arguments. We drank together and we fought about Farrell, yet I saw him. And when I did Bob spent his time in bars, or passed out, in his clothes, on his bed. Farrell took me to small, good restaurants, he bolstered my spirits—all I needed, he insisted, was the right play. No actress was ever finished. One good role could bring one back bigger than ever. Look at Laurette Taylor and so many others . . .

I never knew where he obtained the money he spent on me. He never told me where he lived. "Oh, Mother and I have an apartment around the corner," he said. I never learned where it was nor did he mention his mother again. I couldn't telephone him—he gave me no number—he always called me. Several times a week he drove to Hyde Park, eighty miles from New York, in a flashy blue roadster. Was it his? I never knew. Nor would he explain what took him to Hyde Park.

He had surprising interests. One night we sat for hours listening to records. I put on the Rachmaninoff Number 2 in C Minor—the record Van Heflin and I played together—and Farrell and I sat as one, his arm around me, and neither of us spoke a word throughout the entire recording, not even in the silence when the records dropped.

He was suddenly violent, suddenly tender, completely unpredictable. There was a mystery about him that he never resolved for me. He was uneducated, and self-conscious about it—he spoke abominably and described himself as illiterate—but he could reel off pages of poetry. One day I noticed that his right shoulder drooped. I asked him about it.

"Oh, that's from toting," he said.

"From toting what?" I asked.

He said, "What do you think, baby? A gun."

I said, "Oh, Tom. You don't expect me to believe that, do you?"

But I grew to believe it. He had been married once, he said—to a cousin of Lucky Luciano. I never knew if it was true. He would telephone me at odd hours. I'd hear voices in the background. "Where are you?" I'd ask. "A little business conference," he'd say. "Meet you in an hour at the same place." It was always on the overpass over the East River Drive. He always stood, waiting, silhouetted against the sky as I came up the ramp. I would begin running then, hearing music that wasn't there, thinking, the lover is waiting, the brutal male lover is waiting. He stood, both hands on the stone balustrade, watching me, and when I came near, he would open his arms wide, and I ran to him.

Then, calmly, "Darling, is Bob following?"

"No, dear."

"All right. Come, my love," and he would lead me down the steps to our bench on the water's edge, and for a little while we would sit and watch the lights of the opposite shore flicker in the dark mirror of the river. Then, masterfully, without questioning his right to do so, he would take me where he wanted to take me.

What was there about him, I asked myself, that made me allow this? He was the kind of man who would escort you across the street against the light because he knew where he was going, and why, and by God, no automobile would run into him, he would run into it, and it would be the driver's fault, not his . . . Was it this directness, this simplicity, this sense of impending violence in a world he understood and a world that did not frighten him, that had first drawn me to John Howard? And now Farrell? What *kind* of man attracted me so powerfully . . .

Through it all, Bob suffered. Why, why, why do you go out with that thug? Why, why, why, must I see Farrell? Each time Bob asked why, it was like waving a red flag at me. I really couldn't tell him—I didn't know, and I think he knew I didn't. Once he said, "Asking you why is like asking a little girl to explain why she broke her doll. There's no answer."

"Maybe there is," I retorted, stung. "Maybe this man can take me out of my surroundings and give me hope again. Maybe I'd rather go with someone who can take me to dinner, dine and wine me as I'm accustomed to, than sit in this dreary prison day after day and look at somebody like you who can't afford to do these things."

One night, quarreling over Farrell, Bob slapped me hard across the face, the first time he had ever struck me. We had both been drinking; my balance was precarious: I reeled backward and fell, cracking my head against a table leg. For a moment I was stunned; then I found myself lying there, crying. "For God's sake," I wept, "when I told you about Farrell six weeks ago, why didn't you hit me then or leave me? Why did you wait six weeks and do it now? It doesn't make sense."

Bob looked down at me. He lit a cigarette. "I'm going out for some air," he said and left.

I managed to get to my feet and stumble into the bedroom. I slammed the door and fell asleep. When I woke an hour later, my pillow was soaked with blood. I had bled for a long time. The doctor I called sewed up an inch-long gash in the back of my head. Then I sat down and waited grimly for Bob.

When he came in, I said, "Out! This is it! You've had it! Get out!"

But I couldn't go through with it. When he looked at me, his face gray-white with misery, I couldn't stand it. "Oh, Muzzy," he said. "I didn't mean to hurt you. Don't you know you can walk over my heart and I wouldn't care? Diana, I love you so much, anything you do I will take. I can't help it. Don't ask me to go away!"

I melted. "Darling, darling, of course I don't mean it. It's all been a ghastly mistake. Farrell is a monster. Look how he's making us act toward each other. I don't want any part of him. I'm finished with him. How I could take up with anyone so *common* . . ."

I kept my promise. When Farrell called, I hung up. He telephoned, and telephoned again. Finally I spoke to him. I made it short.

"I can't see you, Tom. I don't want to see you any more."

"Baby, you can't mean that," he said.

Oh, yes I could. "You've **had it**. It's incredible that it lasted this long. Good-by." I slammed the receiver. He called again. "Good-by, baby—for now," he said and the receiver clicked.

Now there was nothing to do but drink and listen to records and watch TV and fight and try not to remain sober long enough to realize where we were heading . . .

A few days later, after spending an hour drinking with a charming young man at the York Inn, I made my way to the apartment. I heard voices. One was Bob's—the other, Farrell's. I stood at the door listening.

"I love your wife," Farrell was saying. "I've got to have her. What are we going to do?"

"I don't know," came Bob's voice, surprisingly calm. "I don't know what we're going to do. She's my wife, actually, and you should quietly pull up your tent and steal away. Leave her alone, Tom. Give her a break."

I'd heard enough. I opened the door. First thing I saw was our casement window, smashed. Glass littered the carpet. Farrell sat in an easy chair on the far side of the room, near the TV. Bob was on the sofa. On the coffee table before him were a couple of cans of beer, some cheese with a knife stuck in it, and crackers.

"What's going on here?" I demanded. "What happened to that window?"

"Hello, Muzzy," said Bob. He was feeling no pain. "Your lover boy just came through it. I'm sitting here, peaceful, having a snack, when all of a sudden—crash, bang!—and here he is. Dove right through the window."

"Good God!" I exclaimed. "This is crazy." I turned on Farrell. "Look, kiddo," I said furiously. "I thought I told you I don't want to see you any more."

Farrell had been drinking too. I could tell it in his slow speech. "Diana," he said, "you gave a bum check for ten dollars yesterday to the York Bar. I came in all the way from Hyde Park to make it good for you. Then I pass the bar and see you sitting there playing patty-cake with another guy . . ."

"So what?" I retorted. "I didn't expect you to show up."

He said, "I know you didn't. Or you'd have been waiting here."

His arrogance enraged me. "Listen, Buster," I snapped, "I wouldn't have been waiting *anywhere* for you." Bob, suddenly insulted, spoke up. "Don't you talk to my wife like that, Farrell. Get out!"

Farrell looked at him. "I certainly will not." His voice was contemptuous. "I've been here plenty of times when *you* weren't around. I'm staying."

Bob snatched the knife from the cheese. It was a long, sharp, wicked-looking thing. He held it in his right hand and put the tip of the blade against the palm of his left hand, weighing it back and forth. He looked at Farrell, "You know something?" he said softly. "I'm going to kill you. I'm a professional knife-thrower. I'm going to put this right through your heart."

I got panicky. "Now, wait a minute," I cried. "We're all grown people . . ."

Farrell laughed at Bob.

It was the worst thing he could have done. In a flash Bob threw the knife. He hurled it, overhand, as a knife-thrower would, with all his might—and, thank God, it missed. It clattered against the wall and fell to the floor.

Oh Christ, I thought, now somebody *will* be killed, and it's going to be Bob. He's no match for Farrell. I rushed screaming into the hall, "Martin, for God's sake, they're in there and they're going to kill each other. Get the police, quick!" Behind me glass and furniture crashed. I was afraid to go back. I thought I'd find Bob on the floor, dead. Then I heard a heavy thump—and silence.

I stole to the door and peered in. Farrell lay sprawled on his face, blood pouring from a gash on his head. Our heavy glass ashtray was on the floor beside him, ashes splattered everywhere. Bob was seated on the sofa, trying to light a cigarette and looking very pleased with himself. "I gave it to him right over the noggin," he said. "That'll hold him."

All at once everything in me exploded. The sight of blood completely unnerved me. First he'd split my head open, and now Farrell's. I screamed at Bob, "You monster! You killed him! Why did you have to do that? Why couldn't you just have him arrested?"

I dragged Tommy into the bedroom and pushed a pillow under his head. He was unconscious. The blood poured out as though it would never stop. I began to cry. If it had been Bob, my sympathy would have gone to him. But it was Tommy who was hurt and bleeding. "Poor Tommy," I wept. "He smashed a window because he wanted me . . ."

Everything began to happen at once. Policemen were in the room—one holding Tommy, another applying wet towels to his head, a third phoning for an ambulance. They carried him out on a stretcher.

"Wait a minute," I shouted. "I'm going with him."

I felt a hand on my arm. "Oh, no, you're not." It was Bob, reeling a little, but determined.

I jerked away. "Oh, yes, I am!" I boiled over. "Now you've done it, Bob! You've had it! Tom wants me and after all, he came to cover my check, which is something you couldn't do. Good-by!"

In the ambulance I pleaded with the police. "Please don't tell anybody who I am. It'll be in all the papers." But a few minutes later at the hospital, when they refused to let me see Tommy, I screamed, "I'm Diana Barrymore! How dare you say I can't see him!"

Finally they permitted me to visit Farrell. He was in flannel pajamas, a huge white bandage like a turban wound about his head. "Get me out of here, baby," he begged. But not until dawn, two hours later, were we able to leave.

We walked out of the hospital into a barrage of flashing bulbs. "Oh, no," I said. A reporter spoke up. "Miss Barry-more——"

I thought, well, it's happened. Face it. I smiled happily

in every direction. I didn't care. I wasn't thinking of tomorrow.

A reporter offered to drive us back to Sutton Terrace. We were followed by a caravan of a dozen cars jammed with newspaper people. We arrived at Sutton Terrace. The York Inn was the only place large enough to hold us all. We had a block to walk to the Inn, and with each step photographers' bulbs flashed as they hadn't since the day I arrived in Hollywood to be met by Daddy. But there hadn't been as many reporters and photographers then as there were on East 63rd Street that June morning. Even Martin came out and stared; people's heads popped out of windows to watch this extraordinary procession. Tom led the way into the Inn.

Then he turned to the crowd. "Please," he said calmly, "let Miss Barrymore and me have coffee alone for a few minutes; then we'll see you."

We drank coffee silently. Then I said, "We better go face them, Tom."

He said, "All right. I'll buy them all a drink when the bar opens."

I was fascinated by his aplomb. He was vital and virile and unconcerned and unafraid, and he wore his bandage about his head like a laurel wreath.

It was like a Presidential press conference. Tom presided standing at the bar, the reporters crowding about taking notes. Were we to be married? Tom was coy. "We don't know," he said. What about Wilcox, they asked me. "I'm divorcing him," I said. "It's no secret that we've been incompatible for some time. But I'm not marrying anyone for a while. I'm only thirty-two and I've had three husbands, and that's enough for now."

The bar opened. Drinks were served. Some time later a man shoved a newspaper in front of me. A huge picture of me stared out from the front page with a blazing headline. I gazed at myself. I was wearing one of my Rory Calhoun outfits—Western pants and a toreador jacket with a bolero—and

I looked foolish and happy. All I could think of was, "What a lovely billing—on the front page!" Not even Cholly Knickerkocker had put me on page one.

The martinis came thicker and faster. It seemed only a few minutes before another newspaper was before me. Different picture, same story. A reporter suggested we go back to my apartment.

Bob was there, lounging on the sofa. The place was a shambles. Broken lamps, broken glass, blood on the floor, chairs upturned . . . Cameras began to flash again. Bob held his own press conference while taking long swigs from a can of beer.

"That man broke up my home," he announced. "As far as our marriage is concerned, we're through. We're finished."

While he talked, I thought, how this place looks! It's disgraceful! I went into the bedroom and called maid service. Finally the last of the reporters trooped out, and Bob and I faced each other.

"Well, you certainly fixed it," he said. "Do you realize you're going to be on every front page tomorrow?"

"*Be* on it? I'm already on it. I saw the papers."

"Are you proud of yourself?"

"No, I am not proud of myself," I replied with a woozy dignity. "Definitely not. I'm ashamed of myself. But you started it all. Really, Bob, you better leave. It's just no good, the two of us. We need a separation. I wish you'd go to Rochester."

He shook his head. He seemed almost indifferent. "Nope. This is my apartment too. I'm not leaving. I'm tired, I'm going to bed." He went into the other room, threw himself on his bed, and fell asleep almost instantly.

The phone rang continuously. Everyone seemed to take it as a lark. "Well, really, darling! How terribly un-chic!" They treated it as a huge joke. "Sweetie, you're all right, making the front page!"

I took the cue from them. A madcap escapade—why not?

Later I met Tom. What were we going to do? I didn't know. I thought the only solution was for Bob to leave. I'd told him so. It was hard, of course, after six years of sharing every kind of experience . . . But how long could we keep on as we were?

"Yeh," said Tom. He wore a much smaller bandage. His head ached a little, he said.

The sun began to set. The waters of the East River grew gray, then inky. The air became chill. "Let's go to the York Inn," Tom said. He grinned and brightened. "We're celebrities now," he said.

We went to the York Inn and sat at the bar and drank.

CHAPTER THIRTY

IT'S A STRANGE THING, but notoriety will bring out old friends as quickly as fame. After an ominous silence of several days the calls began to come from those who had read the newspapers and were horrified. Oelrichs and Mays I hadn't heard from for years telephoned me. "My God, Diana! Have you lost all decency?" Leonard's wife, Yvonne, was on the telephone, but her Gallic sense of humor showed through her dismay: "My dear, this is like the Grand Guignol!" Surely, she hoped, it wasn't as bad as it sounded. Fortunately for me, Leonard was incommunicado, somewhere in the West, prospecting for uranium, and undoubtedly had missed the newspapers. Ann Andrews called, and so did Nita Naldi. Both were salty characters and knew how to speak their minds. Ann said, "You're insane, child, and that husband of yours should have horsewhipped the two of you long ago." Nita was outraged too. She never trusted Farrell. Once, when she came to spend an evening with me, I introduced them. Before she could remove her coat, he had escorted her to a cab, given the driver a dollar, and sent her home. He wanted to be alone with me. Nita never forgave him. I tried to explain, weakly, that Farrell kept me from drinking, helped my confidence . . . "I'd rather be helped by Jack the Ripper," she snorted. "Deen-ya, that man will do you in one of these nights——"

And Bob moved about the apartment like a lost soul, utterly bewildered. "I can't understand it," he would say. "You'll go out with a hoodlum like that and come back in the morning looking perfectly fresh, perfectly charming, singing out gaily, 'Hello, darling!' to your husband . . . I tell myself, 'This woman, she's two people.' I don't understand it."

I didn't either. "Maybe I am two, Bob. What makes me two? I don't know. Or is every woman really that way?"

"They aren't," Bob said. "Maybe they think that way, but they don't live that way. You do."

All right, I thought. Of course everyone's right. It's unbelievable that I should go with that man. Wouldn't you think a woman who was a lady would know how to end an affair? She'd say, "Well, thank you. It's been charming. Good-by."

For the second time I broke with Mr. Farrell. "Okay, baby," he finally said. "If that's the way you want it." "You're damn right that's the way I want it," I said. "Good-by."

A week passed. The night Queen Elizabeth's coronation was to be televised, Bob and I decided to make a cozy little party —just us two. "We'll stay home and watch it. Okay?" I said to him. "I'm going to be a good wife again. It will be like old times from now on, Bob. I promise. I've made an incredible fool of myself—it's all over."

Bob kissed me. "It's that little girl in you," he said. "The one who thinks life is out of a story book—nothing's real except what she wants to think is real."

We were snuggled together in the big easy chair before the set, leisurely drinking beer and watching the proceedings filmed in far-off London, when the phone rang. I didn't want to disturb Bob with my conversation, so I took it in the bedroom.

"Baby." The voice at the other end was low and breathy. "I miss you so much, baby——"

It was Farrell. I cannot explain what went through my

mind. If anything, I thought, "God, but I have a thing about
this man." I went to my closet, took my coat, and like an
automaton walked into the sitting room, putting on my coat
as I came in.

Bob looked up. The blood drained from his face. "You
going out?"

I nodded.

"Farrell?"

I had to be honest. I wanted to shout my honesty. Farrell
wanted me, I wanted him. It was so clear, so certain—anything so clear, so certain, must have its own rightness, its own
justification.

"Yes, Bob, it's Farrell." Before he could say more, I
blurted out, "It's no use, Bob. We've gone all through this
before. I can't help it."

Bob rose slowly, fumbled for a cigarette, and lit it. His
hands shook. "All right. You can't help it. Everything you've
promised me goes down the drain." He spoke with an effort.
"But if you must go with a man, for Christ's sake, go with a
gentleman. Don't go with a thug. Don't go with Farrell.
Oh, Muzzy . . ." I was afraid he would cry. "Please don't go."

Nothing could have stopped me, but my heart went out to
him. Tears sprung to my eyes, a compassion I could not
express wrenched me. I felt so damn sorry for him! He was
my husband, and I was cuckolding him, and he couldn't stop
it, and I couldn't stop it, and how awful it must be for a man!
I walked over to him, raised up on my toes, and kissed him
tenderly on the cheek, and I went out to meet Farrell.

And Bob let me go.

The next day Bob left me. "I'm finished," he said. "I'm not
beat, but I can't go on any longer. I'm going to Rochester
tonight."

At the door he took me in his arms. We both wept. "I
don't know if I'll ever see you again," he said miserably. "But
if I do, I want everything to be friendly."

"Yes, Bob." I couldn't stop crying. "I'll always love you."

"And I'll always love you. You'll never find anyone who will love you as I do." And he left.

I poured myself a drink and then a second and a third. I paced the room. I couldn't telephone Farrell; I still had no number to reach him. I smoked and I drank, and I listened to music.

Bob's plane, I knew, took two hours to reach Rochester. I called there at midnight. Bob answered. "You made it all right?" I asked. "I was worried."

"Of course I did. You all right, Muzzy?"

"I'm all right. I miss you like hell though. I wish you hadn't gone."

"I wish I hadn't too. But it's the best thing. We have to do this."

It was insane. Absolutely insane.

I always knew when Farrell had been drinking. His eyes began to stare, his voice dropped until it was gentle, almost childlike, and he spoke with maddening slowness, like a man in a dream.

He was most dangerous then. One night as I came out of the bathroom, he threw a glass at me. "Are you crazy?" I cried. He grabbed a bottle, smashed it against the iron frame of the coffee table, and lunged at me with the sharp, jagged edge. I ran shrieking into the street. It took two policemen to oust Farrell. I refused to press charges. I was shamed to have more publicity.

Two nights later Farrell went beserk. I came back to the apartment after a chance drink in the York Inn with an old friend to find the words, "I hate you," scrawled in soap on every glass surface in the living room—the mirrors, the windows, even the marble surface of the coffee table.

I looked about, speechless. Unexpectedly Farrell emerged from my bedroom. Through the door I could see my bureau: the drawers thrown open, my make-up box upside down.

He'd gone through all my belongings, read my mail, turned everything topsy-turvy. "Hi-yuh, baby," he drawled softly. His eyes had a faraway look.

I didn't think. I screamed at him, "Have you lost your marbles, Farrell! You bastard——"

I rushed toward him. His fist crashed into my face. I actually felt the small bones of my nose crumble, excruciating pain stabbed at my eyes. Neon lights whirled and exploded in my brain. I began choking on my own blood. Out of nowhere something hard rocked against my left cheekbone. I heard myself screaming, as from a great distance. His fists were pounding me, I began falling backward, I blacked out. For an awful moment I came to: I was lying huddled on the floor and Farrell was kicking me, silently, without a word, without anger, without emotion: my arms, my legs, my ribs, wherever he could reach me as I rolled and twisted madly to escape. I saw him through a red haze, unbelieving; I was watching this on stage, he wasn't doing it to me. Then, all at once, Farrell was gone; the door closed behind him, and I lay retching and choking and gasping. I tried to get up; I reached a kneeling position on my hands and knees; the blood pounded behind my eyes until I could not endure it. I fainted.

When I came to, I was in bed and Nita Naldi sat beside me, a bowl of broth in her hand, trying to feed me. My nose was broken, my eyes blackened, my lips swollen, my body a mass of pain despite the codeine the doctor had filled me with.

"Deen-ya," said Nita sorrowfully, shaking her head. "I told you. Now, here, get some of this in you."

I tried to talk through my bruised lips. I had brought it on myself. It was my own fault. I said I wasn't going to see him again, and I did. Now I was really frightened of him. "Mother Moonbeam—" I began, and fell asleep.

She stayed with me that day and the next, and cared for me. Farrell had vanished. Ann Andrews came with food for me. "Well," she said, "you certainly bring out the chivalry in your gentlemen friends." I had no answer for her.

The third night I looked up and there, incredibly enough, stood Bob. He was going to Los Angeles to stay with his brother. He might find a job there. He had come for the rest of his clothes.

"Well," he said, and he looked at me. "This is a nice kettle of fish. I ought to kill the son of a bitch. But you got what you deserve."

"I know it," I mumbled. "I'm never going to see him again."

"Do you still want me to leave?" Bob asked.

I shook my head, no. "You know when I say things like that I don't really mean them," I said. "Why do you say them then?" he asked. I didn't know. Why did I see Farrell again? I didn't know.

"Diana," he said sadly, "you've just taken this thing too far. There's a point of no return."

"I was stupid," I said. "That man's crazy and I don't want to see him again. He's a monster!" I began to cry.

Bob sat next to my bed. He spoke slowly in his deep voice. "Diana, don't you know that my whole life is centered about you? Sometimes I try to think of myself and my woes as something that happened to somebody else in a book I'm reading. I have to think that way because what you do to me can only make sense in a book, not in real life. Diana, darling, the whole plot of my life is twisting and turning this minute, and I think I'm the hero and you're the heavy, and you think it's the other way around—and then I realize we're both the heavies . . ."

We wept. But he did not stay. He bent down and kissed me and left. If I had said the words, "Bob, don't go—" he would have stayed. But I couldn't say it to him. I couldn't lie.

Six months. Six fantastic months now began. Nothing I had ever read in *True Confessions* in my Brearley days could compare with my weird existence after Bob left. The tone was set by an agent for the Tishmans, my landlords at Sutton Terrace. My lease had expired; courteously but firmly they refused to renew it. No other tenant had guests diving through windows. No other had brought such undesirable publicity. I had to move.

Fortunately a sizable check came from Leonard and I found an apartment on Fifth Avenue. Here, as though I deliberately planned it, I let myself go. Looking back, I can't understand how I slipped into it, why I did it, what I was searching for. Perhaps I was trying to kill myself because I felt someone needed to do it, and I might as well be the one. Bob was gone and I had driven him away. My career was shot; I had made the Barrymore name a ribald jest, a filthy joke; my shame had been spread everywhere.

I drank. I put myself to sleep with blue jackets and yellow jackets and every kind of sleeping pill I could persuade doctors to give me. To ensure my supply I went from doctor to doctor. I woke myself with Benzedrine, took a morning drink to make me retch, so that I could take another drink to set me up. Then I drank through the day. I holed up in my apartment: I never saw daylight. The blinds were always drawn. I didn't begin to function until dusk. Men came to the apartment—men I'd never seen before, men I never saw again. In three months I left my apartment only four times. I didn't want to show myself. I was appalled at the way I was behaving, and I couldn't stop the way I was behaving. My maid Florence shopped for me. My gentlemen callers would order food from a nearby restaurant and literally feed me, spoonful by spoonful, pleading, "Diana, please, you must eat."

I couldn't eat because I drank. The moment I got sober I became so horrified at my behavior that I got drunk again. I thought, my God, Diana, it's too much. If Mother were alive, she wouldn't speak to you, she'd send the men in white for you. If Daddy were alive, he would have said, "Well, she certainly comes by it rightly, but how *dare* she!" Nita Naldi and Ann Andrews took turns visiting me, bringing hot broth and tea and trying to straighten me out. Nita would say, again and again, "Oh, my dear, my dear, my love, my child, what are you doing to yourself!"

As the days passed I dropped from one hundred thirty to one hundred fifteen to one hundred to ninety-seven pounds. I grew so weak I could scarcely walk. One morning when I managed to get out of bed, I tried to stand and my feet crumpled under me. There was absolutely no feeling in them. Florence carried me back to bed and massaged me. The doctor diagnosed it as neuritis. I had to stop drinking. But I didn't. I lay in bed in a nether world of alcohol and nembutal, while the numbness climbed like an evil vine until it reached the base of my knees. There, inexplicably, it stopped.

Fantasies crowded my mind. The walls began to spin and unexpectedly I was backstage a moment after the final curtain fell on opening night. I stood listening to pandemonium out front: the audience standing on its seats, screaming, "Bravo! Bravo!" people stamping and shouting, others looking at each other with tears in their eyes. I had to come before the curtain and stand there, humbly, while the waves of applause broke like surf over my head.

I said, when they let me, "Oh, ladies and gentlemen, I never made a speech in front of the curtain before. All my life I prayed that this might happen to me. I don't know what to say to you, but I remember what my father once told me: 'If you don't know what to say, say simply what you feel in your heart.' And so I say to you, my dear audience, thank you, thank you so very, very much, and God bless you."

At Sardi's that night, while people at other tables glanced in my direction and whispered, almost in awe, I read Brooks Atkinson's review in the *Times*: "Last night's audience underwent an emotional experience such as happens only once or twice in a lifetime of theatergoing. Never have we seen a St. Joan of such moving spirituality, such shattering comprehension of the human soul . . . Diana, you have fulfilled all the hopes I had for you, all the hopes you had for yourself when you wrote me years ago. I am proud that I was one of the first to see the promise in you—not because you are a Barrymore, but because you are you—and you have done it yourself. We are all in your debt, Miss Diana Barrymore . . ."

Then I would awake suddenly to reality, and to a slug of whisky, strong and burning, to keep me from thinking . . .

My sister-in-law, Yvonne, tried to help. If I would go to a psychiatrist, or perhaps to a milk farm and then a psychiatrist, she was sure Leonard would foot the bill. I refused. I'd go mad with boredom at a milk farm. I was frightened of psychiatrists. I didn't know why, don't ask me. I would go to a priest instead. I knew of one, Father Mahar.

But I couldn't face Father Mahar sober. I couldn't lie to a priest. The knowledge of what I must tell him about myself terrified me. Half a bottle of gin dissolved the terror. Father Mahar had to help me up the steps of the rectory and lead me to a chair. I have only a vague memory of our conversation. He was very kind. I told him about Farrell. He asked, is he a Catholic? I said, yes. "Send him to me," he suggested. I shook my head. "No, Father, I'm not seeing him any more." Someone had told me Farrell had gone to Europe. The priest said, "You must return to the Church, Diana. Religion is very important for someone like you who seems to be utterly rootless——" That would be my first step toward finding myself. I left the rectory without making a promise. Had I said, "Yes, Father, I'll come back. I'll go to mass every day," I would have lied. We left it open. Perhaps I would call again.

In the cab I thought, confusedly, what does religion mean to me? I never understood. Miss Gerdes had taken me to church every Sunday morning but Mother went only twice a year—at Easter and to midnight mass on Christmas Eve.

"Mummy," I'd ask, "why must I go to church when you don't?" She would reply, "I don't have to, Catkin. I build a church in my heart. And Jesus understands. He's a divinely understanding Man." To add to my bewilderment, Mother had twice married outside her faith—Leonard Thomas, Sr., and Harry Tweed, both Protestants. And though she reared Robin and me as Catholics, Leonard chose to become a Protestant, like his father. Robin, too, seemed rather cavalier about religion. "If you must go to church," he once told me, "by all means attend a Catholic service—the costumes are superb, and after all, the show *has* been a sell-out for centuries." As far back as I could remember, only Grandma Tibi, of my family, had taken religion seriously . . .

I stumbled into my apartment to find Anna Wiman. Anna, whose father was producer Dwight Deere Wiman, had gone to Fermata School with me and was now a play producer herself. She was about to leave for Bermuda for a month's rest. With warm, quick sympathy she insisted that I come as her guest. Sun and sea air and rest were the medicine I needed too. But her lovely house on the beach was full of guests day and night. My breakfast was gin and orange juice, and though we drove daily to a doctor in Hamilton for vitamin injections, my next stop was a bar. It wasn't sensible, but I wasn't being sensible then. Still, with the sun and the swimming, my neuritis improved, though I gained very little weight.

Back in New York, there was an eviction notice in my mail. I stared at it, unbelieving. The complaints had caught up with me. I had been using my apartment "for purposes other than residential." Oh, no, I thought. Then I exploded. I'll sue them, I cried. I'll make them eat every filthy word!

But I dared not press the issue—I couldn't face more publicity. In a walk-up I took in East 80th Street, I went to the telephone and called Bob, at Ross' home, in Los Angeles. I needed my husband. I knew now that I could not be without him. Without him I simply collapsed.

"Bob, come back," I said. "I've been an incredible fool. I'm sick, I need you—Christmas is coming, I want you with me."

His voice was gruff. "Muzzy, I need you too. I miss you terribly." We talked. Then he asked, "But what about your lovers?"

"There aren't any lovers," I replied. I thought, everyone must lie sometimes. "There are no lovers, no anything—please come back. You don't know what has happened since you've gone."

I sent him money for a plane ticket and frantically, despite my neuritis, in the day it took him to reach New York, I tried to fix up the apartment, hanging a print here, covering an old dried-blood-spattered chair with a leopard throw. I made myself as presentable as possible. Then I waited for Bob. I heard him climbing the two flights of stairs. Then he was at the door. His face paled when he saw me but with a sad smile, he said only, "Have you missed me, Muzzy?"

"Oh, Bob," I said, "I've missed you so incredibly. Look at me. Isn't this enough to tell you the way I've missed you?"

He took me in his arms. "We'll have to decorate this place," he said later. "It looks pretty bare." Then he walked into the kitchenette. "My God, this is tiny. How am I going to cook in here?"

We both began to laugh through our tears and we could not stop.

CHAPTER THIRTY-ONE

No one could have nursed me back to health as Bob did. Day and night he tended me, waking up three and four times a night to feed me soups, eggnogs, special dishes he turned out in the little kitchenette to tempt my appetite. My doctor had been frank. "Your wife has the beginning of cirrhosis of the liver," he told him. "She is suffering from lack of sleep, too much alcohol, and no food." My neuritis lingered: for days I fought back the tears each time I took a step. It was as if a thousand needles had been plunged into my feet.

The bills began to mount. The last five hundred dollars from Mother's estate had gone. I began borrowing again. We economized where we could. Once I was able to remain on my feet again, I shopped. I bought the cheapest cuts of meat and loaded them with tenderizer. On Thursdays, when the supermarkets sold beef liver as low as thirty-three cents a pound, hamburger for a quarter, I stocked up on them. I learned how to whip up a dinner for two for a dollar. I borrowed money from everyone. I couldn't afford to be ashamed. I still had my debutante telephone book and I made use of all the names in it. I simply couldn't borrow again from Aunt Ethel in California and there was no one of the family left. From time to time Leonard sent me a check. It was spent the day we cashed it.

For weeks we literally lived from hand to mouth. I had

nothing more to pawn or sell; we'd virtually given up hope
of work. We were ashamed of our appearance—we hadn't decent clothes, we didn't want to see anybody or be seen by
anybody.

The day came when we stole food. Bob, wearing his trench
coat, and I, carrying my bag, sneaked small packages at the
supermarket to add to our purchases. Mostly we pilfered
cheeses. It was astonishing how affluent a few crackers and
Camembert, after a dinner of hamburger and rolls, could
make you feel. Once, in a supermarket, when I tucked a
Liederkranz in my bag and Bob a fine Brie in the deep
pocket of his coat, we knew terror. Bob was about to push
through, after paying for a bag of potatoes, when the clerk
demanded suspiciously, "What about the cheese in your
pocket?" Bob looked utterly astonished: the actor in him was
superb. "Oh, I'm sorry," he said. He allowed himself an
embarrassed chuckle. "I completely forgot it." I didn't draw
my breath until we were safe on the street. That was all that
had to happen. Barrymore arrested for pilfering food in a
supermarket!

Yet, when we received unexpected windfalls, the money
didn't always go for food. A bottle of Imperial cost about
four dollars—sometimes that was our first purchase. The bottle was the surest way through the little door to forgetfulness.
Once Bob, looking through an old brief case, cried out
triumphantly, "Muzzy, look!" He held up two twenty-five-
dollar war bonds. I remembered: we'd begun with the idea
of buying ten thousand dollars' worth. Two were as far as
we got. We couldn't reach the nearest bank and then a bar
quickly enough. We had been on beer that week, four cans a
day, only two apiece, when our usual quota was twelve apiece.
We played the bowling machines, sinking about five dollars
in dimes in them, and returned to our apartment with ten
dollars. Tomorrow was another day.

We were gay—the gaiety of desperation. Bob went out for
cigarettes one night: we'd been economizing. I was desperate

for one. Even while he was gone I searched frantically for a cigarette butt. I found the stump of a cigar in one of his suits. When he came back, I was sitting up in bed reading the paper, the lit cigar jutting out of my mouth. He almost choked with laughter.

Sometimes it wasn't funny. One night as it grew dark, I pulled the chain of one of my little gold baroque lamps, the last vestiges of my Hollywood grandeur. Nothing happened. The bulb's burned out, I thought. I tried the other lamp; nothing happened. Then a third—it was out too. I grew panicky. Ever since Robin used to tease me in the dark with his tiger, or leap out pretending to be a ghost, I'd had a fear of the dark. I ran about the apartment turning on the lights, but they were all gone.

All at once I knew. Our electric bill hadn't been paid for months. We must have missed the notification that the current would be turned off.

I sat in the darkness waiting for Bob. Nothing that had happened to me so far, not even being locked out of our room in Hollywood, hit me as hard as this. I could only think of Mother. I said to myself, if Mother were alive, she'd never let them do this to me. I'd only have to telephone her and say, "Mummy, the lights have been turned off on me," and immediately there would be someone from the Colony Club with a check to cover it, and Con Edison would have been given a piece of her mind they wouldn't soon forget. She would never let them do this to me. I cried a little.

When Bob came I said, "Will you please go out and buy some candles?"

"With what?" he asked. He had thirty cents left.

We sat in the darkness, saying nothing, and when we were ready to go to sleep, we walked like two blind children into the bedroom, kissed each other, and went to bed.

I telephoned a chic friend next morning. "Darling, do you happen to have any spare candles about? I'm having a candelabra party tonight . . ." She sent them over by messenger. For several nights, until Leonard's next check came and we paid the electric light bill of forty-two dollars, we lived by candlelight.

CHAPTER THIRTY-TWO

I WAS IN FAIRLY good shape—Bob too—when the offer came out of the blue. Day Tuttle, manager of a Wilmington, Delaware, theater, was producing *Moulin Rouge,* a play based on the life of Toulouse-Lautrec. My name had popped into Tuttle's mind. Would I consider the starring role—that of Marie Charlet, the artist's mistress?

I signed immediately. I had no idea that doing so would bring Mr. Farrell back briefly—and send Bob out of our apartment again. I went to work, I learned my lines without too much trouble: I felt encouraged. The actor who portrayed the crippled French artist was Karl Shanzer, a diffident, twenty-one-year-old boy who, like Toulouse-Lautrec, was about five feet tall. He seemed terrified of me, which bolstered my ego. During rehearsal week I tried to relax him, as only a woman can. I spent evenings with him; I sat at bars with him. I was impressed by his performance, by his fanatic devotion to his work. Here was a young actor whose life was the theater. *Variety* found his interpretation "significant." I felt toward Karl as though he were my protégé—I was proud of him. After the play closed he was at loose ends, he had no place to stay. I said, "Why don't you come stay with us? At least we have a sofa and you can sleep there until you do find something." He did—for a week.

Bob, unhappy enough that I'd taken an engagement with-

342

out him, brooded; and a few days after Karl left, he decided
that his home had been violated. We flared at each other. "All
right, get out!" I shouted one night. "No one's asking you to
stay!" If after all we'd gone through together, he was to play
the outraged husband over a frightened, twenty-one-year-old
boy . . .

"Okay," said Bob. With great dignity he found his way to
the door. He would spend the night on a park bench. I immediately got on the telephone and invited a few friends
over—Nita Naldi, young Karl, and others. Unexpectedly, like
Banquo's ghost, Farrell padded in.

"Oh, no!" I cried. He wouldn't leave. The police escorted
him to the nearest precinct, but I refused to press charges.
I'd had enough. After the party, with everyone gone, I was
in the apartment when sirens suddenly screamed outside
and a bewildering array of flashlights played up and down my
walls. I looked out. There, in the street below, was Walter
Winchell in a police radio car.

"Hi, Walter," I called down. "What are you doing here?"

"We got a tip your husband is going to shoot you," he said.

"Really?" I was intrigued. "Come on up and wait for him."
I had considerable Bourbon in me. Walter came up with two
policemen and we chatted for a few minutes. Bob didn't appear. All was peaceful. Walter was getting bored. They left.

As though these entrances and exits were timed, Bob
showed up. He'd come for his coat, he explained. It was cold
in the park.

"Oh, stay here, darling," I said. "Everything's been so divinely dramatic!" I entwined his arm in mine. "You weren't
going to shoot me, were you? Winchell got a tip."

Bob looked astonished. "Of course not. It never entered my
mind." He bent down and kissed me. "Muzzy, you know,
we're crazy," he said. "I don't know why I let you do these
things to me, and even come back for more—but you're crazy,
we're both crazy, and I love you very much."

"Oh, darling," I said. "I love you so much too! I think I'd die if anything happened to you!"

Dawn was creeping in the window when we fell asleep in each other's arms.

Perhaps *Moulin Rouge* was good luck. Bob and I were promptly signed together for summer stock in *The Four Poster*. We pulled ourselves together and made it. After that came *Separate Rooms*. And in Columbus, Ohio, in the middle of the night, Bob woke in agony. Pancreatitis again—the third attack! I was frantic. Hadn't Ross warned that the third or fourth attack could be fatal? I rushed Bob to the hospital and for four days he was out of the play. He emerged pale and chastened. "Ah, but that was bad; there's no pain to compare to it," he said. "From now on it's beer for me—nothing stronger. You watch, Muzzy."

A few days later I found him nipping whisky. "Are you insane?" I exclaimed. "Do you want to kill yourself?" He wouldn't listen. "Just one won't hurt," he drawled. "I've got a hell of a constitution. Do you think only Barrymores are tough?" And soon it was as it had been before.

As though nothing had intervened since the days our summers were full of work, Bob and I once more were traveling from town to town, living out our lives in tiny dressing rooms. We tried to drink only after performances. But often, though we were fine in Act One, in Act Two we were rather playful, and in Act Three definitely high. People were baffled. None saw us at a bar during intermission. They couldn't know that the bottle of "cough medicine" in my make-up case was really Four Roses.

I remember a week in Litchfield, Connecticut. We kept fairly sober and did beautifully. Saturday night we celebrated. There are no Sunday stock performances in Connecticut, and we could relax as we wished. You were prohibited from buying liquor after 12:01 A.M. on Sunday, though you could

finish drinks already on your table. We rushed from the
theater to our hotel, arriving a moment before midnight,
and immediately ordered ten double Scotches set up. They
lasted us through the early hours.

We celebrated the following day, too, as we drove to our
next stand. I vaguely remember the drive; I remember quarreling loudly with Bob in the hotel about getting to the
theater in time. What happened later Jules Ziegler, our agent,
told us. Eight o'clock came—and we hadn't arrived at the
theater. The producer began tearing his hair. Eight-fifteen
came—still no Diana, no Wilcox. The curtain would go up
at eight-thirty, and a full house waited out front. At eight-
twenty we arrived.

"You walked in, Diana, wearing two left shoes," said Jules,
"Bob followed, weaving.

"I led you both to your dressing room. I could think of
only one thing to do. There was a large terry-cloth robe there.
I soaked it in a fire bucket of water, shoved you together
facing each other, arms around each other, threw the wet
robe over your heads and tied it tight around you. You
screamed murder, and Bob kicked and cursed, and while the
stagehands held you, I doused you with buckets of water, and
I outyelled you, 'You're not getting from under for ten
minutes! Goddamn it, I'll sober you up!' "

When he let us free and we were dried off, Jules went on,
"I saw the miracle of my stage experience, Diana. You sat
down and began making up. You were still making up when
the curtain rose. You walked out on that stage and gave a
terrific, a masterful performance. The applause was deafening. I couldn't believe you were the same girl who'd staggered in fifteen minutes before.

"When it was over, my wife said, 'Why don't you tell her
how great she was, Jules?' "

He did. As he told me the story, I listened as if it were an
anecdote about somebody else, not about me. He added,

"Diana, you don't know how proud I am of you. If you'd only given me that performance on stage without your performance in the dressing room!"

I could understand the producer's stipulation when we were signed to do a six months' tour in *Pajama Tops*, a French bedroom farce. We'd get five hundred dollars a week and a percentage, but half our salary was withheld until the tour ended—insurance against my showing up drunk. In addition, if I was unable to perform because of drunkenness, I would forfeit the entire amount held back, as well as a sum equivalent to the theater's total receipts for a week.

These were harsh terms, but all very legal. I was to be ruled too drunk to act only if three persons agreed: the company manager Joe Roth, the producer, and the manager of the theater in which we appeared.

Because it meant steady work for at least half a year and we desperately needed the money, I signed. I did so furious, humiliated, sick at heart. The play was cheap. It was publicized as "The Play That Rocked and Shocked Paris!—Uncut!—Uncensored!" Posters and newspaper ads showed a half-naked brunette wearing the top of her pajamas, and they were cut almost to the navel. I pleaded for a change in the publicity, the sketch: make the girl's hair longer, or blonde—anything so people won't think it's me. Nothing was done.

We opened our tour in November, 1954, in Rochester, New York, Bob's home town. We behaved well. I was proud of the chic manner in which we carried off dinner with Bob's mother—a sweet and understanding woman whom I called "Mom," and who acted like a second mother to me. The tour went on to Cincinnati. There, two hours before the curtain rose Monday night, November 15, the telephone rang in our hotel room.

Bob turned the phone over to me. It was a newspaper. "Miss Barrymore," came a man's voice, "I'm sorry that we must give you this sad news. We've just received a flash that Lionel Barrymore died a few minutes ago in Hollywood."

I listened to the reporter's voice without emotion. I was still in the room when half a dozen photographers crowded in. One slipped a photograph of Uncle Lionel into my hand.

"What is this for?" I asked. I wasn't drunk, but I wasn't sober.

"We want to take you looking sorrowfully at your uncle," he said.

I returned the picture. "I can't do it. I didn't know him that well," I said. "I'm going on tonight, and I can tell you that my heart isn't broken."

They were horrified. One said, "Miss Barrymore, we can't print that." Finally I agreed to pose with the photograph. I looked at Uncle Lionel while the familiar flashes lit up the room again and again. I thought, my uncle is dead, and it means absolutely nothing to me. I felt terribly, bitterly cheated. This moment should mean a lot to me, if only to give me a great sorrow. I was cheated even of that. I had met him five times in my life. Had we exchanged more than one hundred words, he and I? Dry-eyed, I looked at his picture. It would have been good to weep. It's only right to shed tears when a member of your family dies. The tears wouldn't come.

I went on that night and if I wasn't sober when I arrived at the theater, I didn't give a damn. Joe Roth, the company manager, fought and lied for me. I wasn't drunk, he insisted. "Call the doctor!" someone cried. "Let's keep her off the stage." But by the time the physician arrived, Joe had poured black coffee into me, the curtain was up, and I was already playing my part, playing make-believe.

The tour went on. Our notices were abysmal. Yet people came, the play made money. "If Diana Barrymore could only look in the mirror and see her bloated face and figure—" ran a review in an Indianapolis newspaper. Well, Diana, I thought, how much worse can it get? As for Bob—he was drinking as though he'd never heard of pancreatitis.

In Detroit, Tallulah Bankhead was starring in *Dear Charles* when we arrived. Tallulah was a great friend of Aunt Ethel's, she had known Daddy and Mother and Robin: my admiration for her as an actress, as a woman, as a very special human being, had no bounds. I telephoned her several times, but I was drunk; one afternoon when I was sober and got her on the phone, she invited Bob and me to dinner.

Gay, insouciant, incredibly herself, she welcomed us in her suite at the Book-Cadillac with a tall drink in her hand. I didn't know it then, but she had been on the wagon for some time, and to make me feel that she wasn't watching me, that evening in front of me Tallulah took her first drink in weeks.

She hadn't seen me in *Pajama Tops,* but friends told her my make-up was "ghastly." She said nothing about the fact that I was tipsy on stage. "Darling," she said, "you know your face hasn't the exquisite bone structure of your Aunt Ethel. Make-up is terribly important to you. I don't think you've had your best points brought forward. Let me try making you up."

I sat down and Tallulah made up the left side of my face, instructing me how to do the right side myself. I did, and stared at myself in the mirror, unbelieving. Lines had vanished, the heavy curve of jowl had gone—Tallulah had worked magic! I jumped up and ran to Bob in the next room. "Bob!" I cried. "Look at me! I'm beautiful—for the first time in my life! Oh, Bob, look at me!"

And so I was. "I've been in the theater for fifteen years and no one ever told me, no one ever helped me, not even my family," I said to her again and again. I could not get over it.

Later, as we sat alone, there was a moment when Tallulah talked to me as an older sister might. "Diana, you must try to get hold of yourself. Do you know, there's a generation between us, but you look almost my age." She looked at me.

"God knows, who am I to lecture you? But, Diana, like me, you are your own worst enemy; fortunately I've not been caught in a trap—and you have." And she told me, "Darling, you have a soul, you have a rare quality of spirit—I know you have—but it will take you years to prove it because you have spent so many years trying to destroy it."

I knew she was right.

I tried to help myself. In Chicago, during a lucid moment, I actually made an appointment with a gynecologist. Beating at the back of my brain was still the thought, *a baby, a baby, maybe a baby's the answer.* In this very city ten years ago—was it that long?—Flo Reed and I had talked about a baby. To save my marriage with Bramwell. To make my life add up. Now I was thinking the same way. Only it was Bob, not Bram. And if my life was confused then, what about it now? Yet I was only thirty-four—surely I had time.

I never got around to keeping the appointment.

Opening night in Philadelphia—Philadelphia, crowded with the majestic ghosts of the Drews and Barrymores—I was rubbery-legged on stage. Bob couldn't fathom it. He had been kicked off once, protesting doggedly that he was fine, but Bob wasn't the star. Now he said, "It beats me, Muzzy. We play a hick town and you're sober as a judge. We reach Philadelphia, where everybody knows you, and you're crocked. Why?"

I couldn't answer his whys, just as he couldn't answer mine. Perhaps, I thought, *because* everyone knows me and is here to watch Barrymore go down, down, down the skids . . .

Among the letters in my mail I found one from Actor's Equity. It minced no words. I was a star. I had to live up to the responsibility of a star. If I failed that responsibility and the play closed because of me, I would throw people out of work. The warning was clear: I could be expelled from Equity . . .

Shaken, I put down the letter and reread the reviews in the

Philadelphia newspapers. The words jabbed at me: ". . . its shrill and vehement players . . . a dull and tasteless exhibition . . . Diana Barrymore plays its femme fatale with a curious collection of roars and the general restraint of a Jerry Lewis . . ."

H. Clay Blaney, the producer, raged at me. "These shop-girls who work to earn the money to go to the theater—when they come in and see a drunken slut of a dame stagger across the stage, what do you think they think of you and your father?"

I sat, silent.

"You know they don't come to see Barrymore—they come to see you fall flat on your face, not because they want to see you act! They say, why, she wasn't so drunk!"

I sat, silent.

"Your name is up in lights, Diana. Goddamn it, they're up there in letters as big and as bright as your father's ever were: DIANA BARRYMORE."

I sat, silent.

"You're nothing but a drunken bum!"

He slammed the door behind him.

Minutes later he was back. "Diana," he pleaded, "for God's sake, you're ruining me. Time after time I've taken this from you and I haven't made you forfeit your money——"

I spoke. "I don't know what it is," I said. "I can't explain it. I've broken my word to you again and again. You should throw me out."

He shook his head. "You know we already have theaters rented in advance and tickets sold all along the way—if the show closes, you'll hurt me only for the moment, but you'll hurt yourself for the rest of your life."

"I know it," I said dully.

Three-fourths of the theater managers in the country, he went on bitterly, were on record saying they would never permit me to appear in their theaters. "If I close this show because of you, this will mean the rest. Will you tell me what you will do outside the theater? My God, Diana, all I ask of you is to stay sober for two and a half hours a day!"

I burst into tears. "I know, I'm a fool, I'm an ass, I don't know—I'll never do it again. This time I mean it," I cried. "Bob gets me drunk, he starts me off—it's his fault!" I looked around wildly. "And if he doesn't get me drunk, then I get drunk and get him drunk . . ."

Blaney looked at me. He turned and left my room.

Night after night during our two weeks in Philadelphia I tried to console myself at the Variety Club after the show, drinking with other actors. I saw the plays they were in—why can't I be in a good play, not one advertised like French postcards? Why did I sell the name Barrymore so cheap? Maybe if I was in a better play, a decent play, I'd respect myself, I'd try to live up to it, I'd . . . And night after night, so that I could sleep, I took pills, and so that I could stay awake, I took pills, and so that I could be calm, I took pills.

In Boston I paced our room at the Touraine Hotel. Memories assailed me. Here I'd stayed in my first tryout in *Romantic Mr. Dickens,* and from here every afternoon I'd gone to Mother's suite at the Ritz to be coached. "I'd have you stay here with me," she had said. "But I think it's better for you to stay at the hotel where your fellow actors live." Here I'd stayed, too, when I toured *Outward Bound,* with Florence Reed and Laurette Taylor. I'd had my personal maid then. What a fuss they made over me. What a brilliant future, they said.

I drank that night. My pills kept me in a daze and only liquor could snap me out of it. I weaved on stage.

The next night at 6:30 P.M., two hours before curtain, Blaney flew in from New York. He was white-faced when he entered my room. "All right, Diana. You've had your last chance. If this happens once more, I take the money and I bring you up on charges before Equity. You leave me no other choice."

Now events became hazy. Blaney went from my room to

a movie. He returned at 9:30 P.M. He walked backstage. "Hi, Blaney," I said. I pretended I hadn't been drinking.

He walked away. I was sure he didn't know. God, I thought, that was close.

At intermission I hurried into my dressing room for a refresher—and there was my make-up case, open, and conspicuously standing on the table, my medicine bottle. It had been emptied into the sink—the sweetish odor of whisky was still there. Under the bottle a slip of paper fluttered. Penciled on it were two words: "Thanks. Blaney."

I fainted.

In the hotel, later, I fell asleep. I slept a long time. When I awoke, the blinds were drawn, the luminous dial of the clock on the dresser showed four-thirty. That can't be 4:30 A.M. It's afternoon then. I turned to Bob's bed. He wasn't there, but it had been slept in. Of course, he's out walking Fini. As I lay in bed, my mind rambled. Fini, our little French poodle. Incredible that we should have taken him, a gift from —of all people—Farrell.

I remembered the day Farrell called. Bob had been back a week. I was alone. "You monster!" I had cried over the telephone, recognizing the husky voice that always sounded as though he was speaking through several thicknesses of cheesecloth. "How dare you call me!"

"I wanted to apologize, Diana," Farrell said, almost formally. "I'm just back from Europe. I won't bother you any more. I'm sorry for all the trouble I caused you. I told you how I get when I drink." I let him talk. "I'm really sorry, very sorry." And he had a present for me.

"Indeed?" I asked. "Diamonds? Or do you want to pay my doctor bills?"

Oh, no, he laughed. A very special present. Could he bring it up? Well, I thought, it's over with Farrell. Let him give me my gift. I'm curious anyway. And if I don't let him come up, it'll mean I'm afraid there's still something between us.

He came up. The present was Fini, an adorable little
puppy then, peeping out of a blue cashmere sweater he'd
wrapped him in—no collar, no leash, just a naked, lovable
little puppy. Farrell looked so sad, standing uncertainly by
my door, the puppy peeping out, that I couldn't stay indignant. I took Fini.

Farrell had gone away, and though Bob was at first outraged, he, too, melted before that little black bewhiskered
face, and we kept him. We named him "Fini"—French for
"The End"—because it was the end, my accepting a gift from
that monster Farrell. I'd seen him once more, during that
Toulouse-Lautrec affair. And then he faded away and was
out of my life . . .

Suddenly, with a sharp twisting of my very bowels, Blaney's
words came back to me. If he took the money, if he preferred
charges, I'd be finished. Broke, finished, ruined. Shamed,
broke, finished, ruined. I thought, well, Diana, what do we
do? Laboriously I got out of bed and took my morning drink,
threw up, and took the second. As always, that stayed down.
I got into bed with the bottle and took another long, comforting swig. Thirty-four and a has-been. A drunk and a has-
been. If I ever hope to act again, I have to stop drinking. But
I can't give up drinking completely. I don't enjoy it any
more, but the pattern is too strong for me. And Bob won't
stop either. Look at him, drinking like a fish though he
knows it will kill him! Then I remembered—*if* I ever acted
again. If Equity kicks me out, it's all over. The public wants
another Barrymore. They are ready to take you to their
hearts, give you every chance, if you'll let them. They'd love
to see the name go on, as bright, as great as it always has been,
but you don't have what it takes. Frankly, Diana, you're not
worth it. That's about the long and short of it. And since
you can't face the world or yourself, why keep up the silly
game? It's just got too much for you—to hell with it.

I reached over and opened the bedside-table drawer. Eighteen nembutals left. I counted the sodium amytal—nine of

them. Yellow jackets and blue jackets. Let's see—eighteen and nine—I was lousy at math, always good in English, fine in art, in drawing those grotesque faces Daddy liked . . . For a little while I thought of my father. You messed that up, too, Diana. Remember when he first took you through his house? The little curving staircase leading to a turret? He climbed three steps, turned, put up one bent, clawed hand, and mugged fiendishly: "How do you like my lit-tle tower?" He was playing Richard III. Something about the room, something at that moment, reminded him of the past, and he was playing Richard III again. And you said impatiently, "Oh, Daddy, what *are* you doing?" He came right down then, hurt and silent. And when he showed you the room he'd fixed up for you, probably having had to ask for an advance to pay for that yellow chintz spread and the new wallpaper, all you said was, "Oh, charming, Daddy, charming." You should have thrown your arms around that man and cried, "Daddy, I'm moving in with you right now. I won't stay at a hotel, I don't care what Mother says." But all you could get out of that tight little, chic little, bitchy little mouth of yours was, "Charming, Daddy, charming . . ."

I counted the pills again carefully. Eighteen and nine make twenty-seven. Enough. I put them, blue jackets and yellow jackets mixed together, on a Kleenex. They look like succotash, I thought madly. A succotash to oblivion. Rather nice, that, Diana.

What to wash them down with? Well, why not? A double shot of Four Roses.

I managed to stuff half the pills into my mouth. They felt like soft nougat. For a moment I was back in Newport, a little girl, and Grandma Tibi was giving me a nougat bar . . . *Don't be a ham, Diana. Skip the hearts and flowers.*

I swallowed the pills and washed them down with whisky, then swallowed the rest and washed them down too.

Damn, I thought. I won't be able to read my obituary. Who will be at my funeral, I wonder? You can bet I won't

have one like Daddy's. Clark Gable won't be there. Or Louis
B. Mayer. Or Darryl Zanuck. Or Alfred Hitchcock. Would it
be proper for a man to come to your funeral and shout, "Get
that drunken woman out of here!" No, they'd say, "Get,
Buster! You've had it! Good-by——"

Blackness covered me.

CHAPTER THIRTY-THREE

F ROM THE FRONT PAGE of the *Boston Globe,* April 28, 1955:

> Diana Barrymore, member of a famous theatrical family, made a quick recovery today from a brush with death and will return to her role tonight as star of the play, "Pajama Tops." Suffering from a severe head-cold "which I've been carrying these past six months," the actress explained that "I took too many phenobarbital. I took them for no reason at all, except that I'm exhausted . . ."
>
> The actress speculated on what kind of treatment some of the New York newspapers were giving her story, coming as it did on the heels of the attempted suicide by actress Susan Hayward by taking sleeping pills.
>
> "Poor Susan," she said. "Poor Susan."

"Oooh," I said to Bob, "I certainly can't complain of my billing, can I? Page one?" And Bob, who had returned to the hotel just in time to call the police and save my life, only shook his head. "Must you always put on an act, Muzzy? Even for me?"

Of course I didn't try to kill myself. Who, Barrymore? If there's one thing she despises, it's self-pity. She's tough. She can take the rotten with the good. If you try to kill yourself, you're not bouncing around on a stage twenty-six hours later, are you?

Everyone pretended nothing had happened, and to prove I hid no secret morbidity, I was as gay, as buoyant, as charmingly drunk as ever as we played out our tour, closing in New Haven, Connecticut, in May. The play made money. Blaney had to admit that. People came to see Barrymore, drunk or sober, and what was Mr. Blaney complaining about?

I'd even messed up my own suicide, hadn't I? Hadn't I, I screamed at Bob within the four walls of our room, and now that I'd made an even more public ass of myself, what next, in God's name, what next? And when I was by myself I cried a little over the telegram Tallulah had sent me the day after it happened: "We all have these dark moments. Press on, darling, press on."

We found ourselves, that summer, in a west side hotel in New York, a bottle's throw from the rooming house where I'd once climbed a creaking stairs and tiptoed along a creaking corridor with Richie Merino in search of Life and Romance.

It was a hotel, as Bob said glumly, where even the obscenity scrawled on the walls of the men's room was misspelled. Girls in tight dresses and high heels minced with their dogs through the lobby, and heavy-set men with moist eyes followed them across the huge room with its overstuffed leather chairs and scarred furniture. We hated it, but we had a bedroom and sitting room for what one room would cost elsewhere, and the hotel would take Fini and other hotels would not. After all, if Fini hadn't been ready to go back to our hotel in Boston, Bob wouldn't have returned in time. I hugged Fini to me, but I wasn't sure just how I felt about him.

"You see," Lyman Brown, the agent, explained, "they want you. Not Bob." He was talking about two young producers in Canal Fulton, Ohio, near Cleveland. "They have a resident company and they're hiring only two names—you'll open the season; Julie Haydon will close it." They wanted me to star in a comedy, *Glad Tidings*.

I went in the first week of June. Maybe Bob would be driven by boredom to get a job, somewhere, somehow. I went and I kissed Bob good-by. "I'll see you in three weeks," I said. It was the second play I had ever done without Bob in all the time I'd known him.

At Canal Fulton the party was in full swing. I was the guest of honor in a huge, white frame house where I was to live, with a community kitchen where we were all to take our meals. I felt lighthearted. I was on my own again, and my medicine bottle on the plane had been augmented by mellow Bourbon when the two producers, David Fulford and Bill Dempsey, met me. Then I turned to greet someone and the air quivered: I was looking at a tall, dark young man about twenty-eight, with the blackest, most alert eyes I'd ever seen.

"*Who* is this?" I asked, holding out my hand.

"Your leading man," said David. "Cute, isn't he?" He pronounced the name. "Mr. Dan Freeman."

"Well, I certainly approve," I said. Out of nowhere I heard Bram's words the night I came back from my drive with Van Heflin. ". . . these sudden, physical attractions . . . you'll always be attracted by one man or another the moment you meet them . . ."

Mr. Freeman took my arm and led me to a corner and we talked. After the party he carried my bags to my room. It was tiny and charming, all of twelve feet square, with flowery wallpaper. Its single window was propped open with a highball glass. "How divinely perfect!" I cried. I gaped at the bed. It was a mattress supported by four bricks under each corner. It sagged in the middle. "This is a bed?" I exclaimed. "It's a hammock!"

"You're lucky," Dan grinned. "You should see where the

peasants sleep." He took me downstairs. The living room had become a dormitory, with eight army mattresses on the floor. "We don't even rate bricks," he said.

Dan seemed heaven-sent. He was right for the part and right for me. I couldn't drink before a performance or during it, he insisted. He was proud to act with a Barrymore, but he refused to have his performance made ridiculous by my antics. He'd read all about me. And what I refused to take from others, I took from him. After rehearsals, instead of rushing to a bar, standard operating procedure for Bob and me, Dan took me on long walks. We raided the refrigerator, we drank ourselves into a stupor with milk. He was fanatically serious about the theater. His directness and enthusiasm excited me. I felt nineteen again, Diana Blythe with the world before her. I marveled at the discipline I accepted, and my own response. See, I thought, liquor isn't the answer to boredom. Given the job, the right man—or perhaps the right man, and the job——

Bob telephoned that evening. "Muzzy," he began. His voice sounded penitent, like a little boy's. "Muzzy, I'm calling from New York Hospital."

My stomach turned. "For God's sake, what is it?"

The same thing. Pancreatitis. The attack struck in the middle of the night. It had been a bad one: unconscious, rushed through the streets in an ambulance. He had to stay in the hospital for a week.

Instead of sympathy, fury overcame me. "You stupid fool!" I raged. "Won't you ever learn? It's the fourth time. You're lucky you came out of it. You know you shouldn't drink because you know exactly what it's going to do to you!"

He sounded guilty. "You were gone and I just couldn't . . ." His voice faded away. "I missed you so damn much. It won't happen again. This is the last time."

"It better be," I said, "or there won't be a next time."

I hung up, sick and frightened. The same story all over again. The same worn record, played and played again: his helplessness, my being sorry for him and resenting it, hating him and hating myself.

Dan and I were together now all the time. Everything Dan did underscored Bob's weakness. Dan was strong, he was vital, he threatened to walk off the stage if I didn't behave. He was a more facile actor than Bob, and because he was, I was too. I suddenly realized that for eight years I had been acting with Bob and Bob alone: Dan, skillfully handling his cues, throwing me lines, helped me strike sparks too. He played as a man should with a woman, aware that there were two sexes.

"I threw a man-woman challenge at you the minute I saw you," he confessed later. "You're the type of woman who must know where she stands with a man. I had to make it clear that I was your leading man and you had to act with me—not by yourself."

It wasn't conceit, he said. Everyone had trembled before I arrived. Watch out for her—the temperamental, unpredictable star, the bitch on wheels no one can handle . . .

"The key to you is the man," Dan said. "Only the right man will give you peace. If you don't get it, Diana, you're going to fly in larger and larger circles, like a bird with a broken wing, until you turn yourself inside out and simply die—die in an alcoholic ward or fall in front of a truck."

Cruel, harsh—and true, I thought.

The night before we opened Bob telephoned again. His voice was stronger. Unexpectedly he said, "I'll need some money to get out of here. Diana. You'll have to send it to me."

It was like a blow in the face. How long was this going to continue? I found myself crying. "You're upsetting me," I wept. "I haven't opened yet. I'm counting so much on this one to get back with——"

"Now, Muzzy," he said cajolingly. "I'm only asking for a loan of two hundred dollars."

"A loan?" I cried. "You know it's no loan!"

"All right, but it's only two hundred dollars."

"For God's sake, I left you with enough money, and you have Blue Cross—and you're not even out of the hospital!"

"It's just a little extra I need," he insisted.

"Oh, God, all right, I'll send it. I don't want to send it, but I'll send it. Two hundred probably won't be enough. I'm wiring you two hundred and fifty dollars," I said, and hung up.

Now I really am finished with him, I thought. He's not for me, I'm not for him. We'll talk divorce when I get back to New York. Let's face it, life with Bob is get drunk and get undrunk. Why should the future be different than the past?

Dan had brought me down from two bottles of Imperial a day to a few highballs. He was good for me. "You're really a frightened actress," he said, playing my psychoanalyst. "You compensate for your fear by loudness and arrogance. Cut down on both."

Opening night was excellent. I hadn't read such notices about myself in years. "Diana Barrymore Wins Fulton Theatre Raves," read one. I was compared to Tallulah in another. I gave, I felt, a bright, strong, authoritative performance. Yes, I told myself, the key is the man, the man is the key. When Dan took me back to the big white house that night, I removed my wedding ring from my left hand and placed it on my right.

A week after Bob's seizure he called. "I left the hospital this morning," he said. He was shaky but okay. "Haven't touched a drop of alcohol in seven days. You should have seen me this morning, Muzzy, nursing a big shot of ginger ale."

"Bob, if you ever take a drink again . . ."

He resented that. "You sound awfully holier-than-thou. You've got a hell of a right to talk, Diana."

He couldn't make me angry. I felt proud of the way I had controlled my drinking. I couldn't help telling him. "It's because of my leading man," I said. "He keeps me away from liquor—which is more than you could do for me, Bob."

"Oh, I see," he said in an "Oh, I see" voice. "All right. *Who* is it *this* time?"

"For God's sake, Bob," I exclaimed. "What a silly thing to ask. It's nothing like that. Look, Bob, go to Rochester. You've been dry for a week. Get out of New York, away from all those barflies you drink with. You know now that alcohol is pure poison for you. Go up to Mom's and eat three meals a day and put some weight on yourself."

He said, "I get so damned bored in Rochester. I won't stay more than a couple of days."

"If you have any sense, you'll stay a couple of weeks," I said.

"Oh," he retorted, "so you can be with your lover?"

We argued back and forth. Finally I said, "Bob, I've been doing a lot of thinking here. I'm sorry you were sick, but Bob, really, I don't know about us any more. When I get back we'll have to have a very serious talk. We've got to do something before one of us kills the other. *We can't go on this way!*"

He was silent for a moment. "You sound strange, Diana. I know you too damn well. You're sleeping with this man, aren't you?"

"Oh, Bob, please!"

"You are, aren't you?"

I said, "Bob, stop goading me."

Bob said, "Is he attractive?"

"Yes, he is attractive."

"And you're sleeping with him?"

I was silent.

"You are, aren't you?" he went on doggedly, like a man digging at his own wound. "You are, aren't you?"

Then I broke. "Goddamn it, maybe I am! You can think whatever you like, Bob." I rushed on. "And Bob, he's good for me! He doesn't let me drink, he's helping me get back my self-respect, he doesn't ask me for anything, he doesn't make me feel responsible for him, I feel free . . ." The words poured out of me. "I'm sick of supporting you, sick of it! We'll talk when I get back, Bob, and we both know what the outcome will be. I know damn well!"

I could hear him sigh over the telephone—a long-drawn-out sigh.

"Diana, I'm beyond hurt," he said.

"Yes, you're beyond hurt; well, I'm beyond hurt too! We're finished! Good-by!"

I slammed down the receiver.

The knock on the door came at seven minutes to ten the next morning. I fought my way out of deep slumber. The rapping on the door was insistent. "Who is it?" I managed to call out.

It was Bill Dempsey, he said.

"Oh, what do you mean by rapping on my door at this hour in the morning!" I cried. "But come in, darling, come in."

The door opened slowly and Bill came in and closed it behind him. He stood and looked at me. His face was ashen, even more ashen against the bright red shirt he wore.

He said, "I have something to tell you."

I began to crumple inside. "Bob?" I whispered.

He nodded. A tattoo began to drum at my temples. My lips formed the words: "Is he dead?"

For an unbearable moment Bill stood motionless, then he inclined his head. "A heart attack in his sleep," he said gently. "On the train to Rochester."

I felt numb. I knew what he told me, but they were words only. I thought, I must call Bob's mother. I spoke aloud:

"Bill, would you mind going downstairs and seeing if the phone is free. I'll be right down." I put on a robe. I went slowly down the stairs, without thinking. They say a really great shock numbs you. After Robin's death, when Mother was to bring him to Indiana for burial, they threw his body

into a sack before her eyes, and she stood calm, calm, calm.
That's why I'm calm. It will all come later.

I got on the phone to Bob's mother. "Mom—" I began.

"Yes, Diana," she said. And then: "There's no need to
talk. Our boy is dead."

"Do you want me to come?" I asked. No, she said. Ross
was already on his way from the coast. "There's no reason
for you to come," she said. "You are there, you have work—
you do it. Bob would have wanted it."

I hung up. My calmness began to ooze away. My fellow
actors wandered about helplessly. I grew nervous. I took a
drink and then another. Time passed. Dan was beside me.
Part of what he told me and part of what I heard made no
sense to me. They had found Bob dead in his berth just before the train reached Rochester. After our telephone call
the night before he had checked out of the apartment, had
his bags taken down to the lobby, and left word that he
would pick them up at 10:00 P.M. At 10:00 P.M. he had not
shown up. The night clerk saw him reel in at midnight, with
Fini on his leash. Bob had spent hours at the bar around the
corner, speaking to no one, drinking, drinking . . . Somehow
he managed to pick up his bags and take the cab to the station. Just before the train reached Rochester, the porter
heard a dog crying and whining. He investigated. It was Fini,
crying, lying next to Bob, and Bob was dead.

I became hysterical.

"Diana, darling." Dan's voice broke through the haze.
"The worst thing is for you to stay in this house all day.
You've got a show to do tonight . . ."

I said, "I'll go on tonight, I'll go on. Everyone I've ever
loved died while I was working—my father and my mother
and my brother and now my husband . . ." Suddenly it was
minutes later, and Dan was helping me to dress. "Come on,"
he said. "We'll get out of here and walk, just walk anywhere.
Don't think, Diana, don't try to think."

I wanted to walk barefoot. Somehow it would solace me to

feel the earth under my bare feet. Dan refused. "You'll catch cold," he said. He helped me put on socks and loafers.

Then, in the quiet noonday, we were walking by the river. The water rippled softly over the stones. Dan held me close as we walked, supporting me when I stumbled, or slipped on the grass. I talked endlessly. "It isn't true, it isn't true. Eight years, and then last night— Oh, God, why couldn't I have given him one kind word! It isn't true. Why did I tell him those terrible things . . . it isn't true. He's still alive. I'll always love him. He's my husband, I love him, I love him, he's the only man I've ever loved. Dan, I did wrong. I know what I've done. The fates are catching up with me. You are punished for what you do, and I have done a terrible thing and I am being punished . . ."

"You owe the dead nothing," Dan began.

"Don't say that word!" I begged him.

"You owe them nothing, Diana. If you owe them something, you owe it to them to change the conditions that led to all this. Diana, darling, let the death *mean* something. *Be somebody better.*"

I cried, "I've gone too far. It's too late."

No, he said, I was young. "You're too full of vitality to be anything but young. Diana, this may sound ghoulish, but this is the greatest opportunity in your life to create something wholesome and fine out of Diana Barrymore . . ."

His voice turned into words that flowed without meaning. I walked dreamily. How peaceful nature was, and how tormented human beings were. We were walking in a small picnic grounds, and before us was a child's swing, two ropes and a crossbar, hanging between two huge trees.

Dan said, "Come on, baby, sit in the swing." I let him help me into it. "Push me," I whispered. He pushed me gently, and I slowly swung back and forth, back and forth. I put my head back and watched the sky move above me, so that the huge blue dome and canopy of trees rode back and forth . . . I was swinging in my swing in the yard of Grandma

Tibi's house. Dear God, if I could turn the years back . . .

After a little while I said, "I think that's enough."

He helped me off. I murmured, "What a crazy thing. To be in a swing."

Dan touched my cheek with his lips, and we walked down a small incline to the grassy bank of the stream. The summer sun was strong. Dan threw a stone into the water. We watched it strike, heard the soft "plip," and saw it sink. He threw another. I picked up a stone and tossed it into the water. My arm was heavy.

"Let's get some sun here," Dan suggested. We sank to the ground. I leaned against him. "You're a sick girl, Diana," he said. "Don't try to fight everything. Just sit here, look around —maybe looking at God's world, you'll see something else."

I couldn't understand. "Just what I say," he said softly. "You are going to get to God. You are going to understand what this all means."

I began to cry. "I love that man. I'll always love him. I just can't get out of it. I'll never forgive myself."

Dan began gently rubbing my back between the shoulders, as if to massage everything away, and he sang as he did so: "Ei-lu-lu, Bab-en-u, Ei-lu-lu-lu-lu, Baby. Ei-lu-lu-lu, Bab-en-u, ei-lu-lu-lu-lu, Baby." Over and over again. It was an old lullaby, he said, his mother used to sing him to sleep with. I don't know how long we sat there as he rubbed my shoulders and sang the lullaby.

We'd better get back, I said. I had to curl my hair. I had to prepare for my show . . .

When dinner came, though I was under sedatives, I could not eat. I came down and looked at everyone sitting stiffly about the table and I climbed upstairs and collapsed. Dan virtually carried me to the theater. I have a vague memory of my two performances: at 7:30 P.M. and 10:30 P.M. I remember a tremendous ovation when I found myself on the stage. Half this audience, I thought, have come to see a woman whose husband just died, and half have come to see a Barrymore. I shall never know which half started the tremendous hand I received that night.

The play was an unrelieved nightmare. In one scene I played a woman who recalls her husband's death. I managed the lines because Dan squeezed my hand until my fingers were numb. In the second performance I staggered onto the stage. I mouthed the words. When I was called upon to cry, I cried uncontrollably. Dan carried me to my dressing room.

At midnight four of us—Dan and I, and Paul and Nancy, two young actors who played my children, walked to our hill, a grassy knoll about two hundred yards from the house, where we used to go each night to sit and look at the stars. We walked there silently, under a high, starry sky. I felt emotionally drained, completely spent, yet never had I seen the world about me so purely. The night mist made stage scenery wherever I looked. The moon was iridescent, lighting everything pale and blue-white. I saw the dew on the grass, and it was not dew, it was the moon making sequins on the grass. I saw everything but felt nothing.

We lay on our backs and looked up at the stars, enormous and very clear. Nancy asked, "Do you mind if we sing, Diana?" I shook my head. "Sing anything you like."

She sang, "You Go to My Head." Then Paul sang. Then we all joined, and I found myself singing with them. I hadn't sung like that since I was seventeen, singing with Edouard d'Avignon in the woods of Brittany. I wondered, ought I be singing? Here were three friends and for some reason, being with them, this was not a sad night, for all my sadness. Perhaps I should not have been singing, but since I was, they understood.

I tried to look at the stars, but tears blinded me. Looking at the stars meant life, and there was a dead man in my life. I couldn't look at them because I was alive. I could see the stars. He would never see them again.

When we were back in the house, Dan took me to my room

and gave me three sleeping pills left by the doctor. I was suddenly panicky. "I won't be able to sleep, Dan. I know I won't."

I took the pills. But I fought them desperately. Dan sat beside my bed. "Stay here," I implored him. "When I open my eyes I must see that someone is here, watching over me." Despite the pills my eyes opened and closed, only to open again. Something in me fought to keep awake, to cling to consciousness. I was afraid that if I fell asleep, I would sink into the arms of death.

I dreamed. In my dream Bob was alive. We were in an apartment, like the one at Sutton Terrace, with an enormous French window. And in the dream I looked out the window and made an exclamation. "Well, this looks rather ominous."

Bob looked and gasped. High in the sky were rickety, old-fashioned airplanes, hundreds of them, all made of spun glass. We could see into them. Each was flown by a pilot two feet high and carried passengers two feet high. "I don't know what's going to happen, Bob," I said, terrified. "Maybe this is the end of the world."

The planes made a perfect landing on the grass outside our window and the little people spilled out and moved toward us like a swarm of enormous insects, silently, without a word.

I cried, "Bob, let's throw ourselves out the window into the ocean. Maybe they don't know what water is." Inexplicably, the grass outside had become the sea. I hurled myself into the water, Bob with me; but when we tried to swim, the ocean turned into a bed with heavy blankets. We struggled. I screamed, "Get out of the blankets!"

We were surrounded by the little people, prisoners. One said to Bob, "We're going to take you. We're going to make you our size."

Bob said, "Well, all right, if you want our world so much. How will you do it?"

"We tattoo your right foot. That brings you down to our size."

I cried out in panic. "Look, if you're going to do it to him, I want it too. Whatever you do—however he comes out—I want to be the same, because I can't live without this man."

They did it to Bob first. Suddenly he was only two feet high, in a space suit, and he was crying brokenheartedly, "Take me into your arms, Muzzy, please."

"Oh, my darling," I said. "Of course I will." I took him into my arms, like a doll, and caressed him. I begged the little people, "Do the same to me, please. We want to be together."

As I watched, they tattooed my foot, putting a blue potion on with a brush. "Does this hurt?" they asked. I shook my head. "Then the rest won't either." And suddenly I was small, but not two feet. I was three feet tall, and larger than Bob. He was still crying.

I held him in my arms. "It's all right, it's all right," I whispered. "So long as we're together, nothing else matters. Nothing else matters." I carried him into a room, and it was our apartment on East 80th Street, where the lights had been turned off. "See," I said. "We're safe here. No one will hurt us here."

Then two fully sized men entered.

"What do you want?" I asked in alarm.

"We've come to save you, to restore you to your rightful size."

And all at once we were both big again, and Bob wasn't Bob but had turned into Bramwell . . .

I exclaimed, "Oh, dear—you're not expected. You're not supposed to be around." Bramwell held out his arms. "I haven't forgotten you, Diana," he said. "I never will . . ."

And then I was awake, lying in my bed, alone, weeping.

The funeral was to be held at 2:00 P.M. Tuesday, in Rochester. I was unable to leave the play but spoke to Ross on the phone. He said, "We have Bob's effects here. What do you want done with them?"

I told Ross to keep them there for the present.

"One thing, Diana," he said. "Bob was wearing a watch I'd like to have. I'd like to have something of his."

"Whatever you wish," I said. "Go through everything and take what you want."

"There's a sport shirt, if you don't mind."

I said, "Of course, I don't mind." It was as though we were talking about a mannequin, not a human being.

I sent yellow roses to the funeral and a note: "Please place them by his head." Because yellow roses were what Bob always sent me for my birthday.

And at two o'clock on Tuesday I borrowed a rosary and went out walking by myself and prayed.

CHAPTER THIRTY-FOUR

Wнат is dream, and what is reality?
I shuttled between the two. In the terrible weeks that followed, after I returned to New York, I appeared in two plays: *A Streetcar Named Desire* and *Glad Tidings*. How I managed is something of a miracle, even to me. There was no Dan to stop me from drinking; but I knew if I drank, I'd really go to pieces and never be able to do the show. I tried to think of what Bob would have wanted me to do—and I stayed sober. In order to sleep I increased my dosage of pills each night until I was taking five and six seconals at a time. One puts most people to sleep in minutes. Next day I was forced to swallow two and three Dexadrine tablets to keep from stumbling dazedly about my hotel room. I ate hardly anything. My weight began to drop.

Suddenly, one night in August, my temperature shot to 106 degrees, I was rushed to Doctors Hospital. I have a vague memory of struggling against arms pinning me down, of hearing myself screaming profanity, of voices roaring in a nightmare. When I came to I found myself strapped down in bed, my arms and legs helpless, and my physician, Dr. Martin Hemmings, sitting by my bed, watching me.

He smiled when I opened my eyes. "Don't be frightened," he said gently. I had just gone through a convulsion—my second. It was the result of withdrawing sleeping pills. He explained as the afternoon wore on. My fever stemmed from an infection, at other times unimportant, but in my run-down condition extremely serious. I suffered from malnutrition. He was treating me for barbiturate addiction and alcoholism as well.

"It's the barbiturates that concern us," he said. "Taking you off alcohol presents a less serious problem." DTs, after all, could be controlled with medication. But they were still forced to keep me under sedation—they dared not withdraw my pills completely. I had been forced to take so many each night because the alcohol I drank only excited and agitated me. In addition, through the years I had built up a tolerance of barbiturates. "Diana," Dr. Hemmings warned me, "you are on a dreadful merry-go-round—alcohol, barbiturates, stimulants. If you don't get off it quickly, you will die. Your drinking has already given you the beginning of cirrhosis of the liver. Next will be hepatitis, progressive deterioration of your blood vessels, internal hemorrhaging—and death. You simply cannot continue to torment your body as you have been doing." He looked at me sadly. "It took your father sixty years to do it: you keep this up and you'll manage in a much much shorter time."

I *was* frightened. How could I help myself? He recommended that I commit myself to a sanitarium for at least four months to rid myself completely of barbiturate addiction. I listened but said nothing. Dr. Hemmings couldn't know the terrible fear lurking in the back of my mind. My grandfather Maurice died in a mental institution. Daddy's secret fear had been that he might die insane or be committed into an institution because people thought he was insane. I, too, had an unreasoning fear of such places: I was sure that if I found myself in one, I would become insane. I told my physician I would think about his suggestion. I could not promise.

I spent eight days in Doctors Hospital. I walked out at noon: at 4:40 P.M. I ordered a double vodka at the bar of my hotel. Hadn't Dr. Hemmings said sleeping pills were worse than drinking? I can have one drink, perhaps two—never more, I told myself. Surely one, perhaps two, can't hurt me. And if I drink less, I'll be less excited, I'll need fewer sleeping pills—why, I can work my way out of this myself.

Things began to look up when H. Clay Blaney, in spite of his experience with me in *Pajama Tops,* asked if I would replace Veronica Lake in *The Little Hut,* in Detroit. Veronica, suddenly taken ill, had been forced to drop out. "You've just come from the hospital," he said. "You're in good shape. You'll do me a favor." He escorted me to the plane to Detroit. "I'm counting on you, Diana," he said. "Not a drop now." I assured him. "Not a drop, Blaney."

How does one explain such things? I was drunk when I presented myself at the theater in Detroit. I never opened in *The Little Hut.*

I came back to New York.

Martinis in the afternoon, to begin with. Then, gin to hold you until your friends come to take you to dinner. Diana isn't working now, she's still brooding over Bob, she mustn't be left alone too much. By the time they arrive, you've polished off a quart of gin. Time: three hours.

At the bar, waiting for a table, three stingers—brandy and crème de menthe. At the table, waiting for your dinner, a double brandy and soda. You hardly touch food. After dinner a demitasse, from which you pour off half the coffee in order to replace it with brandy. Then, sitting and chatting, eight more stingers before you rise, gay and flushed.

Back to your hotel. "Diana, you don't mean to say you're in the same suite you had with Bob?" Yes. Nothing else available. Let's talk about other things. There's half a fifth of vodka in the pantry—enough for you and your two friends to finish off before they leave.

Two in the morning and you're alone. You wander about,

thinking nothing, while your records play. In the icebox you come upon two quarts of ale. It's pleasant to lounge on the sofa, sipping ale, listening to the theme music from the movie, *Spellbound*. Prodigious capacity, incredible constitution—that's me. I can hold it. I can hold it . . . hold on now. Hold everything . . . I'm listing to starboard . . .

When I awake, I'm lying on the sofa. Must have dozed off. *Spellbound* is still playing. I'm soaked in perspiration. I put both hands on either side of me and push myself up to a sitting position. My head pounds. The walls and furniture fuse together, like a movie dissolve. Shaking, I make my way into the bedroom. The alarm clock is a patch of white: I can't focus on the hands. I get on the phone: "Darling, my clock stopped. What time is it?" Five-twenty. Five-twenty in the morning. I really slept. Good. I need sleep so badly.

I begin to cough. Oooh, I know what that means. I reel into the bathroom and fall on my knees in front of the bowl to throw up, gag, retch, gag again. This is agony, this is the stomach pump all over again: I can't bring anything up but greenish bile. After a while the attack passes. I undress weakly and slip shiveringly into bed, pulling the blankets over my head. I huddle under them. My heart pounds as though it were trying to leap out of my body. My hands are ice. A moment later I burn: I toss the blankets off. On, off, on, off. Okay, Diana, so you've got the hot and cold shakes. Where's that Goddamn white crab? Isn't it due about now? . . .

When I woke again it was 2:30 P.M. I was in a hammock, swinging slowly, widely, from one side to the other. The walls rose and fell. Sweat, thick and oily, poured from me—from my armpits, my back, even my eyes. They stung with it. I worked my way laboriously out of bed and into the bathroom and splashed cold water on my face and eyes. Strangely enough, it seemed only to make me drunker.

I put out one hand against the bathroom wall to hold it

back. Steady. Steady . . . is that you in the mirror? I peered
at what was there. Week after week, drinking myself blind,
and no figure of speech, that, either. I couldn't open my
eyes, not completely. They were half closed with the edema
that puffed out the flesh above and below. My face was
blotched, gray and blue and distorted. Let's see, I thought
painstakingly. What do I look like? Why, as though I saw
myself in one of those fantastic Coney Island mirrors under
a ghastly light that turns your veins and lips blue . . . No.
What you really look like, my dear, is a character who's been
beaten again and again over the face with a rubber hose.

Is this a *face*, Diana? Is this a *human being*?

I stood, swaying.

Oh, Diana, I thought, Diana baby, everything's mixed up.
Your life is like a bad play. Act Three is all balled up. This
is Act Three now. Now's the time to go into the sleeping-pill
bit. But you've played that scene already, in Boston. What
are you going to do? What *will* you do? It's obvious what
you're *trying* to do. Dr. Hemmings told you. You're trying to
drink yourself to death. You don't have the guts to do it any
other way.

I thought of Leonard. He is my rock to cling to.

It was Leonard who arranged for me to enter Towns Hospital for alcoholic treatment. "I've checked everyplace," he
said. He had visited a retreat in Hartford, Connecticut; one
on Long Island, where one of the Oelrichs had been; even
Mattawan, where my grandfather died. In some I would have
to commit myself for at least six months; they refused to ac-
cept me for a shorter period. No, no, no! I cried. I wouldn't
be treated like a mental patient! Leonard understood. He
soothed me. He soothed me even as we drank together, because I could not talk without drinking to give me courage
to discuss what we were discussing. "I'll never commit you
anywhere against your will," he promised me. "I will never

put you anywhere you don't wish to be." He investigated again, and this time he returned to tell me about Towns. It was in New York City. I could remain weeks instead of months. He added wryly, "You might be interested, Diana —your father went there once too."

I thought, how right. How right. Leonard and I, through the years, had been restrained with each other. Now I kissed him and thanked him. We were catkins now as we had never been when Mother and Robin were alive. There was no one else now who really cared whether I lived or died but Leonard.

I went to Towns because it meant salvation.

As I was about to register, Dr. Domenico Paccione, resident physician at Towns, asked, "What name will you use?"

"My own," I replied. "Why?"

He smiled. "Many well-known people prefer to use an alias when they come here."

I said no. "I have nothing to hide." I signed in: "Diana Barrymore." As if everybody didn't know!

From the outside you had no idea it was the place it was. A private brownstone house, overlooking Central Park, with half a dozen steps leading to a small vestibule, an old-fashioned wooden door with highly polished brass letter chute. It might have been our house on East End Avenue where I lived as a little girl. I was ushered into a room on the third floor. The walls were restful green, the carpet green, the bedspread green, the bars on the window green. I tried not to look at them.

At the hospital I tapered off on liquor. Many patients came only to sleep off a drunk and were gone two days later. I wanted more than that. On the first day I was permitted a drink every hour; on the second, one every two hours; the third, one every three hours; presently, one drink a day; and finally only ginger ale. We sat around, patients all, in pajamas and robes, an exclusive little club of our own, watching television, commenting on each other and the latest arrivals; and as the hour neared for a drink, we crowded about the locked liquor cabinet and waited. Then an attendant opened the cabinet, poured one drink for each of us, and locked it again. As the days passed, I was astonished to see that I no longer watched the clock.

No one had to lecture me at Towns. It was a shock for me to learn that I was the youngest guest there: I was the only patient in his thirties. I watched the newcomers enter, all drunk—not charmingly, not entertainingly, but staggeringly drunk. Women without make-up, their hair looking filthy and sticky; one girl in bra and panties under a mink coat; another carried in by a boy friend who staggered as he walked. I'd never really been fully sober in the presence of completely alcoholically soaked human beings. God, I said to myself, is this the way I am when I'm drunk . . . ?

I was given vitamin injections, I exercised, ate a carefully planned diet, walked for hours in Central Park. The day came when I kept the blinds up in my room. Sunlight no longer tortured my eyes. From my window I looked out on the expanse of the park. I drank in the blue of the lake, the fresh green of the grass, the sight of riders taking their horses along the winding bridle paths. I thought, I lived like that, once, among those people, up in the morning, out in the daylight world . . . I tried, during those weeks, in my own way, to sum things up. I had the time, I was sober, I was alone, for the first time in my life.

I thought a great deal about Bob and about men. I wondered—had I ever really been in love as a woman should be in love? I thought it was so with Bram, with John Howard, surely with Bob. But even with Bob it had not been a woman's love for a man. I had been in love as a mother loves a child. What I really sought was a strong man who could father me: I wanted a man to take care of me, and always I had linked my life with men I had to care for. The only strong men I had met were violent men. What I needed, I thought, was a strong man who was gentle, who would be lover and father, not lover and child. Perhaps I was always on this search, and this might explain my constant, almost compulsive, need for the companionship and intimacy of men ... Yes, I had had many lovers, but they meant nothing. They were faceless, like the lovers I dreamed about, the dream lovers I wouldn't tell Dr. Powdermaker about in my Brearley days—I had so many, they were like a deck of cards, I just shuffled and chose the most beautiful and fell into his arms, swooning ...

"I don't know," said Ann Andrews, with whom I discussed this on one of her visits. "Maybe that's your explanation. It's convenient. But I just think, Diana, that you were born without a sense of morals. You are a completely amoral person." Ann, as always, would not spare me. "You are your parents all over again. You have their theatrical attitude toward life, their impulsiveness and refusal to think of consequences." She sighed. "If only you'd inherited less of their weaknesses and more of their virtues!" Their moral behavior, she said, was outrageous too. "But when they had to work, they worked—they exerted the most rigid self-discipline. Now it's up to you to exert that same discipline to overcome the weaknesses and develop the virtues."

I wondered. Was I a projection of my mother and father? Had I been reliving, in a kind of strange reincarnation, the life they began as one and could not live out together?

Once, after the Farrell episode, I thought of writing an open letter to all the newspaper columnists. I wanted to explain to Walter Winchell and Dorothy Kilgallen and Earl Wilson and Leonard Lyons and Ed Sullivan and Louella Parsons and Hedda Hopper, to all the columnists who reported the highs and lows of my career—I wanted to explain to them that there was more to me than the girl on the front page of the tabloids, the girl whose bloated face and silly, drunken grin stared out from all the exposé magazines. Really, I wanted to say, that isn't the whole story. And it came to me, suddenly, that I myself didn't know the whole story. Perhaps if I tried to relive it by telling it—if I searched back into my life and my beginnings—if I laid it all out in front of me, so I could see it from beginning to now—perhaps I would understand—and others would too.

Maybe it would help me find my way. For, God knows, I thought, I have lost it.

When I left Towns Hospital after eight weeks, I looked as if I'd come from a milk farm. I began to organize my life again. I made preparations, frightened but determined, for my first New York play in years. I was signed to costar in *The Ivory Branch* to be presented in downtown New York.

Now and then I took a drink. I had finally reached a conclusion about myself and alcohol. I would never be able to give up drinking completely. I faced that fact. But I told myself that I would never again live as drunkenly as I had in the past.

I rehearsed *The Ivory Branch*—sober.

I opened in *The Ivory Branch*—sober.

I played it through its entire run—sober.

I read Mr. Brooks Atkinson's review in the New York *Times*:

> Miss Barrymore has a good voice, good dimples, a good figure, a good dramatic temperament and a lot of power . . . Any time she wants to stop fooling around and learn the difference between acting and performing, she can be an exciting actress. The stuff is there.

This time I did not write a letter to Mr. Atkinson, as I had done nearly sixteen years ago. Then I was young, exuberant

Diana Blythe Barrymore, with all the world before her. But now I repeat my vow—and mean it: *I promise. You'll see. You will indeed, Mr. Atkinson!*

Perhaps I have begun to find my way.